TEACHER HACKS ENGLISH

**BY
DR HAILI HUGHES & STUART PRYKE**
SERIES EDITOR: MICHAEL CHILES

Together we unlock every learner's unique potential

At Hachette Learning (formerly Hodder Education), there's one thing we're certain about. No two students learn the same way. That's why our approach to teaching begins by recognising the needs of individuals first.

Our mission is to allow every learner to fulfil their unique potential by empowering those who teach them. From our expert teaching and learning resources to our digital educational tools that make learning easier and more accessible for all, we provide solutions designed to maximise the impact of learning for every teacher, parent and student.

Aligned to our parent company, Hachette Livre, founded in 1826, we pride ourselves on being a learning solutions provider with a global footprint.

www.hachettelearning.com

Although every effort has been made to ensure that website addresses are correct at time of going to press, Hachette Learning cannot be held responsible for the content of any website mentioned in this book. It is sometimes possible to find a relocated web page by typing in the address of the home page for a website in the URL window of your browser.

Hachette UK's policy is to use papers that are natural, renewable and recyclable products and made from wood grown in well-managed forests and other controlled sources. The logging and manufacturing processes are expected to conform to the environmental regulations of the country of origin.

To order, please visit www.HachetteLearning.com or contact Customer Service at education@hachette.co.uk / +44 (0)1235 827827.

ISBN: 978 1 0360 1067 6

© Haili Hughes and Stuart Pryke 2026

First published in 2026 by
Hachette Learning (a trading division of Hodder & Stoughton Limited),
An Hachette UK Company
Carmelite House
50 Victoria Embankment
London EC4Y 0DZ
www.HachetteLearning.com

The authorised representative in the EEA is Hachette Ireland, 8 Castlecourt Centre, Dublin 15, D15 XTP3, Ireland (email: info@hbgi.ie)

Impression number   10 9 8 7 6 5 4 3 2 1
Year   2030 2029 2028 2027 2026

All rights reserved. Apart from any use permitted under UK copyright law, no part of this publication may be reproduced or transmitted in any form or by any means, electronic or mechanical, including photocopying and recording, or held within any information storage and retrieval system, without permission in writing from the publisher or under licence from the Copyright Licensing Agency Limited. Further details of such licences (for reprographic reproduction) may be obtained from the Copyright Licensing Agency Limited, www.cla.co.uk

Illustrations by DC Graphic Design Limited, Hextable, Kent.
Typeset in the UK.
Printed in the UK.

A catalogue record for this title is available from the British Library.

TABLE OF CONTENTS

About the authors iv
Introduction v
Foreword viii
    Chapter 1: Teaching vocabulary 1
    Chapter 2: Literary devices 36
    Chapter 3: Structure 56
    Chapter 4: Inference and making meaning 83
    Chapter 5: Context 108
    Chapter 6: Comparing texts 123
    Chapter 7: Rhetoric 133
    Chapter 8: Generating original interpretations and thesis statements ... 142
    Chapter 9: Considering 'judicious' quotations 167
    Chapter 10: Sentence structures and grammar 189
Conclusion 213
Bibliography 215

ABOUT THE AUTHORS

Dr Haili Hughes is a Director of PD at a multi-academy trust and a professor of coaching and mentoring at a university. She taught English for twenty years and now writes books for English teachers. She has written seven books, her most recent being *GCSE English Literature Boost: A Christmas Carol*. She facilitates the ECF and NPQs and delivers CPD all over the world.

Stuart Pryke is an English teacher and Assistant Principal for Teaching and Learning at a secondary school in Norfolk. He is the co-author of *Ready to Teach: Macbeth* and *Ready to Teach: A Christmas Carol* and the student revision guide *100 for 100: Macbeth*. He has worked with Oak National Academy and GCSE English in Action as well as PiXL. Alongside being a leadership coach and NPQ facilitator, Stuart provides a range of CPD to English departments across the country.

INTRODUCTION

Why Teacher Hacks: English?

In today's fast-paced, information-rich world, the study of English is more vital than ever. Admittedly, we may be biased. We are, after all, English teachers. Yet we find ourselves in an era increasingly defined by division, hostility and a breakdown in communication; the ability to express ourselves clearly, thoughtfully and with empathy is, regrettably, becoming increasingly fractured within our society.

English, then, is essential.

At its core, English offers the tools to reopen dialogue, to rebuild understanding, to help us reach out and to reimagine connection in a world that sorely needs open dialogue and communication

English is not only the foundation, the bedrock, of the national curriculum, but also a gateway to academic success, to personal expression and social mobility. How lucky we are to be able to teach a subject where we can help students to articulate their thinking, to craft their arguments and to explore the richness and complexities of the human condition through literature that gives us a snapshot of societal thinking in a particular period of time. English is a subject where we can encourage students to find their voices, to add them to the rich tapestry of thoughts and musings that make our subject the brilliant thing that it is.

Through English, we can help our students to change the world, in small ways that may go unnoticed, or bigger ways that are recognised. English is a subject where, as teachers, we can help students recognise in themselves the adults that they will grow up to be. Beyond identifying verbs and similes, we need to nurture our students to become confident communicators, critical readers and thoughtful writers. We need to think about how we can cultivate their ability to think deeply, to express themselves clearly and to engage meaningfully with the world around them. English is not just a subject, it is a life skill, one that has the ability to change lives for the better.

Yet many learners face challenges when it comes to our subject. It might be they struggle to decode unfamiliar texts, or cannot work out how to get their thoughts down on paper in a clear and coherent way. It might be that they can't interpret literary meaning. Any barrier can feel daunting, and if we think of the personal challenges we have had to face at some point in our lives, we can appreciate why students might 'switch off' at the thought of having to express original views on a text they're studying in an essay we've set them to write in 45 minutes. Reading can be laborious for some. Writing can be threatening. Just because we love a subject, doesn't mean the thirty faces sitting in front of us automatically do too.

We love our subject and we want to impart that love to our students. Even confident students can find English challenging when it comes to expressing the beautiful complexities and nuances of the discipline.

To help all learners, students must be taught how to understand complex texts, how to write with control and clarity, how to use grammar to shape meaning and how to read to access subtext. These are not skills that develop automatically. They require deliberate teaching. We need a set of strategies that are high leverage that aim to make the most of every lesson.

English is a subject under constant scrutiny and review. While debate is good, for it can only push us into new ways of thinking and alternative paths for doing things, it is also easy to get lost in the myriad arguments for what we should and shouldn't be doing. One person on social media argues for one way of teaching, another blogs about another. If they contradict each other, which source are we meant to believe?

Teacher Hacks: English aims to cut through the noise. In this book, we present to you a set of strategies, or 'hacks', that are informed by research and have been tried and tested in the classroom. Of course, there is not one way of doing things, and any hack must be adapted to suit the context in which one teaches, but these are a strong starting point, a 'way in' and an opportunity for us to try things on for size before implementing them in our classrooms, or de-implementing them if they don't work. Some of these ideas may be recognisable to you already and some may be brand new. Some you may agree with and some may challenge an established view of what you believe English teaching to be. Any reaction to these hacks is valid, whether you like or dislike an approach. Our sole goal is to be able to spark a thought, whether one that agrees with the ideas in this book or one that diverges from the book completely but helps you to figure out what you need in order to teach effectively and with impact.

In *Teacher Hacks: English,* you will find a set of strategies that have been presented by a variety of teachers, not just those who teach English, but that have been adapted and used in English contexts. We hope you find these hacks useful for the context in which *you* teach.

Who is this book for?

This book is written for English teachers at secondary level (KS3 and KS4 learners/ learners aged 11 to 16), though many of these approaches will also be relevant to upper primary learners and even A-level. Whether you are an English specialist ECT or someone who has been teaching years, we hope this book provides useful ideas and allows you to reflect on ways in which day-to-day practice could be enhanced further.

Splitting each chapter into a 'What', 'How', 'Why' structure, we discuss common issues faced by English teachers on a daily basis. Through research, anecdotes and resources, you will find information around what these issues are, how we can address these with our set of tried and tested 'hacks', practical tips and resources and why it is important these issues are addressed.

We have picked ten areas of English that can be particularly challenging for both teachers and students. Some of these areas have had entire books written about them. In no way do we seek to replace these. Instead, we offer a way in, which might lead to further research.

We hope that English subject leads and curriculum designers will find this book useful for department CPD, teaching and learning handbooks and whole school literacy initiatives.

What do we hope teachers of English will take away from this book?

Teacher Hacks: English is structured to support the pillars of English teaching: reading, writing, and speaking and listening. We do not champion a single pedagogical approach. Instead, we offer a curated selection of what we think are some of the most effective strategies for teaching English explicitly and with impact. Every chapter is rooted in real classroom experience and not just our own.

We want this book to be a practical companion, something any teacher can have next to them when planning, a book you can read cover to cover or dip into depending on what you are planning on any particular day. Whether you're looking at ways of teaching vocabulary, helping students consider characters as conscious constructs, or thinking about how you can introduce the idea of a thesis statement to your class, we hope you find that the hacks here save you valuable time in your planning, helping you to raise achievement and inspire confidence in both you and your students.

In our work outside of this book, we have always championed for helping teachers, for saving them time, for sharing resources and ideas. We have poured what we know and what we believe into this practical manual for teaching English. We hope you find it useful.

Please note that, while we have written this book together, we change our pronoun choice to 'I' through the hacks for the ease of the reader.

Haili Hughes and Stuart Pryke

FOREWORD

Teaching is complex, and the cognitive demands are substantial. Teachers are seen as masters of their subject from day 1, but teaching requires 'in the moment' decisions to be made when knowledge and understanding of the intricacies of curriculum design may be imperfect. Teachers need to learn on the job to quickly develop an understanding of the most effective approaches to teaching, and skilfully use these approaches to deliver subject matter to their students in a way that they will understand.

In recent years, schools have invested a lot of time and thought into how we can codify teaching pedagogy so that it creates consistency, clarity and a shared understanding among teachers. By establishing clear, research-informed methods for instruction, schools can ensure that teachers know and can apply effective practices that are easily replicable and adaptable, and that can contribute towards maintaining high standards across diverse classrooms and curriculums. However, despite all the research, we still grapple with views on the best pedagogy approaches, and this can make continuing professional development (CPD) somewhat confusing.

One area of professional development that does not seem to get the same limelight is subject pedagogy development. We often assume that once a teacher is qualified, they can automatically teach their subject. However, the role of subject pedagogy professional development in schools is a crucial part to support teaching and learning, as it contributes towards the unique demands of each subject in the curriculum. Effective subject-specific pedagogy enables teachers to break down complex concepts into more-accessible steps, making it easier for students to grasp challenging material.

In this book, Haili and Stuart provide a comprehensive guide on how to approach the teaching of English, considering aspects of reading, writing, and speaking and listening. From vocabulary, through literary devices and comparing texts, this book provides detailed guidance on how you might approach teaching these elements in your classroom.

The aim of this book, as with all the books in the *Teacher Hacks* series, is to provide an insight into a teacher's classroom; a look through the keyhole to see how expert practitioners approach some of the most complex and challenging elements of their subject. In this book, this is exactly what Haili and Stuart have done. Each chapter is split into a 'What', 'How', 'Why' structure to discuss common issues faced by English teachers and highlight the research and their experience to help tackle them through their hacks.

Michael Chiles

CHAPTER 1: TEACHING VOCABULARY

This chapter examines the pivotal role of vocabulary in our English classrooms, demonstrating how it can be effectively integrated across reading, writing and oracy instruction. In highlighting the importance of deliberate word selection and repeated exposure, it makes clear that vocabulary development is not acquired through isolated exercises that are segregated from the wider curriculum; word acquisition must be embedded within meaningful literacy activities. Here, I advocate for instructional approaches that not only nurture the linguistic confidence of our students but enhance their communication too. The chapter, through a set of easy-to-use hacks and strategies, stresses that vocabulary teaching must be intentional, responsive and adaptable to meet the diverse needs of our learners, enabling all of them to access complex ideas, engage critically with language and express complicated, nuanced concepts, particularly in the realm of emotional literacy. In doing so, we can avoid offering what Mary Myatt calls a 'diminished diet' (Myatt, 2021a) to our students when it comes to vocabulary. Ultimately, vocabulary instruction should not be a concern that lingers on the periphery of our awareness as teachers, but a central component of a broad curriculum that is 'unapologetically ambitious [and] unashamedly academic' (Webb, 2018).

READING

What?

'Vocabulary knowledge is fundamental to reading comprehension; one cannot understand text without knowing what most of the words mean. A wealth of research has demonstrated the strength of the relationship between vocabulary and comprehension. The proportion of difficult words in a text is the single most powerful predictor of text difficulty, and a reader's general vocabulary knowledge is the single best predictor of how well that reader can understand text.' (Nagy, 1988, p. 1)

The explicit teaching of vocabulary has experienced a remarkable surge in interest in recent years; I am thrilled by this renewed focus and take particular delight in exploring etymology and tracing how vocabulary has evolved over time. With this focus, educators have been generously equipped with a wide array of strategies for teaching vocabulary effectively in their classrooms. A few more will be offered later in this very chapter! Yet this enthusiasm also calls for caution; with so much emphasis placed on vocabulary instruction, we not only run the real risk of overwhelming students by introducing too many words at once, but also of promoting the misconception that all taught vocabulary needs to be treated as a checklist when it comes to extended writing. It is essential, therefore, to be deliberate and selective in our choices. When deciding on what words to explicitly teach, we might ask ourselves or our subject teams these questions:

- Which words will be the most useful to teach? Why?
- Which words hold relevance across multiple subjects and contexts?
- Which vocabulary will serve students both today and in the years to come?

To ground such discussions and to consider which choices to make, we need to begin by defining the concept of tiered vocabulary. The following definitions are taken from the Department of Education's *Supporting Reading in Secondary Schools: Guidance and Workbook for All Secondary Practitioners*.

- *Tier 1 words are everyday words we usually use in speech like "hot", "nice", "ordinary" and "school".*
- *Tier 2 words are more complex vocabulary found in writing or formal situations like "analyse", "evaluate", "maintain" and "tend".*
- *Tier 3 words are subject-specific vocabulary associated with a particular domain of knowledge like "algorithm", "longitude", "feudal" and "metaphor".' (Department for Education, 2025)*

So where should we start when having these discussions about vocabulary selection? Tom Needham argues that Tier 2 words are where the true value of selection lies:

> 'Like many other departments, we have tried to focus on Tier 2 words, those "that occur across a range of domains, are characteristic of written texts and occur less frequently in oral language". Teaching Tier 2 words is a high utility strategy, allowing students access to vocabulary that can be used across a text, other texts and maybe even other subjects.' (Needham, 2018a)

This is not at the expense of Tier 3 vocabulary by any means. As Mary Myatt says:

> 'The concepts and big ideas [of the curriculum] are generally Tier 3 vocabulary. They are the gateways into the individual subjects. If we want pupils to know more and remember more, it's worth spending time teaching them, talking about them, and showing them in lots of different contexts.' (Myatt, 2022a)

This is precisely why the debate over which words to teach remains so vital, and why we must continually revisit the questions posed earlier.

Alex Quigley advocates for immersing classrooms in rich vocabulary instruction, emphasising the teaching of morphology and etymology as key strategies to develop what he terms 'word consciousness', an active awareness and nurtured fascination with words and what they mean. He explains:

> 'This love of language and continual curiosity about what words mean, where they are from, and their legion of connections, feels like the end-game of great vocabulary teaching. With careful cultivation, this curiosity can be fostered and it can help fuel our pupils' school success.' (Quigley, 2021)

Yet the fundamental question remains, why? Why is it important for students to acquire vocabulary at such breadth and depth? As linguist David Crystal puts it:

> 'Education is the process of preparing us for the big world and the big world has big words. The more big words I know, the better I will survive in it. Because there are hundreds of thousands of big words in English, I cannot learn them all. But this does not mean that I shouldn't try to learn some.' (Crystal, 2007)

While Crystal's observation is expressed in a light-hearted way, he captures an important truth. There is a deeper moral imperative to consider. Data from the Reading Agency's 'The State of the Nation's Adult Reading: 2024 Report' tells us there is significant decline in the number of people who read regularly for pleasure, dropping from 58% in 2015 to 50% today. The report goes further, highlighting that among young people ages 16 to 24, a quarter are not regular readers and 44% of this group can be categorised as a 'lapsed reader', one who previously enjoyed reading regularly but has stopped entirely or drastically reduced their reading frequency (The Reading Agency, 2024).

This becomes particularly alarming when we consider the findings of Dugdale and Clark (2008), who highlight the impact of low literacy levels on someone's life. The profile of someone with low literacy levels includes: more likely to live in overcrowded housing, less likely to vote, more likely to lead solitary lives without any children, more likely to live in a non-working household (National Literacy Trust, 2011). On the other hand, regular readers in the UK reported fewer feelings of stress and depression than non-readers, along with high life-satisfaction levels, and '44% of regular readers said reading had improved their mental health and wellbeing, compared with 23% of lapsed and non-readers' (The Reading Agency, 2026).

This, then, brings to mind the importance of Mark McCourt's perspective around the design of curricula:

> 'There is a lie that continues to circulate in our system, subtle and smiling, dressed in the language of relevance and engagement. It suggests that the children who come from homes without books, without tradition, without stability, need something less demanding. That they should be shielded from the rigour of canonical texts, or complex scientific ideas, or abstract mathematics. That Shakespeare is beyond them. That Bach is meaningless to them … School is not meant to reflect back a child's existing world. It is meant to offer new worlds. It is meant to take the child by the hand and lead them to places they never knew existed, places beyond their postcode, places they have every right to belong.' (McCourt, 2025)

When viewed through the lens of vocabulary, our mission becomes crystal clear: to ensure all students have access to the very best language and literature. We must not restrict what students are allowed to read simply because they struggle. We should not teach different words for different pupils depending on their prior attainment. As Myatt cautions, we should never offer learners a 'diminished diet' (Myatt, 2021a). Reading allows students to transcend their 'existing world' (McCourt, 2025) and explore new possibilities. Yet with a generation of reluctant readers, and students who may never pick up a book at home, it is up to us as educators to open doors to the richest and most challenging texts. Vocabulary instruction is essential in this effort. We must think of thoughtful, impactful ways to help students in accessing complex language. We must ensure no student is excluded or held back, purely because a text is considered challenging and we must continually reflect on our vocabulary instruction to meet the needs of all our learners.

How?

HACK #1.1: I SAY, YOU SAY

Effective vocabulary instruction begins the moment a new word is introduced. As English teachers, we are constantly teaching new words and, unlike other domains where the focus is often placed on Tier 3 vocabulary, English requires us to navigate a large number of Tier 2 words as well. This reminds us of the need to be selective. While we aim to expose students to as many words as possible, this cannot come at the expense of other priorities.

One easy way to support vocabulary learning is the 'I say, you say' approach, which helps students rehearse the pronunciation of new terms. Science teacher Pritesh Raichura says of 'I say, you say':

> 'During an explanation, I teach lots of words that are brand new to pupils because they are highly subject-specific. For example, the words "covalent" or "ionic" or "ionic compound". When I encounter such a word during an explanation, I might say: "I say, you say: covalent!" and pause, and expect 100% of pupils in the room to chant, "covalent!" back to me.' (Raichura, 2025)

This is a strategy that can be adopted across any subject, but I think it holds particular value in English for several reasons. As Raichura highlights later in his blog, the technique is low on accountability. It doesn't take much effort for students to simply repeat a word back to their teacher, especially when a clear cue is given in order for this process to commence. While it may not be a rigorous approach in isolation, it excels at ensuring full participation from every student. Beyond that, it's an easy and effective hack to seamlessly integrate into a lesson and can help maintain or increase the pace of classroom instruction, particularly if things are going slowly (Raichura, 2025).

'I say, you say' is useful for whole-class repetition, but also can work on an individual basis. A student may stumble over pronunciation when reading something out loud to the class, for example, and so the strategy can be used to model to them in a low threat way. It serves too as an effective way to add extra emphasis to words you want students to remember.

While a strategy like this may not be new to English teachers, it is a valuable reminder of the power of repetition. Students need multiple exposures to new words and repeated practice is essential if they are to internalise the vocabulary in question. When I first introduced 'I say, you say' in my classroom, my students took a while to warm up to it, perhaps because it was a strategy they associated more with modern foreign languages than English. Now, they readily participate and are prepared to repeat my selected words whenever prompted.

Beyond pronunciation, the 'I say, you say' approach is also an easy and effective way to recapture students' attention when their minds begin to wander. Let's bring their focus back with vocabulary!

HACK #1.2: READ, RE-READ AND READ AGAIN

One hack that has significantly enhanced the accessibility of texts in my vocabulary teaching is the idea of 'Read, re-read and read again'. Drawing inspiration from Alice Vissar-Furay's research on academic reading, the hack places particular emphasis on the idea of pre-reading. While it's impossible to explicitly teach every word in a text that students might struggle with, we can still approach challenging vocabulary holistically, considering its role within a broader passage that students will be reading. After all, we have to be sure that students understand what they are reading.

The strategy itself embodies the mantra of 'teach fewer things in greater depth', diving deep into the content to ensure pupils secure the knowledge they need. With that in mind, let's consider how it works.

Imagine presenting students with a passage of text known to contain vocabulary that will very likely act as a barrier to their understanding of what is happening. This might be fiction or non-fiction, such as an academic article. For the purpose of this explanation, let's consider an extract from Charles Dickens' *A Christmas Carol*, an appropriate example due to the potential challenge provided by unfamiliar 19th-century language. Consider the following passage from stave 2, where Scrooge is taken to witness his younger self as an apprentice at Fezziwig's workshop.

> "Why, it's old Fezziwig! Bless his heart; it's Fezziwig alive again!"
>
> Old Fezziwig laid down his pen, and looked up at the clock, which pointed to the hour of seven. He rubbed his hands; adjusted his **capacious** waistcoat; laughed all over himself, from his shows to his organ of **benevolence**; and called out in a comfortable, oily, rich, fat, **jovial** voice:
>
> "Yo ho, there! Ebenezer! Dick!"
>
> Scrooge's former self, now grown a young man, came **briskly** in, accompanied by his fellow-**prentice**.
>
> "Dick Wilkins, to be sure," said Scrooge to the Ghost. "Bless me, yes. There he is. He was very much attached to me, was Dick. Poor Dick. Dear, dear."

CHAPTER 1: TEACHING VOCABULARY

"Yo ho, my boys!" said Fezziwig. "No more work to-night. Christmas Eve, Dick. Christmas, Ebenezer. Let's have the shutters up," cried old Fezziwig, with a sharp clap of his hands, "before a man can say Jack Robinson."

You wouldn't believe how those two fellows went at it. They charged into the street with the shutters -- one, two, three -- had them up in their places -- four, five, six -- barred them and pinned then -- seven, eight, nine -- and came back before you could have got to twelve, panting like race-horses.

The length of the extract provided may vary depending on the focus and purpose of the lesson but, as teachers, it's important to anticipate the elements students are likely to find difficult. To support understanding, we should identify words that we believe will benefit from explicit, deliberate attention before reading begins.

With this in mind, and before presenting the passage itself, I introduce students to a vocabulary grid containing the selected words alongside student-friendly definitions. The accessibility of these definitions is extremely important. They must be written to open the door to the text, not to create another barrier, for if they are overly complex or abstract we risk alienating students further from the very material we want them to access. From the *Carol* extract, we might draw out the following words.

Word	Definition
capacious	Having plenty of space inside; very large or roomy.
benevolence	A kind and caring attitude toward others.
jovial	Cheerful and full of good humour.
briskly	Quickly and with energy.
-prentice	A shortened form of 'apprentice,' meaning someone learning a trade or skill from a master.

Figure 1.1 Words and definitions

Once students have been introduced to the selected vocabulary and their definitions, you can follow-up with a range of activities, depending on the needs of the class and your context. These aim to help reinforce and consolidate understanding, promoting retention and preparing students for the deeper engagement with the text that is about to follow.

1. **Pronunciation with 'I say, you say':** Go through each word using the 'I say, you say' technique. Model the correct pronunciation, then have students repeat it back. A student cannot truly understand or use a word confidently if they are unsure how to say it.

2. **Visual representation:** Ask students to draw a simple image or icon to represent each word. One can easily assess their understanding of the terms based on their justifications of what they have drawn.

3. **Context-free sentence construction:** Have students use a selection of the words in sentences unrelated to the current text. In this case, sentences would have nothing to do with *A Christmas Carol*. This helps reinforce word meaning and encourages students to consider how words can be applied in different contexts. For this activity, you might want to pick two or three words for students, especially if the text itself contains archaic language that is not appropriate to put into sentences now.

4. **Inference and prediction:** Ask students to predict what they think the extract might be about, based solely on the vocabulary grid. Encourage them to verbalise their reasoning, make inferences and justify their predictions using the vocabulary as evidence.

5. **Interleaving and retrieval practice:** Use the vocabulary to create links with prior learning. Are there any words that connect to earlier topics, texts or themes? For example, students studying *A Christmas Carol* at GCSE might recognise that the word 'benevolence' (in this example) connects to *An Inspector Calls*. They may identify that the Birling family lacks benevolence at the start of that play, whereas the younger generation begin to learn its value, highlighting an emerging dichotomy when it comes to the moral path each character treads. This activity, then, turns vocabulary into a tool for revision and cross-textual thinking.

Regardless of which activities you choose, the core aim remains the same: students must actively engage with the vocabulary, whether that's discussing it, debating it or transforming it. Students may not flawlessly understand at this point, but *doing something* with these words is important. Inferences and predictions may be correct at this stage, but that's okay. Clarification will come in time. What matters at this stage is the interaction with the language.

With these foundations in place, the reading can begin. As you read through the text for students, pay close attention to the vocabulary that has been pre-taught. Be prepared to pause when these words appear. This is where the 'Read, reread and read again' strategy really comes into its own. The process may look something like this.

> **Teacher:** [Reading the text] 'Old Fezziwig laid down his pen, and looked up at the clock, which pointed to the hour of seven. He rubbed his hands; adjusted his **capacious** waistcoat ...' There's that word 'capacious' that we discussed previously. Who can remind me of what 'capacious' means again?

Student 1: Large? Having plenty of space.

Teacher: In full sentences please.

Student 1: If something is 'capacious', it means having plenty of space inside. It is very large or roomy.

Teacher: Good work. So let's read that again, but this time we'll replace the word with the definition. 'Old Fezziwig laid down his pen, and looked up at the clock, which pointed to the hour of seven. He rubbed his hands; adjusted his large and roomy waistcoat ...' What do you think Dickens is saying about the character of Fezziwig here? Student 2?

Student 2: He's physically big? So he needs bigger clothes?

Teacher: What else? What about his personality?

Student 2: He has a big personality. His physical size mirrors his big personality? Just like Scrooge's harsh physical description mirrors his personality.

Student 3: Could it also show that he's eating well compared to the poor in London? It shows he's getting enough to eat or has the money to purchase the resources he needs to live?

Teacher: Excellent. We'll discuss those ideas in greater detail in a bit. So... 'Old Fezziwig laid down his pen, and looked up at the clock, which pointed to the hour of seven. He rubbed his hands; adjusted his capacious waistcoat ...'

When we foreground vocabulary in this way, we enable ourselves to model for students what it means to be intellectually curious about language. While it will not be practical to do this for every passage we encounter, intentionally slowing down and spending more time on a carefully selected section of text can be incredibly powerful.

Through this approach, we complete the strategy of 'Read, re-read and read again'. We start by reading the original text, then re-reading with key words substituted for their student-friendly definitions, and finally read again, this time reverting back to the text as originally written, alongside a brief discussion of the word's effect or connotation, or inferences around why the writer has chosen that particular word at that moment.

A common and understandable critique of this sequence is that it disrupts the flow of the reading experience. Pausing frequently (especially during a good bit!) can feel frustrating, but the solution isn't to abandon the approach, but to apply it judiciously. Be selective with the passages you choose, or maybe think about reading the extract through in its entirety once before returning to the text to revisit the vocabulary in more detail, allowing for both analysis and immersion in the story.

This kind of structured repetition is valuable and 'really helps when a lack of understanding, or misunderstanding, of the vocabulary has the opportunity to hamper comprehension ... a lesson spent reading is not a lesson wasted' (Pryke and Staniforth, 2022, p.58).

HACK #1.3: CHORAL RESPONSE

Once definitions have been established, whether through explicit instruction or more holistic approaches like 'Read, re-read and read again', it can be valuable to engage students in active retrieval of vocabulary in order to strengthen understanding and retention. For example, one could ask students to write words on mini whiteboards in response to vocalised teacher definitions, encouraging 100% class participation. However, in moments where maintaining the pace of the lesson is important, a choral response may be more useful. This is another technique used by Raichura, who says:

> 'Choral response is about posing a question to the class which has a short answer, pausing and then saying: "On 3...1, 2, 3!" And the class will chant the answer in unison after "3". For example: "Plants make a sugar called glucose during photosynthesis. What sugar do plants make during photosynthesis? On 3 [Pause] 1,2,3!" The class shouts out 'Glucose' in unison.' (Raichura, 2025)

I've chosen to include this technique in a chapter on vocabulary because, as an English teacher, I've found it particularly effective for consolidating word knowledge. As Raichura rightly notes, the key to choral response is that answers must be short and precise because you are expecting and wanting students to say the same word or phrase. It would not be suitable for questions requiring extended or interpretive responses, as distinct answers would be an impossibility. However, for vocabulary retrieval, it is ideal. If I were to ask, 'Which word means a kind and caring attitude towards others? 3...2...1...' and held my hand to my ear to signal for a collective answer, the whole class would respond, in unison, 'benevolence'.

Unlike 'I say, you say', this technique places more of a cognitive demand on students because they are not simply echoing the teacher but recalling and producing vocabulary independently, even though they are saying it all together as a group. As such, 100% participation may not be achieved. Students may falter or hesitate, but these moments give you immediate data, for they signal the need for reteaching or revision of particular terms.

As a side note, this strategy also works particularly well for checking student knowledge of characters and key literary terms. It is essential, however, to establish clear expectations around accountability. Students need to understand that a response is always expected, otherwise it is likely the strategy will not work. They can murmur with uncertainty, yes, but not responding is not an option.

HACK #1.4: FRAYER MODEL

No chapter on vocabulary instruction would be complete without mention of the Frayer Model. It remains one of the most effective tools for helping students build a solid and nuanced understanding of words. By asking learners to explore a word's definition, characteristics, examples and non-examples, the model supports deep and lasting knowledge of vocabulary. What makes it particularly useful is its adaptability, something I think is needed in a subject like English. It can be changed to suit a range of tasks and texts.

Figure 1.2 shows the traditional Frayer Model, originally developed by Dorothy Frayer.

Definition:	Characteristics:
Examples:	Non-characteristics:

Frayer Model

Figure 1.2 Traditional Frayer Model

The word to be taught is placed in the middle of the model. I will always have the definition pre-prepared in the first box. I ask students to copy this model into their books before filling it out together as a class:

> 'Initial instruction about the Frayer Model is heavily teacher-directed and requires teacher modelling. Teachers should demonstrate how to complete the graphic organiser by talking through what they are doing and how they are coming up with the information they enter into the different sections.' (Center, 2026)

The characteristics of a word refer to its key features, traits or qualities. Encourage students to consider what actually makes the concept what it is. Figure 1.3 show a completed example of a Frayer Model which I use when teaching William Wordsworth's *The Prelude*. I want students to understand the significance of the speaker re-evaluating their thoughts on nature, and so I teach the term 'introspection' to help them see this.

Definition:	Characteristics:
• Self-examination or reflection on one's thoughts and actions.	• Can lead to personal growth or insight. • Deep thinking. • Reflection on personal thoughts and feelings. • Often leads to greater self-awareness.
Introspection	
Examples:	Non-characteristics:
• A person reflecting on their actions after making a mistake. • Reflecting on your motivations before making a decision. • A therapist guiding a client to explore their feelings. • Journaling to understand your emotions. • Taking time alone to think about personal goals.	• Impulsive decision-making. • Ignoring one's feelings. • Distraction or lack of reflection. • Avoiding self-awareness.

Figure 1.3 Frayer Model for the word 'introspection'

Alex Quigley argues that Frayer Models can even be adapted for more suitability with literature teaching (Quigley, 2018). His suggested adjustments look like the completed example in Figure 1.4.

Definition:	Connotations:
• The state or situation of being alone.	• Quiet, calm, peaceful, reflective, sometimes lonely or mysterious.
Solitude	
Examples:	Linked ideas and themes:
• The speaker's time alone on the mountain lake, feeling awe and fear. • The silence of nature around him. • Moments where solitude leads to imagination and self-discovery	• Nature's power, personal growth, imagination, memory, self-reflection, the sublime (awe mixed with fear), the journey of growing up.

Figure 1.4 Adapted Frayer Model for the word 'solitude'

This example explores connotations of the word which could then be used as a guide for literary analysis in an extended written response. This version also allows students to connect the term explicitly to the text they are studying, an example of how flexible the model can be.

It's important to draw attention to how this model can be adapted; we can sometimes be reluctant to modify established strategies to better suit our classes. While it is crucial to avoid the 'lethal mutation' of an idea, that is making changes that end up undermining the impact of an established method, thoughtful adaptations that result in stronger student understanding should be encouraged. Making adjustments like those seen in the previous example are especially useful for the scaffolding of essay writing. They enable students to plan focused, close analysis with greater confidence. As Quigley says:

> 'Does the "Frayer Model" alone transform understanding of words? Well, no – not really. Still, I found it a quick and handy strategy to explicitly closely analyse important vocabulary choices in English.' (Quigley, 2018)

Something else which is important to note here is that:

> 'The Frayer Model is not intended to be used as a worksheet for homework, something that would be no more effective than asking students to simply look up the definitions for a list of assigned words. Discussion is an important element of this practice. By filling out the Frayer Model with their classes, teachers help students ... contextuali[se] terms, actively processing information, and experiencing multiple exposures to terms.' (Center, 2026)

Eventually, as students master the elements of filling out the Frayer Model, begin to strip away the teacher support.

HACK #1.5: VOCABULARY × THINKING HARD

An effective follow-up to a Frayer Model is the use of vocabulary activities aligned with the 'thinking hard' strategies. Unlike the Frayer Model, which is more teacher led, 'thinking hard' sheets can be completed by students independently and then used as the basis for discussion later. Originally developed by Simon Hardwick and Martin Jones, these strategies promote deeper cognitive engagement with the word in question.

An example resource employing these techniques is shown in Figure 1.5.

TEACHER HACKS ENGLISH

VOCABULARY CHECK

Revise the key vocabulary by completing the tasks.

altruistic (adjective) *Being kind and caring by helping others, even if it doesn't help you.*

TASK ONE: READ IT	TASK TWO: TRANSFORM IT
Read about the etymology of 'altruistic'. Highlight key information.	Transform the adjective 'altruistic' into an image to help you remember it.
1853, 'unselfishness, devotion to the welfare of others, the opposite of egoism,' from French altruisme, coined or popularised 1830 by French philosopher Auguste Comte, with -ism + autrui (Old French altrui) 'of or to others,' from Latin alteri	

TASK THREE: DEBATE IT	
'True altruism does not exist because all actions have selfish motives.' To what extent do you agree?	

TASK FOUR: USE IT	TASK FIVE: LINK IT
Can you use the following words in a sentence? altruism, altruistic	Explain how the word 'altruism' links to *To Kill a Mockingbird*.

Figure 1.5 Thinking Hard vocabulary sheet example resource

These resources follow common structures.

1. **Read it:** Students read the definition and etymology of the word being studied. Students highlight key information that helps increase their understanding of the word.
2. **Transform it:** Students transform the word into a small image to help them remember it. This helps them put the definition into practice and is a surprisingly useful tool in helping us see if they have understood the word, especially when they have to justify why they have drawn what they have.
3. **Debate it:** Students are given a statement that they have to agree, partially agree or disagree with. The statement uses the word in question to help students engage with the vocabulary and form an opinion around it. This is also a great way of modelling how the word might be used.
4. **Use it:** Students apply the word, and its various forms, in a series of sentences that are removed from the original context in which the word has been introduced. For example, if the word is being explored because of its use in *Checking Out Me History*, the sentence itself doesn't need to reference the poem. This helps students understand other ways in which it could be applied. To support this, teachers can model the process by sharing their own examples and non-examples.
5. **Link it:** Students are required to link the word to the text they are studying so they can rehearse with it before they use it in a more formal setting.

The 'Debate it' task, in particular, is a great way of sparking classroom discussion and debate. We want to create language-rich classrooms where students aren't using new vocabulary only in their writing but in their speech too.

HACK #1.6: EXAMPLES AND NON-EXAMPLES

Examples and non-examples can be covered in the Frayer Model, but other exercises can also be completed by students to ensure this area of vocabulary instruction is covered. This example from *Bringing Vocabulary to Life* focuses on two target words which presents challenge in a different way:

> '[This activity] asks students to choose which of two target words represents a situation that is described. This is somewhat more challenging as it asks students to bring to mind meanings of two target word and decide which fits.' (Beck et al., 2013, p. 186).

For example, you might ask your class the following questions. The words in italics are ones that have been explicitly taught, possibly through using other teacher hacks described previously.

1. 'If you just won the lottery, would you be *jubilant* or *melancholy*? Why?' (Beck et al., 2013, p. 186) These words, hypothetically, may have been introduced as Tier 2 vocabulary in context of *A Christmas Carol*, yet here they are purposefully out of context. We need to show students how words are transferable, that they can operate in a range of settings beyond the text in which they are first encountered. If we only ever present vocabulary in the context of the text, we risk limiting a student's understanding, leading to the sort of linguistic narrowness we do not want or need to foster, and making it harder for them to apply the words flexibly elsewhere. In fact, addressing misconceptions about use of vocabulary later on can be far more challenging to tackle than encouraging that versatility from the start. Another useful example might be:
2. 'If you were in need of help and support, would you want someone to show you *benevolence* or *malice*?' These questions can form really quick retrieval tasks and often work as a good instigator for discussion, as the justification of student ideas is the most important part.

HACK #1.7: MORPHOLOGY AND ETYMOLOGY

This is a significant area of vocabulary instruction, which cannot simply be dropped into a 'one-off' lesson. Morphology instruction requires repetition, consistency and deliberate and careful integration into schemes of work across all year groups. Of all the approaches to vocabulary, this has always been the area where I personally have felt the least confident, most likely because I never remember looking at words through a morphological lens when I was at school. My degree is in literature, which means I've passed through my education with only a peripheral awareness of what morphology entails, and I bet I'm not the only teacher who feels that way. As I've built my understanding of morphology, however, I've come to appreciate just how vital it is, and also how fun it can be! It's also through this method that I've realised just how much students *enjoy* words. Words can make students genuinely curious; they are keen to learn new words, to show off knowledge of words they already know and to think about how words evolve and connect. Morphology and etymology absolutely deserve a central place in our classrooms. To begin, it's important we distinguish between the two:

1. **Etymology** is the study or the origin and development of words. Etymology looks at where a word comes from and how its form and meaning have changed over time and the languages it has passed through.
2. **Morphology** is the study of the structure of words, specifically how smaller units of meaning combine to form words.

CHAPTER 1: TEACHING VOCABULARY

Let's consider the basics of morphological terminology first as this is always the best 'way in'.

Type	What it means	Example
Root/Base	The main meaning; the core of the word. Can be combined with prefixes and suffixes to form new words.	*walk* in *walked*
Affix	A prefix or suffix added to the beginning or end of a word or word part that forms new words and can change meaning, part of speech, and usage	*dis-* in *disappear* or *-ed* in *worked*
Prefix	An affix that comes before the root	*un-* in *unkind*
Suffix	An affix that comes after the root	*-ing* in *running*
Free root	The main part of a word that can stand on its own and be combined with prefixes or suffixes to form new words (examples: *form, port, tract, script*)	*book, run, kind*
Bound root	The main part of a word that must be combined or 'bound' with affixes to form new words	*rupt, spect, struct, flect*

Figure 1.6 Morphological terminology

So why is the act of fostering morphological awareness with our students so vital? Alex Quigley says:

> 'We know that around 60% of our English lexicon is drawn from a combination of Latin and Greek origins, with the more technical vocabulary of school reaching even higher, to something like 90%. When children learn the story and the deeper meaning of a word, it can prove memorable and revelatory. Given the consistent origins of our academic vocabulary, we cannot miss out on the power of teaching with morphology in mind.' (Quigley, 2024a)

Marcia K. Henry offers a further understanding of why morphemes matter, saying:

> 'Since morphemes are the smallest units of meaning in words, and meaning (comprehension) is the goal of reading, morphemes are of prime importance. Most English words are polysyllabic and often contain prefixes and suffixes to extend and expand the meaning of the base element (often called the root ...). These morphemes provide students with numerous strategies for decoding (reading) and encoding (spelling) as well as enhancing vocabulary (Henry, 1988, 1993, 2010a). As children learn the common prefixes, suffixes, and Latin

and Greek bases, they gain new understanding of these meaning-based building blocks in English words.' (Henry, 2019)

If you're completely new to teaching morphology or still building your confidence with it, here are a few simple steps that worked well for me. As always, feel free to adapt these to suit your own context and learners.

1. **Start with common prefixes and suffixes**: Teach students a core set of affixes along with their meanings. These can easily be found online.
2. **Introduce root words**: Provide students with a list of base words and model how adding suffixes like *-ed*, *-s* or *-ing* can change the form and function of a word. These are gentle starting points because they're inflectional suffixes, suffixes that adjust tense, number or degree without completely changing the word's core meaning or part of speech.
3. **Use colour coding**: This can help students visually distinguish between the root, prefix and suffix.
4. **Sort and classify**: Give students a mixed list of words and ask them to identify which contain prefixes, suffixes, or both.
5. **Break it down**: Choose one longer, unfamiliar word and work with the class to dissect it into its root, prefix and suffix. This is an excellent opportunity to model your thinking aloud as to how to complete this process and deepen word awareness.

These are just the basics, but as a teacher hack, they are a strong starting point, especially if you're feeling less confident in this area. Morphology isn't something that can be 'ticked off' in a single lesson. Students, instead, will benefit from frequent bite-sized exposures. In my experience, it sticks best over time, with repeated opportunities for practice and application.

Let's have a look at what this might look like in practice. As you read, consider how this could be adapted to suit your own context and a word of your choosing.

1. In a lesson titled 'What is subversion?', part of a scheme on *1984*, but supported by supplementary texts (in this case an edited version of the opening of *The Handmaid's Tale*), I wanted to explicitly teach the word 'subversion' through its morphological structure. Given the meaning of the word, I decided to focus particular attention on the prefix 'sub-'. To introduce it, I gave students both the word and its definition (this could have also been framed within the context of a Frayer Model).

CHAPTER 1: TEACHING VOCABULARY

---

subversion
the undermining of the power and authority of an established system or institution lessening the power or effectiveness of a large, important and powerful organisation.

sub-
from the Latin, 'under'.

What other words begin with 'sub-'?

submarine	subconscious	subscription
a warship designed to operate under the sea	mental activity that takes place even though you are unaware of it	an amount of money that you pay regularly to receive a product or service

Figure 1.7 Subversion vocabulary check

2. As you can see, I underlined the prefix to segregate it from the rest of the word.
3. The next part is a simple but effective activity that I really like; it allows students to show off their word knowledge. I asked students to generate as many words as they could that related to the target word by sharing the same morphological feature, in this case, words that began with the prefix 'sub-'. Not only does this build morphological awareness but also strengthens student ability to make connections between words.

subjugate	submit	suburb	subsidiary
bring under domination or control, especially by conquest	accept or yield to a powerful force or to the authority of another person	an outlying district of a city	less important than but related to something
subatomic	**substitute**	**subway**	**subsequent**
smaller than or occurring within an atom	use or add in place of	a tunnel under a road for use by pedestrians	coming after something in time
subordinate	**subjects**	**subliminal**	**substandard**
lower in rank or position	(a person or country) under one's control	existing or functioning below the threshold of consciousness	below expectations

Where does the idea of subversion appear in *1984*?

Figure 1.8 Subversion vocabulary check: words with 'sub-' prefix

19

4. We then explored the prefix 'sub-' and how it influences the meaning of each word, drawing out the shared meaning of 'under', 'beneath' or 'below'. From this, we can begin to see why teaching vocabulary through morphology can be so powerful. A strategy like this will go some way in helping students consider and decode unfamiliar words in different contexts when they're reading independently. If a student comes across a word with the prefix 'sub-', it's likely they will be able to decode it through the prefix and by reading around the word, increasing their understanding of the text as a result.

5. With this understanding, I linked the discussion back to the focus of the lesson by asking 'Where does the idea of subversion appear in *1984*?' so students could consider the word with a familiar, foundational knowledge of a text. Students focused on Winston's quiet rebellion, his decision to open his diary, as a clear act of subversion against the ominous threat of Big Brother's surveillance.

6. To deepen this thinking, I then introduced our additional text, an edited extract from *The Handmaid's Tale*. Rather than diving in immediately, I first presented various editions of the novel's cover and asked students to predict how this text might connect to our key concept of subversion – another way of generating conversation around their morphological understanding of the word. Some questions prompts I used alongside the cover variations were:
   - What can we tell about the world of *The Handmaid's Tale* based on these covers?
   - What do the covers have in common? Why might this be?
   - What can we tell about the characters?
   - How might we link these covers to the idea of subversion?

7. After our initial discussion around our inferences, we read the opening, where we witness subversion in action. Characters surreptitiously reach for human connection, mouthing their names between their beds and lip reading in defiance of an enforced silence.

This is just one example of how one might begin to introduce the concept of morphology in the classroom. In my experience, starting small (focusing on one prefix, for example) and linking it to rich and authentic classroom texts, can make a real difference. Over time, as confidence grows, so too will opportunities for deeper, more meaningful morphological instruction.

Marn Frank, in *Morpheme Matrices*, suggests a matrix can be a really tool to help students increase their morphological awareness (Frank, 2018). Figure 1.9 shows an example.

CHAPTER 1: TEACHING VOCABULARY

Figure 1.9 Example morpheme matrix

As you can see, the root is placed in the middle box. On the left-hand side, we have common prefixes one might 'attach' to the root. These are used to form new words or change the meaning or part of speech. On the right-hand side, we have the most common inflectional suffixes that are shown in the top box. These change the number of a noun or the tense of a verb without altering the core meaning of the word itself. In the bottom-right box, we have common derivational suffixes. These are used to form new words and may change the meaning of the word or the word class itself.

Morpheme matrices can be used in this manner:

1. Present students with a matrix like this one. Ask them to create as many words from the matrix as they can.
2. Discuss how affixes can change the meaning of the word by modelling different prefix and suffix choices. Use this opportunity to talk about what the different affixes mean.
3. Ask students to use some of these words in sentences of their own.
4. Link to the topic of the lesson.

For further examples of matrices, I would strongly recommend looking at *Morpheme Matrices*.

From here, you could explore the etymology of a word, discussing origins and development of vocabulary over time. *Etymonline* (www.etymonline.com) is an excellent resource for this.

WRITING

What?

Vocabulary is fundamental to students' development, not only as readers but also as writers. When students build their 'word consciousness', they are better equipped to understand texts and, as a result, to consider how they can use these words effectively in their own writing. Stahl and Nagy define word consciousness as 'the knowledge and dispositions necessary for students to learn, appreciate, and effectively use words' (Scott and Nagy, 2009, cited in Quigley, 2024b). It enables students to develop a feel for how written language works while also cultivating an awareness of other elements like syntax.

Vocabulary allows students to express their thoughts with sophistication, whether they are writing creatively or analytically. In English, we teach vocabulary not only to expand students' knowledge of words but also to enable them to communicate complex ideas, evoke emotion and construct meaning with purpose. When taught through the lens of writing, vocabulary supports students in making deliberate and impactful language choices. A repertoire of vocabulary means students can vary tone and register and can develop a voice of their own. Without it, students will struggle to translate their thoughts into writing, often reverting to vague, repetitive or cliched expressions that fail to convey their intended meaning. In academic contexts, vocabulary is essential for precision in thinking and writing. It helps students to articulate ideas and interpretations and construct arguments that mirror the complexities of the texts being studied.

Teaching vocabulary for writing is not a separate task from teaching writing itself. It is embedded within it, shaping choices students make. It is more than handing out a list of words. It is about helping students develop the ability to make intentional choices about the words that best convey their message. There are countless strategies one could explore when discussing vocabulary instruction, enough to fill an entire book. In this section I have included those I believe are most effective and beneficial for students.

How?

HACK #1.8: TEACHING EMOTIONAL LITERACY

One thing I've found students really struggle with is the idea of emotional literacy. Anecdotally, in the settings in which I've worked, students rarely have the vocabulary to be able to express their emotions and feelings in the ways we would want them to, and probably the ways in which they would want to. 'Emotional literacy has a simple definition that belies its difficulty to acquire: the ability to understand why you feel what you feel and adapt yourself accordingly; the ability to be attuned and responsive to the feelings of others.' (Evans, 2023)

Students' lack of knowledge around emotional literacy seems particularly pronounced in our post-Covid world, though I doubt experiencing the pandemic is the sole cause. Still, it's hard to ignore the impact of sending students home during lockdown, away from the structure and stimulation of the school environment, and away from important social interactions that help shape cognitive and emotional development, even all of these years later.

In the absence of these experiences, students turned to social media to stay connected, becoming increasingly accustomed to a constant stream of rapidly changing content, a new stimulus every thirty seconds. This shift in how young people engage with the world has surely compromised the ability to pause, reflect and consider their own thoughts and feelings, feeding on a diet of influencers from TikTok instead.

The consequences of this are becoming increasingly clear; many students lack emotional literacy, and this has significant implications for both reading and writing. It seems harder for them to empathise with characters in literature, making it challenging for them to grasp motivations and relationships and emotional subtleties. If they cannot recognise and understand these emotions in themselves, how can we expect them to identify them in others, whether those others are fictional or real?

The impact of an emotional literacy deficit on writing is equally concerning. When students struggle to articulate their own perspectives, it limits the authenticity and depth of their written expression. Addressing this issue isn't just about improving performance in English, it's also about helping students better understand themselves.

Some may argue this falls within the remit of PSHE instead of English, but I would disagree. To see ourselves reflected in literature, to connect with characters on a deeply human and emotional level, is a profound and joyous experience, enhancing not only how students approach our subject, but how they make sense of the world and their place within it. To be teachers of emotional literacy is a role we should fully embrace.

To help with this, resources such as an emotion wheel can be really useful when introducing the concept of emotional literacy to students.

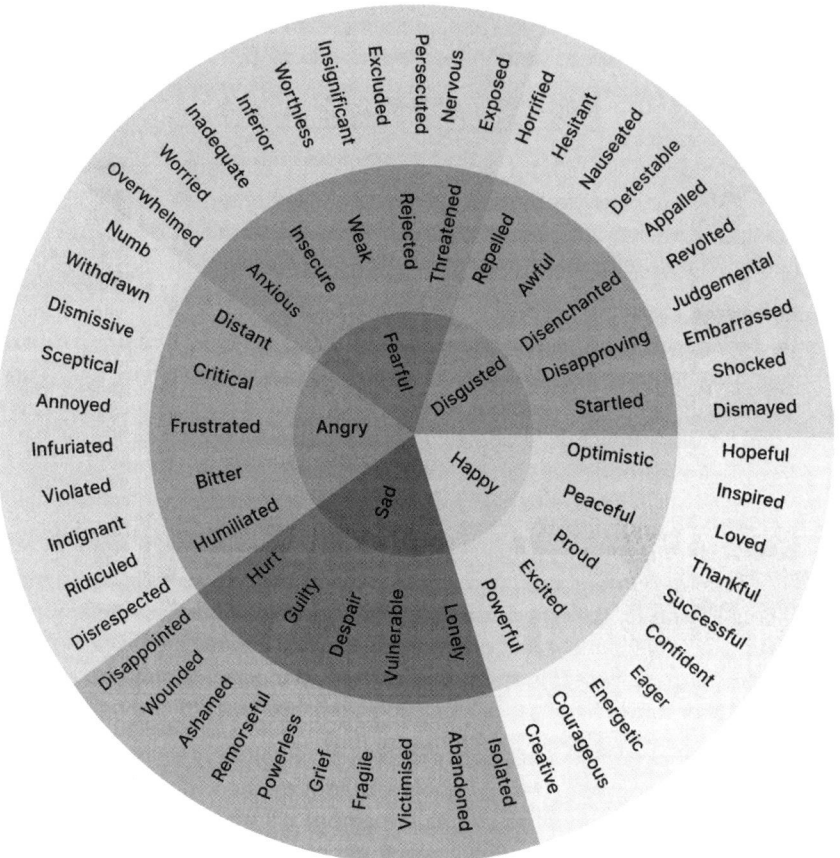

Figure 1.10 Emotion wheel

These types of resource are often criticised when used, but I really think their impact depends on the way in which they are approached. I would never advocate for treating the wheel like a thesaurus. For example, if I asked 'What's another word for anger?', students may just pick another random term from the outer ring like 'exasperated' or 'resentful', but this surface-level swapping does nothing to foster an understanding of real emotional literacy because it completely overlooks the nuance of each emotion.

Instead, this is how I use a resource like this effectively.

1. Introduce the wheel thoughtfully.

I begin by displaying the wheel and explaining its structure, starting with core emotions in the centre and gradually expanding outward to more specific and nuanced feelings. I explain why this emotional precision is important, not just when analysing characters in literature, but also in real life. The ability to identify and articulate emotions in this specific way helps emotional self-awareness *and* writing.

At this point, I might ask students to choose an emotion from the outer ring that describes their current mood and to complete the following sentence.

I feel _____ because _____.

The aim is to begin building emotional vocabulary and help students think more deeply about their own experiences.

2. Apply it to literary analysis.

Next, I'll apply the wheel to a moment from the text we are studying. Let's take an example from *A Midsummer Night's Dream*. I'll ask students to read the opening scene and select a character, in this case, Egeus. We'll begin by identifying a core emotion from the middle and justify our choices. From this, I make known to students that I want a more specific emotion born out of 'anger'. We are tracking from the general to the specific, with students explaining their choices every step of the way. When Egeus is furious that Hermia refuses to marry Demetrius, we might map his emotions like this:

anger → *exasperated* → *frustrated* or *hostile* or *resentful*

This can stimulate debate, but that's not a bad thing. Debate allows us to consider each word in turn and think about the differences between the emotions, which is exactly what we want to do.

3. Justify the choices with textual evidence.

At this stage, I want students to justify their choices of emotion with textual evidence, so they can support their selection. Questions like these may help students in generating thoughtful responses.

- How are your word choices similar to each other?
- How are they different?
- At what point does 'anger' become 'hostility'?
- Does this character experience all three emotions in the text, or just one?
- Can you think of other characters from different texts, games or films who have experienced these emotions? How do you know it was that specific emotion? What happened? How did they act?

4. Use the Frayer Model.

Next, I might ask students to consider which word best fits the character at that moment (in this case, Egeus) and create a Frayer Model (see Hack #1.4) focused on that word. While these models are often used to understand definitions, here the goal is to deepen students' appreciation of the nuance and difference between the related emotions.

5. Connect emotion to students' own lives.

Finally, it may be appropriate to link this back to students' own lives, asking if they have ever experienced a particular type of emotion. This would have to be a controlled and monitored conversation of course, and may not be suitable for all contexts, but is a valuable opportunity to build emotional awareness and empathy while also connected more with the material being studied.

HACK #1.9: VOCABULARY ACQUISITION FROM PRE-EXISTING TEXTS

A big challenge I encounter often when teaching creative writing is students feeling they lack the necessary vocabulary needed to succeed. I find this an interesting perception, particularly because we don't know what we don't know. Yet something about creative writing triggers student awareness that there are 'other words' that they feel they should know but don't. While emotional literacy and related vocabulary are important, building a broader range of descriptive and expressive words is equally vital.

The good news is that students often know more words than they realise. One effective strategy I've found is to encourage students to draw three or four words from a text they have already studied to apply appropriately to their own work. I limit them to only three or four, as this is definitely a hack that needs to be approached with caution. Sometimes students will attempt to copy entire phrases, which is not the goal; we need them to borrow vocabulary thoughtfully, not plagiarise. If students can incorporate select words from memorable quotations, however, why shouldn't we think about how this might work in a piece of creative writing? Why restrict vocabulary to only the original context where students first encountered it?

To illustrate this idea, let's consider an example from a GCSE student's work.

> The sky tore open with a crack like splintering glass as the storm rolled in. All day, the air had felt heavy and still, the **heat oppressed** every movement, making it hard to breathe. Now, at last, the tension snapped. Rain lashed the ground in sheets, each drop **biting** against skin like tiny stones.

Tom stood frozen in the lane, **stunned** by the sudden violence. Wind howled around him, snatching at his coat and flinging grit into his eyes. A fork of lightning lit the rooftops, revealing shadows twisted like broken limbs. Thunder crashed overhead, deep and raw, like the roar of some unseen beast.

Somewhere in the distance, a dog barked with a sharp, panicked sound, like it knew the storm would not pass gently. In that moment, the world felt carved open, exposed like meat on a **butcher**'s table.

There are clear areas for improvement here, but as you can see, the words in bold have been deliberately chosen from other texts on the GCSE syllabus to be used in new, different contexts. Phrases like 'heat oppressed' and 'butcher' come from *Macbeth*, 'biting' from *A Christmas Carol*, and 'stunned' from Simon Armitage's poem *Remains*. The student has effectively used these words as a springboard for ideas and to help them shape their writing. What I like particularly about this method is that it promotes the idea that sometimes the best words to use are not always the longest. In this sense, the hack serves to alleviate some of the pressure students might be feeling to use 'big words'. Students need to show they can use increasingly impactful vocabulary, yes, but repetitive use of longer vocabulary will equally disrupt the fluency of what a student is trying to say.

As a planning exercise, I sometimes display an image as a writing stimulus and ask students to recall words or phrases from the texts we've studied that might help them describe the scene. Not only does this serve as useful retrieval practice for literary quotations, it also encourages students to think selectively about which words they will include and why. The discussion around word choice can be rich and it can also act as a sense check to ensure students won't include whole sentences or passages.

This approach requires careful modelling to ensure students use the borrowed vocabulary accurately and meaningfully and don't go over the top with it. However, as a tool for sparking ideas it can be highly effective.

🔒 HACK #1.10: VOCABULARY SPECTRUM

A strong follow-up hack to the consideration of emotional literacy is the idea of a vocabulary spectrum (Beck *et al.* 2013, p.191). This helps students ensure they're using the right word at the right time in the right context. Providing students with vocabulary spectrums is a great way of helping to teach them that words have power, while also allowing them to consider the differences behind these words.

A vocabulary spectrum may look something like these examples.

1. Happiness

content ────────────────────────────────── ecstatic
(possible route students could follow: *pleased* → *happy* → *joyful* → *thrilled*)

2. Scared

nervous ────────────────────────────────── terrified
(possible route students could follow: *anxious* → *uneasy* → *afraid* → *panicked*)

3. Hot

warm ────────────────────────────────── scorching
(possible route students could follow: *hot* → *sweltering* → *boiling*)

4. Dialogue intensity

murmured ────────────────────────────────── screamed
possible route students could follow: *mumbled* → *said* → *exclaimed* → *shouted*)

5. Movement

flew ────────────────────────────────── soared
(possible route students could follow: *flitted* → *drifted* → *glided* → *soared*)

Two extremes are placed opposite one another and students must add three or four pieces of vocabulary to the middle, working from one extreme to the other.

HACK #1.11: MARKING VOCABULARY

A brief but important point to highlight. When marking and giving feedback on vocabulary, avoid vague phrases like 'use more sophisticated vocabulary.' What does a comment like this even mean? What counts as 'sophisticated vocabulary'? Even if a comment like this could result in something tangible, if a student doesn't know any, how can they meet such a target without intervention from their teacher? Is there a clear line between sophisticated and unsophisticated words? Most likely, students are left confused and unsure of how to improve.

Instead, be precise and clear with feedback. For example, say something like 'Try to use vocabulary that helps the reader understand the character's anger.' This kind of specific guidance provides a clear goal and direction, rather than leaving students trying to guess what we actually mean.

HACK #1.12: VOCABULARY FOR ACADEMIC WRITING

When being selective with what vocabulary to teach, we should leave room to consider words that deepen students' analytical skills, helping their writing align with conventions of modern literary criticism.

For instance, when exploring a writer's purpose, I want my students to use language that allows them to thoughtfully investigate authorial intent. They need to write like literary critics, articulating a clear and precise analysis of a text. To support this, I explicitly teach sentence stems and a range of analytical verbs.

> Perhaps the writer does this:
> - To criticise.
> - To expose.
> - To challenge.
> - To celebrate.
> - To imply.
> - To celebrate the importance of.
> - To manipulate.
> - To consider.
> - To intensify.

There are many analytical verbs to choose from, perhaps too many to teach all at once or expect students to retain immediately. However, explicit teaching of these verbs is essential; we want our students to internalise them because of the clear pathway they offer into understanding a writer's purpose. Once introduced, we can support students in applying these to the texts they are studying. One effective strategy is to start with a brief cloze exercise that helps students frame their ideas, gradually removing this as they gain the confidence and ability to record their analysis independently.

> Perhaps Shakespeare uses Macbeth in this way **to expose** _____.
>
> Dickens positions Fred opposite Scrooge in this moment **to criticise** _____.

Once students have good oversight of these verbs, they can use one analytical verb to lead them into a second, which then extends their thoughts and ideas.

> Through **exposing** this, Shakespeare is also **considering** _____.
>
> Through **criticising** this, Dickens is also able to **manipulate** _____.

Notice the words I use in the first examples: 'Shakespeare *uses* ...' and 'Dickens *positions* ...'. This is absolutely deliberate. Another type of vocabulary we should be encouraging our students to use is that which allows them to discuss characters as the conscious construct of a writer, as opposed to writing about them as if they are real.

Students need to understand that characters have been intentionally created by a writer to help them convey a particular message or theme. They are not autonomous individuals, but vessels, designed to serve a purpose. By teaching vocabulary that reinforces this understanding, vocabulary that foregrounds authorial intention, we can equip students to write more insightfully about literature.

> Dickens **positions Fred** opposite Scrooge in this moment to criticise Scrooge's selfish parsimony; Fred has little to give, yet **he is deliberately placed** as an opposing force next to his uncle to highlight to a reader Scrooge's miserly and malicious personality.

The best way to teach this concept is to explain it in context. Live model the process of analytical writing, or provide students with a well-crafted section of a model response. Then break it down, step by step, clearly articulating why the use of this vocabulary is effective in elevating literary analysis.

Once students understand the technique and begin to use this type of vocabulary in writing, you can take it further by presenting them with a contrasting non-example, an answer that refers to characters as if they were real people. Ask students to critique the example.

- What's missing?
- What assumptions are being made?
- What needs to be revised to reflect a more analytical, literary approach?

A comparison like this helps students internalise the expectations of academic writing and reinforces the idea that precise, selective vocabulary can shape the depth and sophistication of their interpretations.

Other vocabulary that can help students write about characters as conscious constructs includes:

- The writer utilises [Character A] to ...
- [Character B] serves to ...
- The writer constructs [Character C] in a way that ...
- The writer deliberately crafts [Character D] to ...

Teach students a variety of tentative language choices too, alongside effective discourse markers, to support the development of an analytical voice. Tentative language is particularly important in English, for it encourages students to present their ideas with caution rather than as indisputable facts. This, of course, reflects the notion that literature invites multiple, valid readings (as long as they are rooted within the texts themselves). Common tentative language words and phrases I teach are:

- It **could** be argued that ...

- **Perhaps** the writer is suggesting ...
- This **may** insinuate ...

Discourse markers are essential tools to aid the cohesiveness of an essay. They guide the reader through the progression of a student's argument, ensuring that points build logically and fluidly rather than appearing as a series of disjointed observations that have no relation to each other. Students are advised not to overuse these, but to sprinkle them through their essay where appropriate.

Discourse markers can include:

- Furthermore.
- In addition.
- Nevertheless.
- In contrast.
- As a result.
- Consequently.

Again, the best way to teach these is to model the approach and to be specific as to their function. 'Furthermore', for instance, should be used to add to an existing point whereas 'In contrast' tells a reader that an opposing reading of a text is about to be introduced. Used too many times the writing can begin to sound artificial, like a list, with no hint of fluency. Use them too little and the arguments won't connect.

ORACY

What?

Voice 21, the UK's oracy education charity, states 'that oral language is the most effective vehicle for learning new words; it is through hearing new language and using it in speech that children become able to read it, write it and deploy it with fluency' (Voice 21, 2023). Oracy plays a particularly important role in the classroom as highlighted by the brilliant Mary Myatt. I've already shared part of this quotation earlier in the chapter, but let's look at the next part too:

> 'The concepts and big ideas [of the curriculum] are generally Tier 3 vocabulary. They are the gateways into the individual subjects. If we want pupils to know more and remember more, it's worth spending time teaching them, talking about them, and showing them in lots of different contexts.

> It is important to do this, because most of the conversations in classrooms use Tier 1 and Tier 2 vocabulary. There is nothing wrong with this, however it does mean that it's important for pupils to have the chance to talk about and explore these. A rich vocabulary is likely to lead to better outcomes for all pupils, and particularly for those who might not be exposed to them outside school.' (Myatt, 2022a)

The strategies explored in this section can cover both Tier 2 and Tier 3 vocabulary teaching. Of course, oracy in terms of vocabulary teaching cannot just be relegated to talking about words. As Voice 21 states, oracy needs to be carefully planned, ensuring that 'scaffolded exploratory talk for learning provides students with multiple, low-stakes opportunities to hear and practise using new vocabulary in context, deepening students' words knowledge and promoting "word ownership"' (McBride, 2023). The hacks here are about how to prompt this talk in the classroom, but the preplanning of this should have already happened.

How?

HACK #1.13: INPUT AND OUTPUT

Oracy is an excellent way of allowing students to rehearse a word once introduced to it. When they are able to use this newly learned vocabulary correctly in a given context, we might feel that they finally 'own' the word. However, this takes time, and we need to ensure we provide opportunities for students to able to use the words correctly. Voice 21 says that the process of vocabulary instruction:

> 'can be split between an "input phase" and an "output phase". During the input phase, students are introduced to new vocabulary and are given multiple opportunities to hear and begin experimenting with new language. During the output phase, students are encouraged to use recently learned language independently in speech as they build towards word ownership. This process creates a depth of word knowledge as well as creativity with new vocabulary.' (Voice 21, 2024)

In this case, then, we need to give students the opportunity to practise vocabulary and explain the idea of a vocabulary's definition for themselves. The following sequence shows how one could do this.

1. If explaining the term 'metaphor', begin by introducing the main components of one. Talk about the following:

    - Tenor = the subject of the metaphor and its intended meaning.
    - Vehicle = the language used to described the tenor. (Didau, 2022a)

2. From this, get students to rehearse this first step with their partners. Give an instruction like 'Tell your partners a sentence that contains the words "metaphor", "tenor" and "vehicle". You have 30 seconds between you. Go.'
3. Once this time has passed, ask a student to share their thoughts with the class.
4. At this point, repeat the main ideas: 'the tenor is the subject of the metaphor, the vehicle the source of its imagery' (Didau, 2022a). Then you might explain the following concept:

- Ground = the relationship between the tenor and the vehicle.

You might then offer an example. Let's look at one provided by David Didau, taken from Christina Rosetti's poem *My heart is like a singing bird*.

- Tenor = Rossetti's heart.
- Vehicle = 'a singing bird'.
- Ground = we think of singing birds as beautiful and peaceful so we're invited to think that Rossetti's heart (here a metaphor for her emotional state) is in a beautiful peaceful place. (Didau, 2022a)

5. Ask students to tell their partners something else about metaphors now they have this new piece of information.

Notice how many Tier 3 words have been introduced at this point: metaphor, tenor, vehicle, ground. These are subject-specific terms that can deepen students' understanding of literary methods and allow for more precise analysis. Introducing these words isn't enough, however. We must ensure students have repeated opportunities to *rehearse* their use.

This approach, championed by Pritesh Raichura, is all about structured rehearsal while exposing students multiple times to key terminology. It is about providing deliberate moments in a lesson for students to apply vocabulary in context. One might say, 'Have a look at another example. Discuss the ground of this metaphor. Use the labelled tenor and vehicle to help you. Off you go' to a class, to help them move from a phase of recognition to one of active application.

In this particular example, such a discussion could be followed with more advanced discussion, such as how the tenor in a metaphor is often unstated and how that might affect our interpretation as a result. A sequence like this can help us layer our planning to help build student understanding incrementally.

As Raichura sums up: 'give two facts ... rehearse both ... give the third fact, rehearse it, give a fourth fact, rehearse all four etc.' (Raichura, 2023). This works particularly well for vocabulary because it offers that repeated exposure that we need, giving students a chance to try out words. Although the example here is for Tier 3 vocabulary, a variation of this process could work really well for Tier 2 vocabulary too.

HACK #1.14: BUILDING KNOWLEDGE OF WORDS STUDENTS ALREADY KNOW

One idea that I've explored with my classes from *Bringing Words to Life* is about teaching students more about words they already know. As Isabel Beck *et. al* (2013, p. 179) say, 'there are many words that are in students' environment and that they have some passing familiarity with but may not really know much about.' Having that discussion as a class can be really useful.

> 'Studies have demonstrated that people with more extensive vocabularies not only know more words but also know more about the words they already know (Curtis and Glaser, 1983), and that people with high and lower vocabularies differ as to their depth of knowledge about even fairly common words (Van Daalen-Kapteijns and Elshout-Mohr, 1981).' (Beck et al., 2013, p. 179)

An imagined conversation that we might have with a Year 7 class, for example, looks like this.

> **Teacher:** In the story, the girl said, 'I hope my mum comes home soon.' What does hope mean?
>
> **Student 1:** She wants her mum to come home?
>
> **Teacher:** So is hope just about wanting something?
>
> **Student 2:** Kind of, but more like really wishing for it.
>
> **Teacher:** Do we hope for things we already know will happen?
>
> **Student 3:** No. You hope when you're not sure, but you really want it.
>
> **Teacher:** Can you think of something you've hoped for?
>
> **Student 4:** I hoped it wouldn't rain on my birthday because we were having a barbeque.
>
> **Teacher:** So how can we describe 'hope'?
>
> **Student:** It's when you really want something to happen, even if you're not sure it will.
>
> **Teacher:** Or in the case of Student 4?
>
> **Student:** That something won't happen!
>
> **Teacher:** And so what do we now know about the girl who hopes her mum will come home? What can we infer about her?

Why would we talk more about familiar words? If students know them, surely they know them? This is mostly to do with relationships between words, for word knowledge doesn't exist as isolated pockets but as 'networks of words clustered into categories' (Beck et al., 2013, p. 179). Exploration of familiar words can then lead to new words to teach that students may not have encountered before. For example, 'optimism', or even 'realism' might be follow-up words to discuss if we were the teacher leading this conversation. This is something that then helps students to have a more nuanced understanding of the word they originally already knew: 'hope'.

Why?

So why should we teach in this way? Why should we choose words to teach that are carefully selected and sequenced? Voice 21 reveals that:

> 'During our Voicing Vocabulary study, participants benefited by teaching fewer strategically chosen words in greater depth. Teachers found that the quality of vocabulary mattered more than quantity.'
> (Voice 21, 2024).

Many of the justifications for the approaches laid out in this teacher hack have already been explored through the chapter. As a result, I'll end with this: taking time to teach vocabulary explicitly is not an optional extra. It is vital. It equips our students with the tools they need to make sense of language once they no longer have the safety of the classroom to aid them. Teaching students about morphemes empowers them to make sense of the unfamiliar. For example, if a student knows that 'photo' means 'light' and '-graphy' means 'writing or drawing', they could infer that 'photography' is about creating pictures using light. This kind of morphological awareness nurtures curiosity, confidence and, above all, independence.

Vocabulary knowledge underpins success across all disciplines, not just English. If we turn to subjects like science or geography, we can see how they rely heavily on content-specific vocabulary, and without understanding terms such as these students can struggle to access and retain knowledge, let alone begin to make connections across all domains.

When all is said and done, vocabulary is part of the very foundations of teaching and learning. It gives students the best opportunities to ask better questions and engage in academic discussions from which they might otherwise be excluded. Awareness and understanding of vocabulary for our students is like inviting them to have a seat at the table. Our students deserve to have that seat.

CHAPTER 2: LITERARY DEVICES

Teaching literary devices is a staple part of an English teacher's role. Yet, too often, we see students being taught the definition of the devices and then feature spotting them in texts. What students really need to know is how devices work to create meaning, and to be able to use them purposefully in their own writing and speech to create meaning themselves. Knowing the difference between personification and anthropomorphism is only the start, but deep and meaningful learning comes from understanding the effect of the phrase on the reader and how that effect makes the author's intent more clear. However, literary devices can be abstract and complex, making them difficult for students to understand. Terms like 'metaphor' or 'irony' might not be immediately graspable without concrete examples and detailed explanations. Therefore, teachers need to explicitly teach students to go beyond the simple recognition of literary devices and model their own thinking when analysing and interpreting them. This will act as a scaffold for students to have the confidence to formulate and articulate their own personal responses, leaving behind the superficial understanding of just feature spotting.

CHAPTER 2: LITERARY DEVICES

READING

What

There are few certain things about the subject of English. You only have to head over to any social media platform to find English teachers bickering about ideological differences over the best way to teach English language and literature. It is a highly contested field, and quite rightly as it has a rich and varied history, with a well-defined disciplinary, substantive and hinterland canon of knowledge and skills, which can often seem at odds with some explicit instruction methods (Clay, 1956). Yet there are also teachers who have used research on cognitive science to improve their English teaching and are confident that it has improved outcomes for their students (Needham, 2020). As Sam Gibbs said in the brilliant book *The Trouble with English*, 'How do we apply a scientific approach to a subject full of abstractions and emotions? (Gibbs and Helman, 2022, p.15). Yet one thing is certain, regardless of whatever camp English teachers belong to, which is that reading is an essential tenet of the subject.

Reading a text in English can serve many purposes: to gain knowledge and information; for pleasure and entertainment; to understand the thoughts, feelings or intentions of others or to learn about other cultures. Of course, these reasons can also overlap and intersect – every English teacher would hope that their students get some knowledge and enjoyment from every text they read! However, the kind of reading that runs like a 'golden thread' through most English curricula is the kind of reading that students need to employ critical thinking and analysis skills to interpret. To engage with such texts requires interpretation, broadening their understanding and fostering empathy. Sometimes this may require students to find an emotional connection to the text or to imagine what the writer is thinking or feeling. This can be something that students find immensely difficult as, when they are asked what the effect of the text may be, they are unsure or lack the confidence to give a personal response, for fear of it being wrong. It is here that we often see the sentence that makes every English teacher shudder, 'The use of the metaphor makes the reader want to read on.'

Literary devices, sometimes referred to as techniques, or figurative language, are specific techniques that allow a writer to convey a deeper meaning that often goes beyond what's on the page. They work alongside plot and characters to elevate a story and prompt readers to reflect on life, society and even what it means to be human. When we ask students to identify and analyse the writer's use of literary devices, we are essentially asking them to zoom into the granular choices of the writer and to analyse how these devices contribute to the writer's authorial intention or big ideas. Sounds simple right? If only! As examiners and teachers of many years, we often observe that close language analysis is something that students often struggle with, often reverting to feature spotting and providing generic analysis, struggling to elicit the kind of deep exploration and detail required in the GCSE exams. This is a worry of course, as the ability to analyse literary devices is part of the wider skill of close analysis that forms the bedrock of all four English exams. If students can't get this right, it will seriously limit their ability to demonstrate the understanding that will signal to the examiner that they have fully engaged with the ideas in the text.

The aim of analysing literary devices, either in a fiction or non-fiction text, is to unravel layers of meaning and examine how these different subjective meanings might contribute to the thoughts, feelings and attitude of the writer. I often hear English teachers say that there are 'no wrong answers' when trying to encourage students to form their own interpretations, especially when analysing literary devices. I have learned at my own peril that this is not the case! Leonard Bernstein reportedly said that 'a work of art does not answer questions, it provokes them; and its essential meaning is in the tension between the contradictory answers' (quoted in Berger (2024)). Of course, this is true, but we have also seen some absolutely bonkers interpretations from students, which are not rooted in evidence from the text and make it difficult for them to craft a cogent argument.

Analysing literary devices is rooted in both AO1 and AO2. According to the AQA exam board, AO1 requires students to write informed and relevant responses, which use appropriate concepts and terminology, and AO2 requires students to analyse ways in which meanings are shaped in literary texts. So it makes sense that the more that students are given the opportunity to develop nuanced and sophisticated ideas about the writer's use of literary devices, the more they will be able to extrapolate ideas about a text either through writing or talk. Ideas and analysis are inextricably intertwined and for students to be able to make the leap between their ideas and analysis and back again, they need to move away from the confines of single-word analysis (which they seem obsessed with) and explore the text more holistically through the writer's craft. This reframing of the writer as the creator of the text means that students consider more carefully why a literary device might have been used, how it creates meaning and will then find it easier to generate a greater range of ideas to discuss. This method is also supported by AQA's 2019 Examiners' report (AQA, 2019), which states: 'there is an overreliance on word level analysis ... students should be aware that methods mean anything the writer has done deliberately.'

So, how can teachers support their students to be able to do this? I like to think of it as a process of unravelling. During lockdown, Haili decided to learn to knit and, inevitably, her grasp of pattern following went terribly wrong, as well as the tension when knitting, resulting in some very misshapen scarves! Yet as she began to pull them apart to start again and the strands loosened, she could analyse how the knitting was made – both the patterns and the individual threads that formed them. The same can be said about a text: the literary devices a writer chooses form just one example of a thread they might use; this thread could contribute to a recurring pattern in the text. Unravelling helps us understand the message of the writer and how the choice of technique contributes to something bigger and much more conceptual.

How?

When teaching students how to identify and analyse literary devices in a text, it's key that students have the prerequisite background knowledge to be able to identify a device, not just by knowing what it is, but also by having the knowledge to be able to comprehend the effect of the device's use. A review of research on the role of background knowledge in reading comprehension suggests that explicitly teaching background knowledge is foundational to increasing pupils' reading competency (Smith *et al.*, 2021). For example in Act 1 Scene 7 of Shakespeare's *Macbeth*, when Lady Macbeth is chastising her husband for not having the courage to kill King Duncan, Shakespeare has her use the simile 'like the poor cat i' th' adage' to describe Macbeth. Without the explicit teaching of the meaning of the word 'adage' as a proverb or saying, and the sharing of the proverb about the cat who wanted a fish but didn't want to get his paws wet, it is unlikely that students would be able to analyse this literary device. This would be a shame, as it forms part of a pattern of Lady Macbeth emasculating her husband and goading him towards action through questioning his manhood. In turn, this then feeds into more conceptual ideas about the Macbeths' childlessness during the play, which becomes a motif and spur to his ambition. It is clear then that key concepts and vocabulary used in literary devices have to be understood to appreciate the meaning of the words that are read (Rupley *et al.*, 2012). According to the Ofsted English Subject Review:

> 'inference depends on a reader's vocabulary knowledge, contextual knowledge and knowledge of language structures. The reader needs this knowledge to make links between different parts of the text and construct a robust mental model of it.' (Ofsted, 2022)

Readers use the background information and knowledge to fill in details that are not explicitly stated by the author (Cain, 2010). Therefore, a pupil with limited academic or cultural knowledge will find it difficult to make inferences about non-everyday topics about which they know little.

HACK #2.1: BUILDING A SHARED MENTAL MODEL OF DEVICES

To initially build knowledge, it might be useful to begin by compiling a list of common literary devices that students may come across in a range of fiction and non-fiction texts and, after they understand the definition, getting them to come up with possible examples. This bridges the knowing/doing gap (Kennedy, 2016) which can emerge when students are exposed to an idea but aren't helped to understand exactly what to do about it, or how to put it into action. It also makes the abstract concept of literary devices much more concrete, as students can see how they might be constructed and used. This might then be followed by students reading a text and being able to find and identify the literary devices in it. Gibbs and Helman (2022) suggest that English is more about thinking than doing and it's true that a great deal of thinking and talking may go on in lessons before students go on to communicate their ideas on paper. It is important that students have the chance to practise identifying literary devices and understanding their use before they can then move on to the mastery skill of thinking about the effects the literary devices create. Efrat Furst's model of memory representation in the long-term memory store (see Figure 2.1) illustrates this well. Before learning, students might have a vague idea of what a literary device is. With a presentation and explanation by the teacher, the new concepts form connections, which leads to deeper understanding. As students gain fluency and confidence in identifying the literary devices, the mastery skills of analysing can be introduced.

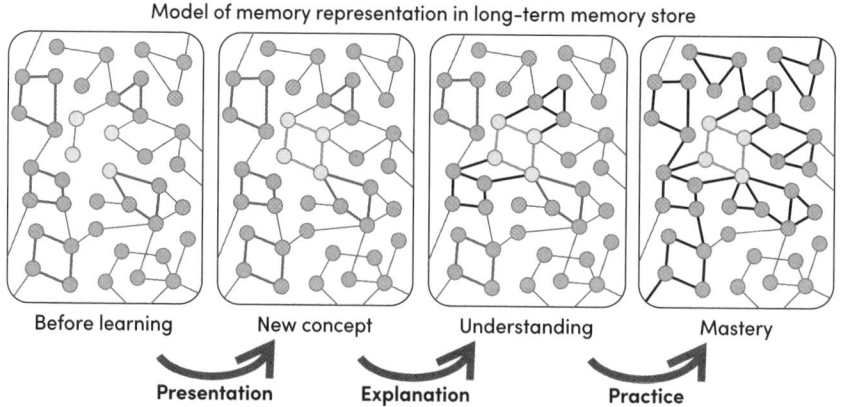

Figure 2.1 Efrat Furst's model of memory representation in long-term memory story

However, just getting the students to feature spot turns them into English's version of trainspotters, with paragraphs full of disparate sentences in their essays about a quote containing sibilance, without saying anything about how it works or why the author put it there. This sometimes happens because lots of introductory lessons to analysing literary devices might involve tables with techniques, definitions and examples that can seem quite overwhelming and meaningless to students. Rather than overwhelming students with a huge list, we may want to introduce in clusters, grouped by common intended effects, such as 'comparison,' or 'symbolism.' Teachers can do this through starter activities/do now tasks, where students have to:

1. Label the literary devices being used.
2. Identify the juiciest words in them to analyse.
3. Analyse the effect of the individual word choices, considering connotation and significance in relation to the device.
4. Analyse the effect of the word or device in the sentence and in context.

This gives students the opportunity to notice things in an extract and have some autonomy in choosing what stands out for them and why. Then ask them to think about how those special words or phrases affect the reader. This kind of activity can then be developed and scaffolded through questions: 'What emotions are evoked by the highlighted sentences?', 'How do the author's choices make them feel?', 'What point is the author making about people or the world in general?', 'How does the literary device contribute to this point?'. Some students might need more scaffolding with this process than others, so a resource such as Figure 2.2 might be helpful, until they have gained confidence and automaticity.

Steps to success: Analysing literary devices
1 Label the literary devices being used. 2 Identify the juiciest words in them to analyse. 3 Analyse the effect of the individual word choices, considering connotation and significance in relation to the device. 4 Analyse the effect of the word or device in the sentence and in context.
What emotions are evoked by the highlighted sentences? How do the author's choices make them feel? What point is the author making about people or the world in general? How does the literary device contribute to this point?

Figure 2.2 Example of a scaffolded resource

These activities don't need to look like summative assessment-style GCSE texts. Too often, schools are only feeding students on a diet of mini-GCSE texts for their whole time at secondary school, and not only is this limiting and teaching to the test, it also completely ruins the enjoyment of our glorious subject. Mini-tasks can only focus on tiny snippets of the text such as the demonstration in Figure 2.3.

Macbeth	
How does Shakespeare use sound imagery, alliteration and plosives to highlight Macbeth's turmoil?	I see thee still, And on thy blade and dudgeon gouts of blood, Which was not so before. There's no such thing: It is the bloody business which informs Thus to mine eyes.

Figure 2.3 Example of a mini-task resource

HACK #2.2: MODEL FOR MASTERY

Once students are familiar with the first steps of analysing, it is useful for them to see the teacher modelling how they might analyse literary devices. Modelling is incredibly powerful as it allows an expert to make their thinking visible and demystify the process of analysis (Rosenshine, 2012). Here is an example of a teacher thinking out loud when analysing the metaphor of mushrooms in the Sylvia Plath poem of the same name.

> 'At first reading, this poem might seem to just be about mushrooms, but actually I think it might be about something deeper than that. Let's go back and look for some clues. So Plath uses personification, to talk about the mushrooms' "toes" and "noses" so perhaps it refers to a person or even a group of people, as she uses the inclusive pronoun, "we." She writes that "We are shelves, we are Tables, we are meek." I am trying to visualise the metaphor here and what it could mean. We put things on shelves and tables, load them up with things they have to bear the weight of. But the people she is referring to don't complain about it as they are "meek", which could suggest they are depressed. Perhaps they are women? Which seems to make sense as she ends the poem with a more positive stanza, "We shall by morning Inherit the earth Our foot's in the door." I know that the poem was written in the middle of the 20th century, when there was a renewed interest in feminism, so that could account for the assertion about women's "foot's in the door", implying that things are changing. Now that I understand she is using this poem as an extended metaphor, I wonder why Plath is choosing to compare these women to mushrooms?'

When we model literary analysis, we can break down our thought process verbally like this, or if we model a written response, we can scaffold by colour coding our thoughts, in order to highlight the necessary critical thinking steps.

HACK #2.3: IMAGES

Images can also be a useful resource when helping students analyse literary devices. Using an image can even show students how to differentiate between summarising and analysing and we can use them to walk through the steps of making observations, applying decoding strategies and questioning for deeper meaning. Using AI tools can be brilliant here, as you can type in examples of literary devices from the texts you are studying and use them as a stimulus to help students discuss the deeper meanings. See Figure 2.4, which captures the metaphor Romeo uses about his love for Rosaline near the beginning of the play, 'Love is a smoke made with the fume of sighs.' Students could analyse the shifting and changing nature of love, which moves stealthily, like the smoke in the picture and has the ability to choke passion. The darkness symbolises the sometimes depressing nature of love, indicated by the 'sighs.'

Figure 2.4 'Love is a smoke made with the fume of sighs.'

HACK #2.4: SENTENCE STEM SCAFFOLDS

When students reach the stage of commenting on effect and communicating this through analytical paragraphs or essays, they may need some support to avoid the dreaded 'it makes the reader want to read on.' Explicitly modelling this and providing sentence stems through a scaffolding worksheet such as in Figure 2.5 can be helpful.

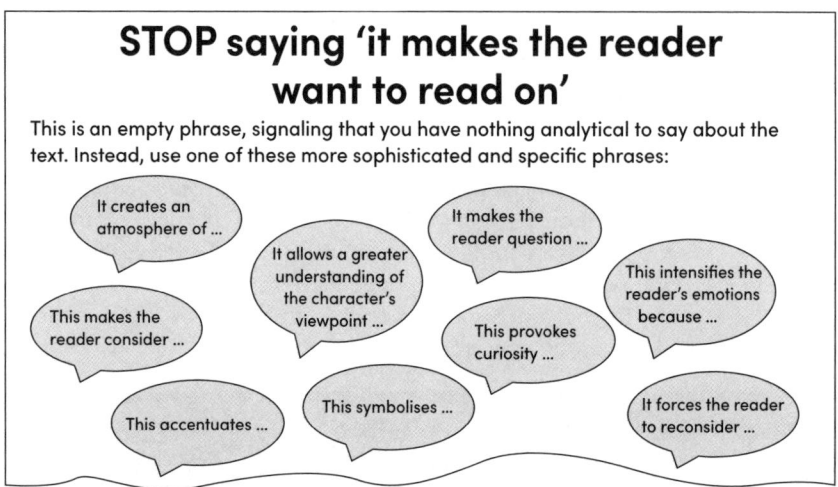

Figure 2.5 Scaffolding worksheet

WRITING

What?

As the Ofsted English Subject Review highlights, students can use the knowledge learned in the context of one modality in English to help them in another. For example, they can use literary devices learned through reading when they are speaking and writing, both in school and their wider lives (Ofsted, 2022). This is because the teaching of reading and writing are not discrete skills and they overlap significantly across all topics studied in any English curriculum. Even the GCSE English Language papers themselves are designed on this premise. Paper 2, for example, would contain two non-fiction sources and a transactional writing activity that is thematically linked to the sources. Some English teachers advise their students to begin with the writing task, as they struggle with timing and the writing task is worth the same number of marks as all of the reading tasks put together. However, we would always advise against this as the reading sources provide a wealth of great knowledge, ideas and information that can help students construct a convincing and compelling argument.

Students will be asked to write for a range of different purposes in English, including descriptive and narrative writing, analytical essays and more transactional writing, such as letters, speeches and newspaper articles. The use of literary devices in all of these types of writing is encouraged – the top of the mark scheme states that there will be evidence of a 'conscious crafting of linguistic devices'. However, it is important for students to think carefully about the purpose, audience and format of the text that they are writing when deciding which literary devices they might include. For example, using irony might not be appropriate in an analytical essay, and imagery such as onomatopoeia might be more suited to a piece of descriptive writing than a letter. Like the danger of becoming a feature spotter when reading literary devices, the same danger is inherent when students use them in their own writing. They can fall into the trap of using devices for the sake of it and littering their writing with so many disparate and unconnected techniques that the ideas and meanings suffer. If we go back to the knitting metaphor, it is useful to think of using literary devices as part of a bigger pattern, which all contributes to an overall message. Remember, that all texts are constructs, which are carefully put together by writers. This time, it is the student's turn themselves.

How?

Helping students use literary devices intentionally in their own writing might once again start with some explicit instruction, where a teacher shows various different examples of pieces of writing for different purposes and discusses how and why the devices have been employed by the writer. This crosses over with reading, as you might analyse these examples with the class, highlighting how the devices function within the text and what they contribute to the overall impact. It might be useful to look at the linguistic devices of a poem such as *Flag* by John Agard, alongside a piece of non-fiction and to discuss how they are used to elicit different emotional responses.

HACK #2.5: MATCHING DEVICES TO PURPOSE

Teachers should spend lots of time modelling how they might use literary devices in different kinds of text, including during the planning phase. When planning, deciding on what mood and message you want to impart is the first step in beginning to consciously craft the use of devices. A few carefully-chosen devices are better than using a device in every sentence. So it is important to match the device carefully to the reader. The example that follows illustrates this well.

'A visit to the seaside is a positive and enriching experience.' Write an argument in which you agree or disagree.

If a student wants to argue that the seaside is not positive, that it is dreary, tedious and depressing, the words and stylistic devices the student uses need to contribute to this mood and tone. An interesting way of practising this skill might be for the teacher to model an anecdotal opening, using some literary devices, in response to the question and then asking students to guess whether the opening agrees or disagrees with the statement and to highlight the words and devices that make it clear (see Figure 2.6). This might then lead to students writing their anecdotal opening, responding to the same question, but this time for the opposite point of view. This can focus on the literary devices used and how their use contributes to the overall effect.

> Feeling the scorching sand shift underneath my feet, I was desperate to sense the cool Atlantic water bubble over my skin. My brother was already in the sea, as confident as a seal, navigating the choppy waves which seemed to grasp hold of him like helping hands. With the support of my dad, who was up to his knees in the water beside me, I took the plunge; I will never forget the excitement of the chilly water rushing over my skin. Swimming for the first time at Treyarnon Bay in Cornwall was a truly energising experience. I felt so proud of myself. Who hasn't had a positive experience like this at the seaside?

Figure 2.6 Model anecdotal opening

HACK #2.6: WORKED EXAMPLES

Worked examples of literary devices in use, in a variety of different types and purposes of texts, are also really useful. The worked example effect suggests that if we want more novice learners to succeed in a task, it would be more beneficial for them to study the solutions to problems, rather than attempting to initially solve them themselves. Asking students to produce a piece of extended writing, without the well-developed background knowledge of how to use vocabulary and literary devices for effect, 'unnecessarily adds problem-solving search to the interacting elements, thus imposing an extraneous cognitive load' (Sweller, Ayres and Kalyuga 2011). This often manifests itself in students saying that they don't know how to start, or asking for sentence starters. To be most effective, worked examples need to be used 'systematically and consistently to reduce the influence of extraneous problem-solving demands' (Sweller, Ayres and Kalyuga 2011).

So using worked examples of literary devices being used can help students build a schema of different ways they can be used effectively, which will help develop their expertise more holistically than if they had just completed lots of writing tasks. Worked examples are also a lot more concrete than just talking in a vague way about how a writer might use literary devices. Teachers can then talk through the worked example, deconstructing and analysing it as they go along. Once this has been done, students could deconstruct another worked example themselves working with a peer, before they do this independently. Pre-populating a worked example with questions can also be useful and allows students to focus on teacher explanations rather than on taking notes. A resource like that shown in Figure 2.7 could work well.

What is the overall mood created in the opening paragraph? Zoom out: How do the literary devices contribute to that mood?	The superiorly thick smoky clouds rolled in like boulders, ready to crush anything in their way. The darkness was engulfing and seemed to fully consume any spec of light. Any last hope was gone... Without warning water came gushing down – throwing itself onto the jagged knife-like rocks.	What does the use of the simile in the first line suggest? If the clouds were being described as delicate, how would this simile change?
Is there a semantic field in this paragraph? How does it contribute to the mood?	The rocks seemed to slice the water from its many thousands of sharp daggers, embedded all over it. The water came gushing down like a waterfall along the jagged surface of the wise rock. The merciless winds caused the enormous waves to crash and erupt like lava coming down from a raging volcano. It splits like an aggressive wild animal, angered by the vigorous storm. The waves punching and beating the rocks with all of their might and the wind gusts knife the piercing thorns of branches.	How has the simile been used differently here through the use of a hyphen? What does it suggest about the rocks?
	Branded upon the colossal tree trunk was a single blinding white light, which had cut through the immensely thick cloud and fog – like a laser. Its source could vividly made out to be an inferior and small lighthouse, perched on the top of a cliff, which was like a bird sat upon its nest, just watching its home shatter to a thousand pieces.	Highlight the personification. Why does the writer make this comparison?
Why has the writer used sibilance here? How is it appropriate for the focus of the description?	The murky water below was an opaque block, of which only faint ghost-like shadows of sea creatures could be seen. With each wave, the fragile bodies of sea creature were thrown carelessly onto the surrounding shore and rocks. Those that survived, has seemed to have lost all will to live; were too exhausted from fighting with the merciless waves to flap their limbs and fins, even desperately.	
	Up above, hiding in any sort of shelter from the ice-like winds they could find, were a flock of seagulls. They had seemingly lost their way because of the greatly thick opaque clouds. Despite this, the vigorous, superior wind remained forcing everything out of its way, with no struggle shown – only complete ease.	Underline the colour imagery. Annotate the connotations of the different colours the writer has chosen to include.
How does the use of the simile change here?	The boulders of clouds remained to loom over the coast like an overprotective mother over its misbehaving child. No end was in sight; not a hint of the immensely powerful wind giving up any time soon. Or seemingly ever.	

Figure 2.7 Worked example

Finally, giving students the opportunity to deliberately practise using literary devices in their own writing can help them gain confidence, develop clearer mental models and use them more fluently. Deliberate practice involves students taking part in 'structured and purposeful behaviours under the guidance of a teacher, to improve their ability' (Busch, 2026a). 'Deliberate practice' is different from 'independent practice' (studying without seeking external feedback or guidance) or 'naive practice' (studying without the main goal to improve). This is because it involves a teacher giving granular and specific feedback on work, so that students know exactly what to improve and how they can do so. Therefore, providing students with structured exercises, which encourage them to use specific literary devices, and giving them immediate feedback on their work, will enable them to complete a similar task again more independently. Chunking tasks, by using scaffolds such as structure strips, can help students move towards independence when these scaffolds are then gradually released. A 'gradual release of responsibility model' (Fisher and Frey, 2013) is an instructional model where teachers strategically transfer the responsibility in the learning process from the teacher to the students. They might start off by using the visualiser to write a paragraph using literary devices themselves, narrating their decisions and thought processes as they go. This is commonly known as the 'I do'. They might then either co-write another paragraph, which leads on from the first, with the whole class, asking for contributions. Alternatively, they might ask students to work in pairs to compose a paragraph. A scaffold such as a structure strip (Figure 2.8) might act as a bridge between the 'We do' and 'You do' stage of the 'gradual release model'.

DESCRIPTIVE WRITING
Hook your reader by describing the setting using sibilance and a metaphor to set the mood.
Move out to a wide view and use personification to reiterate and build on the initial mood you set.
Describe the main character using a semantic field. Get inside his head and describe his thoughts and feelings.
Return to the wider view and build on from the mood in paragraph 2. Use onomatopoeia to include sensory imagery.
Zoom in on a small detail and use a simile to describe it. Connect it to a macro idea, such as the thoughts of the character.
Return to a detail from the start such as the metaphor and change the mood and tone to finish on a cliffhanger.

Figure 2.8 Structure strip scaffold

ORACY

What?

As the EEF states, 'children's language development benefits from approaches that support communication through talking and non-verbal expression' (EEF, 2023). In the last fifteen years, oracy has seemed to fall out of favour in many subjects, with even the Minister for Education referring in 2012 to oracy as 'idle chatter in class' (Rackley and Bradford, 2022), which would divert teachers from their much more important task of raising standards in literacy. As the former CEO of Voice21, Becky Francis said, 'oracy currently has meagre status within our education system' (quoted in Whittaker 2016) and this is proven by a YouGov poll, which saw 57% of 900 teachers polled claiming that they had not received any training in oracy in the last three years, while 53% said they would not know where to look for more information if they wanted it. (Whittaker, 2016)

Yet, over several decades, research has made compelling cases for students' classroom talk as a vehicle for learning. These include improving the communicative competence of students (Bruner, 1978) and the proficient and appropriate use of language for a given purpose (Alexander, 2019). Vygotsky also researched the potential of talk as a tool for thinking (Vygotsky, 1978) and the cognitive benefits of spoken language. For example, well-structured dialogue between students, or between students and teachers, has been linked to improved attainment in a range of curriculum areas (EEF, 2017). Neil Mercer (2013) has also extensively written about the value of exploratory talk, which helps students use features of reasoned arguments and construct engagement with different points of view. This might extend to lifelong empowerment, as Alexander's work on dialogic teaching goes beyond dialogue as a form of talk to outline an overarching ethos that values multiple perspectives and collective-meaning-making (Alexander, 2020).

Recently, there has been renewed interest in oracy, after Keir Starmer announced it would be a key part of Labour's education plans (BBC, 2023). Approaches that support both cognitive and linguistic aspects of communication, such as interactive reading or collaborative talk, are a great way of analysing literary devices. Barbara Bleiman, from the English and Media centre, recently spoke to Geoff Barton, as part of his work for the Oracy Commission, about 'Talking Classrooms.' She pointed out how important oracy is for preparing students for their future lives. But she also stressed that oracy is talk for learning and that subjecting ideas to scrutiny and thinking together is just as vital, but not talked about as often as the more functional use of talk (Barton 2024).

There is often a bizarre ideological dichotomy created between oracy and traditional teaching, with some thinking that oracy and explicit or direct instruction will not work together. However, oracy is not 'prog' or 'trad'. Explicit knowledge, information and thinking from a teacher is always needed, but the interactive aspect of having whole-class or paired discussions where a teacher teases out and probes student thinking is also key. This might look like the sharing of interpretations when analysing the literary devices in a poem, or the spoken personal response to a piece of non-fiction. There is a body of research that explores the benefits of using dialogic talk as a generic pedagogy (Howe and Mercer, 2007). However, Ofsted does warn that this should not be 'conflated with the prior teaching of the structures of language that would allow effective communication in the first place' (Ofsted, 2022). This suggests that students may need pre-teaching or guidance on how to talk for different purposes, through modelling by the teacher or more structured activities, with clear roles for students.

When students are writing and using literary devices in their own work, metacognitive talk can also be a really useful tool in helping them be aware of, and in control of, their own mental processes. Metacognitive talk involves a person saying out loud what they are thinking while they are carrying out a task. This helps the learner make changes and adapt strategies, if the monitoring through the metacognitive talk indicates they are not doing so well on a certain task. Maths teacher, David Thomas wrote:

> 'When I solve a problem in maths, I am constantly talking to myself. This self-talk narrates my problem solving. It is how I test out ideas, challenge myself to think differently and encourage myself to keep going. Talk is the start of reasoning.' (Thomas, 2024)

The power of self-talk in English too can not be underestimated. This might involve an element of modelling, where the teacher would talk through their own interpretations about why literary devices have been used and then this would act as an internal scaffold for students, who could practise how to think in a similar way.

As well as verbally analysing and sharing interpretations about literary devices and the metacognitive talk about using them in their own writing, students can also use literary devices such as rhetoric for the purpose of arguing, persuading or advising. Although Speaking and Listening no longer contributes to the overall GCSE grade for students, they must still perform a spoken language presentation where they will be given a 'Pass', 'Merit' or 'Distinction' grade. At 'Distinction' level, the mark scheme states that the student should achieve the purpose of his or her presentation. Often, their purpose will be partly to inform and engage the audience but also to persuade them of a particular line of argument. Therefore, encouraging students to use literary devices judiciously in their spoken language will make their talk much more effective.

How?

HACK #2.7: USING FILM

When it comes to asking students to deliver a more formal speech, it is useful for them to be exposed to a range of effective speech transcripts and also videos of these being performed. They can then discuss how the literary devices were used judiciously and how it contributed to the overall effect. Many films have persuasive speeches in them, which work well for this, and students often find this engaging, for example, *Independence Day*, *Gladiator*, *Any Given Sunday* or even Lady Macbeth's speech in *Macbeth*. Reese Witherspoon's 'Woman of the Year' speech is also an excellent transcript to discuss, with the whole video also being on YouTube, so students can see the transcript brought to life through intonation and other techniques. Watching a range of different speeches, delivered for different purposes and audiences, will also enable students to come up with a kind of success criteria, which they can then measure their own efforts against. AQA also provides useful videos on YouTube of real GCSE students giving spoken language talks which can be discussed using the mark scheme.

When debating, students again might need a scaffold to help them structure their contributions. A debating bookmark (see Figure 2.9), including some sentence starters, organised by their purpose in a debate, might help less confident students gain more confidence and contribute more meaningfully.

HACK #2.8: METACOGNITIVE TALK

For metacognitive talk, where students discuss and evaluate why they have used literary devices in their writing, questions can be a really useful tool. This goes beyond the simple call and response that some tasks require and instead encourages students to use discussion as a way to build knowledge, instead of just proving what they already know. This builds on both Piaget (1959) and Vygotsky's (1962) research on children being active participants in the construction of knowledge and co-constructing knowledge through social interactions. Talking with their peers about their writing, asking each other questions about their choices, and debating what the best approaches might be, help students develop more complex thinking and reasoning skills. Students can act as critical friends here, helping one another develop multiple perspectives, which in turn can lead to deeper learning. Teachers may need to explicitly teach students how to examine their thinking processes.

This could start with the teacher talking through their thought processes and providing a scaffold such as a question, set of sentence starters or a strategy to help students do this themselves. Taking on a specific role such as 'talking like a writer' can help students structure their metacognitive talk more effectively. Figure 2.10 might act as a useful resource for students who lack confidence in this.

DEBATING

1 Starting off a debate I am increasingly starting to believe ... It is my opinion that ... I know ... therefore ...
2 Agreeing I agree ... because/due to the fact that ... I would like to support ... because I also am of the opinion that ... Following on from ...'s point ... You have persuaded me because ...
3 Building on a point I agree with ... and I want to add ... Building on from what ... said ... Extending on from ...'s idea ... Linking to ...'s idea ...I would like to add ...
4 Justifying I know ...therefore ... I think / feel / know this because ... I know someone that ... I predict ... because ... I bet you're thinking ...
5 Disagreeing I can see your point, but ... While I understand what you're saying, I also think ... That's a valid point, but have you thought about ... I would like to challenge ...

? Did you know that ...? Have you thought about ...?
Can I check that ...? Can you expand on ...?

Figure 2.9 Debating bookmark

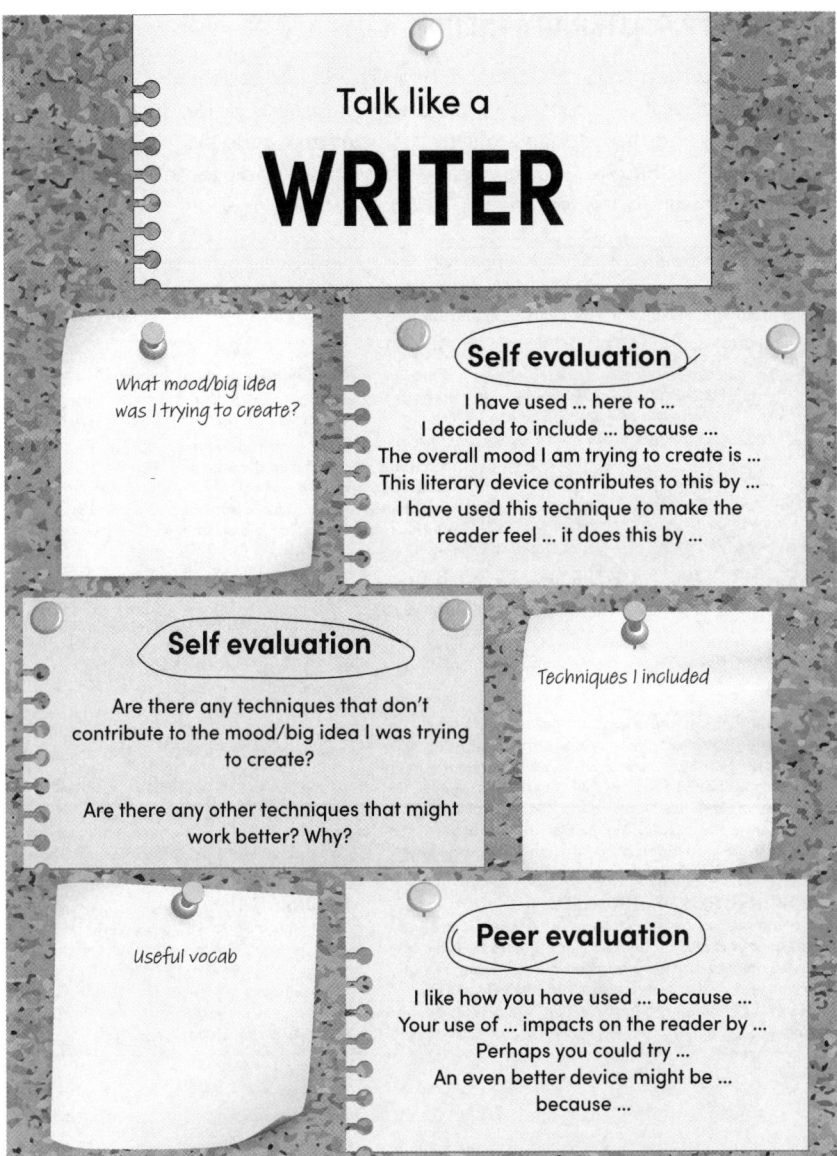

Figure 2.10 Talk like a writer display board

HACK #2.9: LITERARY THEORY

Group and paired talk can also be a great way of teaching literary theory through collaborative inquiry. You could take a famous simile, such as 'solitary as an oyster', and give students a stimulus from an academic journal (see Figure 2.11) and ask them to discuss whether they agree or disagree with the critic's interpretations and whether they can add ideas of their own.

Oh! but he was a tight-fisted hand at the grindstone, Scrooge! a squeezing, wrenching, grasping, scraping, clutching, covetous old sinner! Hard and sharp as flint, from which no steel had ever struck out generous fire; secret, and self-contained, and solitary as an oyster.	
SOLITARY Scrooge is isolated from his fellow creatures as an oyster's body is by its enclosing shell. He edges his way 'along the crowded paths of life', 'warning all human sympathy to keep its distance.' By identifying reclusiveness and misanthropy with miserliness, Scrooge's habitual shunning of other people is a denial of the human commerce upon which a healthy society depends.	**SECRET** There is something hidden inside of Scrooge. The comparison with an oyster implies it is something good, equivalent to the oyster's tasty flesh or cradled pearl. At first this seems confusing as we are told by Dickens that there was 'more cold within him.' But the good is buried deep and we get clues about its existence with his craving for love at Christmas as a child and his gleeful celebrations as an apprentice at Fezziwigs.

A FLEETING GLIMPSE OF THE SECRET WITHIN Within the first stave, Scrooge cracks his shell for an instant:
     'But why?' cried Scrooge's nephew. 'Why?'
     'Why did you get married?' said Scrooge.
     'Because I fell in love.'
 	
 The question about marriage is inappropriate to the conversational context and it betrays his passionate involvement with marriage which still presses down on him. His repetition of Fred's answer marks Scrooge's remastery of what is within and the 'Good afternoon!' is the shell snapping shut again. Just like the potatoes bubbling in the saucepan at the Cratchits, Scrooge's goodness is beginning to bubble up and try to get out.
	SELF-CONTAINED Like an oyster, Scrooge has a crusty shell, which contains an organism quite shut off from the world around him, prevented from finding its way to the outside. Restriction defines Scrooge: his physique, his physiognomy and the stiff gait, as well as the small path he treads through London, on the margins of society.
	
	 Scrooge's restraint is in marked contrast to Bob Cratchit's elaborate celebrations on leaving the office, the frenzied activities of Belle's many children and Topper's tactile behaviour while playing 'Blind Man's Buff.'

BREAKING OPEN OF THE SHELL At the end of the novella, Scrooge's shell breaks open and his behaviour is also no longer restricted; he flails his arms while he dresses and dances as he shaves. When out on the street, he shakes hands rather than sticking to the edges of the pavements. In short, Scrooge passes beyond his shell.	**TO SUMMARISE:** Scrooge is lodged within his world and his story as a grain of sand against the fleshy part of an oyster. Like the grain of sand, he undergoes a transformation, through the visits of the three spirits, then finally emerges as the story's pearl.

Figure 2.11 Scrooge worksheet

Why?

Teaching literary devices is really important, so that students are able to analyse the writer's craft and intention and also so that they are able to produce their own writing, which engages the reader and evokes emotion. It is also a great way of helping students develop their spoken language, as it gets them to think deeply about the ways they are communicating for different audiences and purposes. Researchers have compared a number of methods in teaching literature and all of these methods included some instruction in the use of literary devices to interpret literature. Authors use literary devices and expect their readers to be familiar with the devices if they are to understand what they are reading. Another study pointed to the possible importance of students knowing literary devices. In discussing teaching literature thematically, Thompson concluded analysis of an author's idea without regard to other devices like plot, character or device choice might make analysis more shallow (Thompson, 1973). Finally, teaching literary devices has been stressed in some literature anthologies as a method for improving students' reading, or for interpreting literature (Chase, Jewett and Evans, 1965).

CHAPTER 3: STRUCTURE

In reading, understanding structure helps students grasp how texts are intentionally organised to affect reader experience, supporting comprehension and analytical skills. Writing instruction involves explicit teaching of structural techniques, improving clarity, coherence and impact in students' own work, supported by iterative feedback practices. For oracy, structuring speech equips students to articulate thoughts clearly, enhancing understanding, memory retention and metacognitive skills. The chapter highlights strategies like explicit modelling, the integration of reading and writing, structured discussions, and scaffolded oracy tasks, reinforcing the interplay of structured communication skills as essential to literacy development, cognitive engagement and academic success.

READING

What?

GCSE specification changes always bring fresh surprises for teachers and 2015's offer was no different. Analysing language is an English teacher's bread and butter, but structure? When teachers saw Language Paper 1's Question 3 focus, even the most experienced teacher had a bit of a head scratching moment...I know I certainly did.

The AQA GCSE English Language Paper 1, Question 3, focuses on analysing the structure of a text. It explores how the writer's choices in organising the text (beginning, middle, end) impact the reader's experience and understanding. This begins with an understanding of structure, meaning the way a text is arranged and how its parts fit together, as well as the fact that writers deliberately structure their texts to create specific effects on the reader. If you have been teaching literature well, with an understanding of the text as a construct, then this will help here. Students need to understand that the text is a living, breathing thing, which speaks to them and imparts a message, feeling or tone. It also requires a knowledge of structural devices – the techniques the writer uses to shape the narrative, like changes in time, location or pace. What does the writer draw attention to and where? Is it key details, characters or themes? Then what do these shifts in tone, atmosphere, pace, setting or character make us think, feel, imagine or experience? For many teachers and students alike, this is a far departure from the PEE/PEEL-like structure previously relied on to analyse language. For those first Year 10 students encountering this question for the first time, it must have seemed an odd thing to focus on. In an ideal world, they would have already had the foundations laid for engaging with this task early on in their secondary career.

Bruner proposed that any subject can be taught effectively to any child at any stage of development, provided it is structured properly in a spiral curriculum (Bruner, 1960). The key features of the spiral curriculum are:

- Repetition with progression, where key ideas are revisited at regular intervals.
- Increasing depth, as each encounter with the topic increases in complexity and abstraction.
- Cumulative learning, as prior knowledge is built upon and refined, not simply repeated.
- Transfer and application, because concepts are explored in new contexts to promote flexible thinking.

Therefore, planning a spiral curriculum implies that re-encountering a concept after a gap in time allows for stronger retention through spaced repetition and deepening schema by adding new layers of understanding. Bruner also believed that spiralling back to a concept helps learners restructure and reframe their thinking, which aligns closely with how teachers promote mastery through low-stakes retrieval, cumulative assessments and deliberate revisiting of key knowledge and skills. With a new specification, that backwards, intentional planning was, of course, not possible and in addition, the details about the focus of the questions were not made public to teachers until quite late on in the school year for teaching in a few months time. This meant teachers didn't have time to upskill properly before they had to hit the ground running … it is perhaps no wonder then that teachers find this one of the most difficult questions to teach.

The question asks: 'How has the writer structured the text to interest you as a reader?' Even the wording of the question sometimes flummoxes students as it gives them no steer on what they should think or feel, or even what the tone of the text may be. This is, of course, something the exam board has picked up on and, from 2026 onwards, the question will have a more specific focus, which will direct students to analyse how the writer has structured the text to create a particular effect, such as suspense or tension (AQA, 2025). This will certainly provide students with a clearer direction to help them analyse the writer's specific choices. Many students struggle to move beyond simply summarising the text and instead focus on identifying and explaining the writer's choices. Or even worse, commit the cardinal sins of writing 'the writer does this to make the reader want to read on' or 'paint a picture inside the reader's head.' There are also many examples of the student who exclaims that they don't know what to write as 'it doesn't interest me.'

Question 3 is assessed using AO2: 'Explain, comment on and analyse how writers use language and structure to achieve effects and influence readers, using relevant subject terminology to support their views' (AQA, 2026). So, let's break this down, starting with 'Explain, comment on and analyse.' This phrase reflects a progression of depth in thinking.

- 'Explain' means that students give a basic description of what the writer is doing, for example using a flashback.
- 'Comment on' suggests a slightly more developed view that begins to hint at meaning or effect, for example, the flashback shows the character's nostalgia for a time before this.
- 'Analyse' suggests a much deeper, more layered, interpretation that explores how techniques work and why they're used: 'the flashback evokes isolation as the character withdraws from the present day, reinforcing the theme of alienation, and positioning the reader to sympathise with the character.'

It is clear from this AO that stronger answers go beyond identifying features; they probe the reasons and effects, offering interpretations rooted in the focus of text. This is highlighted in the second part of the AO which focuses on how writers use their structural choices '... to achieve effects and influence readers ...' This makes it clear that writers make choices for a reason: to create an emotional impact, build tension, shape the reader's view of a character or issue or guide interpretation. There are a myriad of different effects beyond the 'interest' the question focuses on. Effects might include: surprise, suspense, humour, sadness, empathy or dramatic tension. Again, the lesson for students here is that they must not just spot techniques. Instead, they need to say why the writer used them in that part of the extract and what impact they have on the reader's experience or understanding. Of course, knowing the correct names for the techniques is helpful, as it creates a shared language and, again, this is also reinforced in the AO, which talks about 'using relevant subject terminology.' This refers to the technical vocabulary that demonstrates knowledge of literary and linguistic concepts. For structure, this might include techniques such as in media res, flashback, foreshadowing, shifts in focus, cyclical structure, juxtaposition, cliffhanger and zoom-in/out (see Figure 3.1). Terminology should be accurate, purposeful and embedded naturally, not used as a checklist. Overusing jargon without analysis does not meet AO2 at a high level and there are many examples of where this is referred to in examiner's reports, such as this from 2020: 'structural terminology need not be complex' and that 'failure to use structural terminology' leaves students 'writing about content rather than structure.' (AQA, 2020)

Structural technique	Definition
Exposition	The introduction of background information, such as setting, character, or conflict.
Narrative hook	A compelling opening that grabs the reader's attention.
Climax	The moment of highest tension or turning point in a narrative.
Resolution (denouement)	The final part of the story where conflicts are resolved.
Chronological order	Events are presented in the order in which they happen.
Flashback	A scene set in a time earlier than the main story.
Foreshadowing	Hints or clues about what will happen later in the story.
Juxtaposition	Placing two contrasting elements side-by-side to highlight difference.
Shift in Focus	A deliberate move in the narrative's focus (e.g. from setting to character, or external to internal).
Zoom-in	Moving from a wide perspective to a detailed close-up in description or narrative.
Zoom-out	Moving from detailed observation to a wider context or overview.
Cyclical structure	When a text ends in a similar way to how it began, creating a full-circle effect.
Analepsis	Another word for flashback – a past event inserted into the present timeline.
Prolepsis	A flash-forward; a scene that jumps ahead of the current timeline.
Pacing	The speed at which events unfold – can be fast (action) or slow (description).
Paragraphing for effect	Deliberate use of paragraph length or breaks to build tension or control flow.
Withholding information	Deliberately delaying key facts to create suspense or tension.
Repetition	Repeated words, phrases or structures for emphasis or rhythm.

Structural technique	Definition
Dialogue	Use of character speech to reveal information or drive the plot.
Contrast	Opposing ideas or tones placed close together to highlight difference.
Binary oppositions	Conceptual pairs (e.g. light/dark, good/evil) used to create conflict or structure.
Perspective shift	Change in narrative viewpoint (e.g. from one character's thoughts to another's).
Time shift	Change in time period within the narrative.
Internal monologue	A character's thoughts presented directly to the reader.
Foil character	A secondary character who contrasts with the main character to highlight traits.
Symbolic structure	The use of motifs or repeated symbols to add layers of meaning to the narrative.
Structural irony	When the organisation of the text creates a contrast between appearance and reality.
Embedded narrative	A story within a story; a character recounts a separate tale.
Circular ending	The conclusion mirrors the opening to suggest completion or futility.
Motif development	A recurring idea or image developed throughout the structure for thematic emphasis.
Tension and release	Alternating periods of suspense and resolution to shape emotional flow.

Figure 3.1 Suggested subject terminology for structure

In practice then, students should aim to:

- Select short, precise textual evidence that illustrates a writer's technique.
- Use subject terminology confidently but only when it supports analysis.
- Explore how the structure creates meaning or influences the reader.
- Interpret possible effects, ideally suggesting more than one impact or reading.
- Link their ideas to the wider purpose, tone or theme of the text and how that shifts.

AO2 is not just about finding techniques, it's about understanding choices. Students who excel are those who think like writers, considering how each detail shapes the reader's journey. For us as English teachers, encouraging curiosity about the why and how of writing, not just the what, is the key to mastering AO2. So, how might we do this?

How?

As we've discussed, this question directs students to examine the organisation of the text: how it begins, develops and ends and to understand how these structural choices impact the reader's experience. Therefore, we can scaffold this process by breaking it down into a series of questions.

1. **Beginnings:** How does the text open? Does it start in media res (in the middle of action), with a description, or with a dialogue? Why has the writer constructed it to start in this way?
2. **Shifts in focus:** Observe how the writer transitions between settings, characters, or time periods. What do these shifts make us think, feel, imagine or experience? Does it change the mood or atmosphere?
3. **Paragraphing:** Note the use of single-sentence paragraphs or changes in paragraph length and their effects. How do they contribute to an existing feeling or mood or how do they change it? Why at that place in the text?
4. **Pace:** Identify where the narrative speeds up or slows down and the purpose behind these changes.
5. **Endings:** Analyse how the text concludes. Does it resolve the narrative, leave questions unanswered, or return to earlier themes?

Yet, even before we get to this point, depending on the structure of our KS3 curriculum, or if we are teaching pupils lower down the school, we may need to first lay the foundations for thinking about structure, as it is a different skill.

HACK #3.1: BUILDING A MENTAL MODEL OF WHAT STRUCTURE IS

In a 2019 blog, Stuart outlined a useful structure for building the skills of analysing structure cumulatively (Pryke, 2019), which we will explore here in more detail. It begins with a discussion about what the term structure actually means, as it gives students something tangible to work with. Students might begin with crafting their own definitions on a mini whiteboard and then taking part in a think-pair-share to refine their definitions with a peer before holding them up for the teacher to scan and read. After crafting the definitions, they would compare them with the teacher's definition on the board, which might look something like:

> The structure of a text is how it is organised by a writer and how its parts fit together.
> Writers structure their texts deliberately to make the reader think and feel certain things.

Although this is quite a simple definition, it can be demonstrated in action by the next activity which came from an idea by Amy Staniforth. Students are asked to imagine a school that has positive and negative qualities and that they need to 'put together' a tour of their imaginary school. This tour must leave their imaginary visitor with a positive impression and the teacher then asks students *why* the various stops on their tour would leave visitors with a good impression of the school. This emphasises the idea that writers 'put together' their text to create certain effects. This can then be flipped to be a tour that would leave their imaginary visitor with a bad impression of their imaginary school. Again, it is vital that the teacher asks students *why* their various stops would leave a negative impression on their visitor. This can be really effective, as it works in helping students to realise that we are shown things in a text for a reason and the things we are shown will leave an impression on us.

HACK #3.2: USING FILM TO EXPLORE STRUCTURE

Next, students could examine how directors structure scenes in films. This is one of my favourite things to do and, as I have a penchant for a scary movie, I love to use *Jurassic Park* or *Jaws* clips – obviously age appropriate. Stuart uses *Harry Potter* for this intro to structure, as it has four distinct edits that students can say a lot about. Students watch the scene twice; the first time, students simply watch it and the second time, students complete the following questions.

- How many edits are there?
- What is the first shot?
- Why do you think the director begins the scene focusing on the character's eyes?
- Why does the director then pull away so we can see the whole of the character's face?
- What is the last shot?
- How is it different to the first shot?
- What is effective about this shot?

The purpose of this task is to help students discuss structure on a basic level and to start thinking about what the director is showing us, how they're showing us and why (see Figure 3.2). This process can be repeated with the opening of *Back to the Future* (an idea by Amy Staniforth) to embed basic knowledge of the 'What, how, why' structure which students will be asked to use later on.

CHAPTER 3: STRUCTURE

QUESTION 3 – LOOKING AT THE DIRECTOR'S CHOICES	
Harry Potter	
How many edits are there?	
What is the first shot?	
Why do you think the director begins the scene focusing on the character's eyes?	
Why does the director then pull away so we can see the whole of the character's face?	
What is the last shot?	
How is it different to the first shot?	
What is effective about this shot?	
BACK TO THE FUTURE	
Note down everything that you can see.	
What does the viewer learn from these camera shots?	
How does the director capture our interest and make us want to keep on watching? What does he reveal?	
What does the director keep secret? Why could this be?	

Figure 3.2 Film worksheet

To make the link between film and text clear, Stuart does stress that writers have the same jobs as directors. Their job is to show us certain events to make us think and feel certain things. A director has music, edits and camera angles to help them create their effects and a writer has their own tools too. He introduces a limited amount of subject terminology here and is explicit about how students should use it and not become too preoccupied with it. This introduction to terminology and the tools a writer can use helps shift the focus away from structure in film to structure in writing. The AQA English Language Paper 1 resource booklet (AQA, 2016) has a great range of extracts you can use for this, as does the generous TES account of Matthew Lynch (TES Resources, 2026), who produces a huge amount of practice papers free for the English community. Stuart often chooses *I'm the King of the Castle* for this intro stage, because the extract provided is relatively easy to understand while containing lots to talk about in terms of structure. Reading through the extract, he asks students to title each paragraph to summarise what is happening, asking questions to do with plot and character as he goes to check understanding (see Figure 3.3).

Extract from *I'm the King of the Castle* by Susan Hill	1. Read each paragraph.
	2. Add a title for each paragraph.
	3. Summarise each paragraph in two to three bullet points.
	4. Summarise what happens in the extract as a whole in no more than six sentences.

Figure 3.3 *I'm the King of the Castle* worksheet

HACK #3.3: WHAT/HOW/WHY?

It is fair to say that Becky Wood's seminal *What/How/Why* blog has really transformed many English teachers' practice (Wood, 2018). It is useful for all questions in language and literature but it is the structure question where it really comes into its own. In his blog, Stuart condenses Becky's idea into three key areas.

- What is the writer showing us?
- How are they showing us this?
- Why are they showing us this?

The first of those three questions is simple to answer and can be summed up in one or two sentences maximum. It is with the 'how' question that students can add in their quotation containing a structural feature. This may need to be made explicit to students as many struggle with how they should include quotations in Question 3, particularly as they won't be analysing any language in them. This gives them a clear format they can use to help them add quotations to their answer in a way that will strengthen the quality of their response.

The 'why' question is the most challenging one for students, as they really struggle to articulate why they're being shown something. To help direct their thoughts, Stuart suggests asking a sub-question: 'Why are they showing us this?', or 'What does the reader learn from being shown this?' By considering what the reader learns about the setting, character and plot, students are able to articulate clearly why the writer is showing them what they are. When modelling with the 'I/we/you' method, it is useful to begin with the 'why' by selecting from the following sentence structures.

- Perhaps the writer shows the reader X to help them learn ...
- This is structurally significant because the reader learns ...
- The writer does this so the reader can learn ...

Eventually, students will find their own ways of expressing the 'why' part of the structure question and many will be able to do so without using the word 'learn'. But to begin with, it can be a really effective way of nudging students in the right direction when helping them comment on the effect of structure.

HACK #3.4: WORKED EXAMPLES

A worked example can help students see what this looks like in action, where they can highlight the 'what', 'how' and 'why' in an answer that focuses on just one small paragraph from the extract. Focusing on the structure of a paragraph before the structure of an entire source allows students to gain the knowledge and skills needed on a smaller scale first. With this in mind, you might discuss each section of the answer before choosing another small paragraph from the extract and writing about that together as a class. Again, a strong focus on the 'what/how/why' structure allows students to clearly express their ideas.

When students get to the 'we do' of the modelling process, you can choose a third paragraph for them to focus on. At this point, students' use of subject terminology is still limited with most focusing on 'zooming in/out' and 'shifts in focus' but students who focus on the 'why' more than the 'how' tend to be more successful anyway, and an answer stuffed with terminology can run into problems very easily. This focus on the structure of paragraphs before looking at the whole text allows students to understand what is required of them and hones their ability to analyse structure on a smaller scale before moving to the text as a whole.

This can then be followed up with a side-by-side look at Questions 2 and 3 with a new extract, so students can see the different requirements of each question and clearly separate them in their mind (see Figure 3.4).

Question 2: Language	Extract (Paragraph)	Question 3: Structure
How does the writer use language to present the boys riding on the bikes? Meaning first: What is the writer saying about the boys riding on their bikes? Method second: How are they being presented? What language features have been used and what is their effect? Why are they being presented in this way? How does the writer want the reader to feel? The writer presents the boys in the extract as being energetic and spirited. When describing how the boys ride on their bikes the writer says 'we charged'. The _____ 'charged' suggests…	We charged through on our bikes. Bikes became important, our horses. We galloped through the garage yards and made it to the other side. I tied a rope to the handlebars and hitched my bike to a pole whenever I got off it. We parked our bikes on verges so they could graze. The rope got caught between the spokes of the front wheel; I went over the handlebars, straight over. It was over before I knew. The bike was on top of me. I was alone. I was okay. I wasn't even cut. We charged into the garages— –Woo wooo wooo wooo wooo wooo wooo! and the garages captured our noise and made it bigger and grownup. We escaped out the other end, out onto the street and back for a second attack. We got material from our houses and made headbands. Mine was a tartan one, with a seagull's feather. We took off our jumpers and shirts and vests. James O'Keefe took off his trousers and rode through Bayside in his underpants. His skin was stuck to the saddle when he was getting off, from the sweat; you could hear the skin clinging to the plastic. We threw his trousers onto the roof of a garage, and his shirt and his vest. We put his jumper down a shore. The garage roofs were easy to get up onto. We climbed up on our saddles and onto the roofs when we'd conquered the forts. –Woo wooo wooo wooo wooo wooo wooo! A woman looked out of a bedroom window and made a face and moved her hands, telling us to get down. We did the first time. We got on our bikes and hightailed it out of Bayside. She'd called the police; her husband was a Guard; she was a witch. I got straight from the roof onto the bike without touching the ground. I pushed off from the wall. There was a wobble but then I was gone. I circled the garages to make sure that the others had time to escape.	How does the writer structure the text to interest you as a reader? What is the writer showing us at the beginning of the extract? How are they showing us this? Find a quotation/structural feature to help you explain your ideas. Why are they showing a reader this? What is a reader learning from this? What does the writer change our focus towards? How are they changing the focus? Find a quotation/structural feature to help you explain your ideas. Why are they changing the focus? What is a reader learning from what they have been directed to focus on? At the beginning of the text, the writer focuses the reader's attention on…

Figure 3.4 Questions 2 and 3 examples

CHAPTER 3: STRUCTURE

AQA English Language, Paper 1, Question 3
Do it now task: List ten structural methods a writer could use in a text. **Extension:** Define them.
1. _____   6. _____
2. _____   7. _____
3. _____   8. _____
4. _____   9. _____
5. _____   10. _____

Activity 1: Read the text twice. The first time, read for meaning. The second time, start searching for examples of the structural choices you have listed above. Highlight and annotate what you find.

Activity 2: Now consider the important question: Why? Why has the writer used these structural methods? Complete the sub-questions below. Use the example to help you.

1. What is the reader being shown here?
2. How is the reader being shown it? (quotation + structural method)
3. Why has the writer shown it? What does the reader learn from being shown this? What will the reader think, feel or imagine?

This extract is from the beginning of a novel by Ken Follett, set in the year 1123 AD.

The small boys came early to the hanging.

> The writer begins the extract by focusing on the 'small boys' who, we are told, have arrived early at a public hanging. Follett establishes the setting, 'a little town' with 'huddled wooden huts', and tracks the boys as they make their way to the site of the execution. Perhaps Follett begins by showing the reader the boys because their presence is surprising. We wouldn't expect young children to witness such a violent event. This juxtaposition of innocence and death, combined with the 'frozen mud' and the 'gallows' creates a bleak tone. It is clear this world is harsh and as such, readers may question how children can survive in this bleak place.

It was still dark when the first three or four of them sidled out of the hovels, quiet as cats in their felt boots. A thin layer of fresh snow covered the little town like a new coat of paint, and theirs were the first footprints to blemish its perfect surface. They picked their way through the huddled wooden huts and along the streets of frozen mud to the silent market-place, where the gallows stood waiting.

The boys despised everything their elders valued. They scorned beauty and mocked _____

Figure 3.5 Paper 1 Question 3 practice

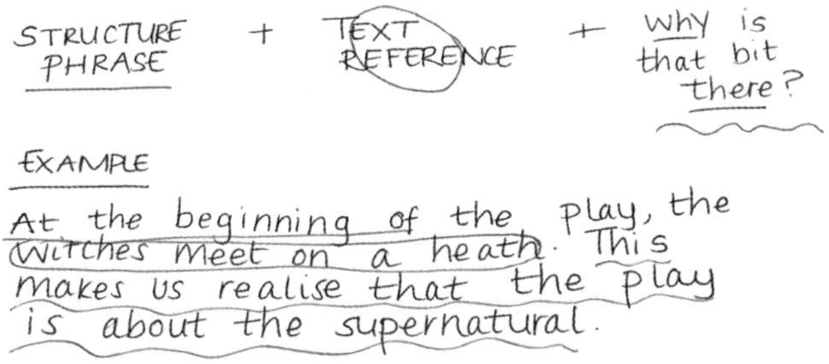

STRUCTURE PHRASE + TEXT REFERENCE + Why is that bit there?

EXAMPLE

At the beginning of the play, the witches meet on a heath. This makes us realise that the play is about the supernatural.

Figure 3.6 Example start of question response

HACK #3.5: PRACTICE

Of course, practice is key, as is ensuring that students do not overcomplicate their answers, so that they become technique-soup, or concentrate on the content rather than the effect. Again, Stuart has produced another useful resource where he breaks the process down with a short model paragraph that students can use as an anchor for their own writing (see Figure 3.5).

Tom Needham (2022) recommends starting with literature texts that the students know well, as it reduces the difficulty. Because they know the content, they can entirely focus on the elements needed for success. When teaching these elements, Needham highlights that providing an abstract representation of what an answer requires helps students to develop a transferable mental model that they can then apply when practising. According to Heal and Berlin (2025), 'a mental model serves as a cognitive blueprint that guides our actions.' They also serve 'as a reference point for our performance,' so that we can refine and adjust till we hit the bar. For the structure question, Figure 3.6 shows how to start a response to the question.

Students can be explicitly taught these phrases and should have numerous different practice opportunities to use these independently. As Tom Needham states:

> 'Initial practice should be guided and the teacher can remind students of what is required in their response. This support should be faded out as quickly as possible and the goal of guided practice is accurate performance. Students will begin to develop their fluency and later trials should require students to finish in incrementally shorter time periods. Guided practice should involve students making specific checks when they finish the task. Students should label their answer, demonstrating where they have included the three elements (structural phrase + text reference + why is that bit there).' (Needham, 2022)

Looking at sample answers and dissecting them for their active ingredients is also an important part of building a mental model. Emma Lee's brilliant *Madame Anglais* blog has some sample answers you can use for each level in Question 3 (Lee, 2018) and you could even print these out and ask students to order them, comparative judgement style, before explaining why they are better or worse than one another.

WRITING

What?

If English teaching involves giving our students the opportunity to take part in the great discursive threads and debates in our subject, then in writing this may look like helping our students stand on the shoulder of giants when it comes to producing their own writing. To be able to understand how they might employ structural techniques themselves, it is useful to see how experienced writers do it – yet another argument to teach both language and literature interchangeably, not as discrete subjects. How has Priestley employed a cyclical structure? Why did Shakespeare begin Macbeth with the stormy witches scene? How does Dickens employ flashbacks through the spirits to evoke a sense of sympathy for Scrooge? All of these are useful questions for students to consider when they begin to understand the text as a construct.

Yet it isn't just structuring fiction writing that students need instruction on. The Ofsted English Subject Report details that the teaching of non-fiction is less well planned than fiction in many schools and this aligns with our own experiences. The report states that 'Individual teachers make decisions based on the needs and interests of their particular class, following on from their assessments. In these schools, it is less clear how pupils are specifically taught to analyse texts in detail or replicate the style of writing themselves.' (Ofsted, 2024). To develop proficiency in writing, pupils need opportunities to write frequently for a range of purposes and audiences, including academic writing. This includes explicit teaching on sentence construction, vocabulary, grammar and syntax, which will allow them to write with confidence and increasing flair. They also need to be taught how to plan, draft and revise their work, to reflect on the choices they make as writers, and to draw on the models of writing they study and encounter in their reading.

AQA's writing mark scheme states that top students must have:

- Varied and inventive use of structural features.
- Fluently-linked paragraphs with seamlessly integrated discourse markers.

Essentially, structuring writing is a fundamental skill for students learning English, as it enhances clarity, coherence and the ability to evoke specific effects, moods, tones and feelings in their writing. A well-structured piece of writing allows readers to follow the writer's ideas logically and ensures that the introduction sets the stage, the body develops the argument or narrative and the conclusion provides closure. This logical flow is not only essential for effective communication, but also helps maintain the reader's interest by presenting information in a digestible and organised manner. It allows for the strategic placement of key points, building suspense and emphasising critical information.

The structure of a text also influences its tone (the writer's attitude) and mood (the emotional atmosphere). For instance, short, abrupt sentences can create a tense tone, while longer, flowing sentences may establish a more relaxed mood. According to the *English Composition Handbook*, tone is conveyed through word choice and sentence structure, impacting how readers perceive the text (Shelby, 2021). This means that writers can manipulate structure to achieve particular effects, such as surprise or suspense. For example, placing a critical piece of information at the end of a paragraph can create a dramatic impact, or the strategic use of structural elements like foreshadowing or flashbacks can also enhance a character's depth. However, as the Ofsted Subject Report cited previously states, understanding structure is not limited to narrative writing; it is equally important in transactional writing. Each genre has its conventions and mastering structure enables students to adapt their writing to various contexts effectively.

Arthur Applebee also emphasised the importance of teaching students how to structure their writing. In his collaborative work with Judith A. Langer, *How Writing Shapes Thinking: A Study of Teaching and Learning*, they argue that effective writing instruction, particularly in academic contexts, enhances the quality of students' thinking (Applebee and Langer, 1987). They note that writing tasks focusing on the relationships that give structure and coherence to information lead to better retention and understanding. They suggest that traditional writing instruction often emphasises the final product over the writing process and advocate for a more process-oriented approach, encouraging students to plan, revise and edit their work. They observe that students who engage in these process strategies tend to be better writers, suggesting a strong link between writing processes and writing achievement .

David Didau (2021a) goes even further than this, by stating that teaching students how to structure writing is essential for developing clarity and coherence. He advocates for a deliberate, scaffolded approach that integrates writing into the broader curriculum, ensuring students not only learn writing techniques but also understand their application within various contexts. This challenges the notion of treating writing as a standalone skill or discrete unit within the curriculum and centres it as an ongoing process, intertwined with content learning. Drawing parallels between writing development and physical training, he introduces the 'Couch to 5K' analogy. Just as novice runners build endurance through incremental challenges, students should develop writing proficiency through regular, manageable tasks that gradually increase in complexity. This approach fosters confidence and skill over time (Didau, 2022b). This might include using thesis statements to structure an argument in essay writing or an inventive structure in creative writing.

Yet, Barbara Bleiman from the English and Media Centre emphasises that teaching writing structure should prioritise meaning-making and the writer's intent over rigid adherence to form and structure. In her blog post 'Teaching Writing: Putting Intentions Before Techniques' (Bleiman, 2024), she critiques approaches that focus excessively on mastering specific sentence structures or writing formulas without considering the underlying purpose of the writing. She argues that such methods can impede genuine expression and the development of a writer's voice: 'Teaching writing at the level of the sentence, focusing on form divorced from meaning, and critically from writers' own intentions, seems like a dangerous blind alley.' Instead, she advocates for a more holistic approach to teaching writing, where students are encouraged to explore and experiment with language to convey their ideas effectively. This perspective is further elaborated in her book *What Matters in English Teaching: Collected Blogs and Other Writing*, where she discusses the importance of balancing form and meaning in writing instruction. She emphasises that while understanding structural elements is valuable, it should not overshadow the writer's purpose and the need for authentic communication.

Like all of these dichotomies in English, somewhere in between the two approaches lies a sensible approach. Education is both enriched and suffers from the wide range of stakeholders it attracts as commenters. While external experts have a place, those who are on the front line teaching in schools must have the last say in what is best for their students, in their context. Teaching how to structure writing can be a fine balance between providing limiting frameworks such as drop/shift/zoom in/zoom out/link or letting students just choose their own adventure. Where do we start?

How?

HACK #3.6: EXPLICIT TEACHING

Although it is American, the What Works Clearinghouse (2016) 'Teaching Secondary Students to Write Effectively' publication is a great place to start. They advocate three evidence-based strategies that will help students learn effective ways to structure their writing.

1. Explicitly teach appropriate writing strategies using a model-practise-reflect instructional cycle.
2. Integrate writing and reading to emphasise key writing features.
3. Use assessments of student writing to inform instruction and feedback.

Let's explore what these approaches might look like in more detail.

Explicitly teach appropriate writing strategies using a model-practise-reflect instructional cycle

This recommendation suggests teaching structure through explicit or direct instruction and through a model-practise-reflect instructional cycle. Therefore, we might teach students different strategies for components of the writing process explicitly, so that they learn how to select a strategy, how to execute each step of the strategy, and how to apply the strategy when writing for different audiences and purposes. You could use the list of strategies from Figure 3.1 in the reading section of this chapter for these. Using the components of the writing process diagram (Figure 3.7) to help with planning may be helpful.

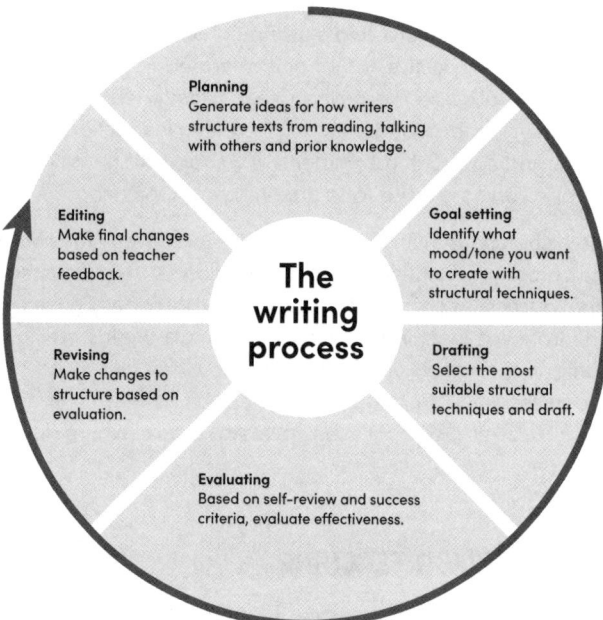

Figure 3.7 Writing process diagram

The model-practise-reflect instructional cycle involves students observing a strategy in use, practising the strategy on their own and evaluating their writing and use of the strategy using success criteria. An example of this might be the teacher modelling using a Freytag pyramid (Figure 3.8) to diagram the plot of a story she is writing.

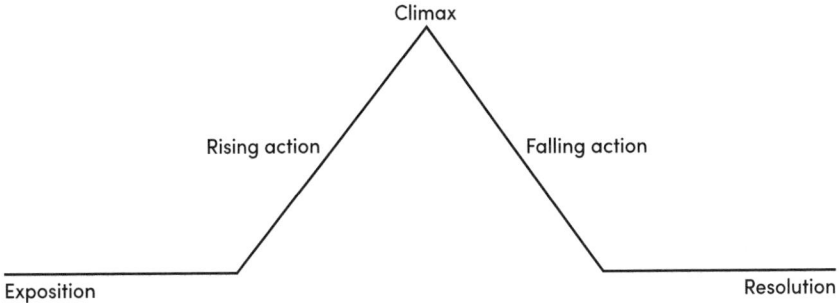

Figure 3.8 Freytag pyramid

To structure her diagram, she follows a framework that includes an exposition or introduction, rising action, climax, falling action, and resolution or conclusion. She discusses how she might complete each section, using a book the class recently read together as an example. Students then select a book to read independently and are asked to produce a plot diagram to analyse the structure and story, before emulating the same structure in their own writing. This also combines reading and writing, which is the second recommendation.

Integrate writing and reading to emphasise key writing features

As highlighted throughout this book, reading exemplar texts familiarises students with important features of writing, which they can then emulate. Writing with a reader in mind and reading with the writer in mind strengthens both skills (Graham and Hebert, 2010). Reading and writing share four types of cognitive processes and knowledge.

'1. Metaknowledge, which involves understanding the reading and writing processes in relation to goals and purposes.

2. Domain knowledge, which is about the substance and content that is revealed from reading and writing.

3. Important text features, which include text format, organisation, and genre, as well as spelling and syntactical combinations that are accepted in a particular language or culture.

4. Procedural knowledge, which includes integrating complex processes to write compositions and using strategies for accessing information when reading text.' (Shanahan, 2016).

The shared knowledge model conceptualises reading and writing as two buckets drawing water from a common well or two buildings built on a common foundation. Therefore, teaching students to understand that both writers and readers use similar strategies, knowledge and skills to create meaning shows students themselves how to create meaning through methods such as structure.

One easy way to do this is to use mentor texts and expose students to high-quality examples of well-structured writing. One particular favourite is the opening of *The Mangler* by Stephen King, where I might scaffold student's analysis of King's use of structure and then support them to use the same structure, with a picture stimulus at the end for some creative writing (see Figure 3.9).

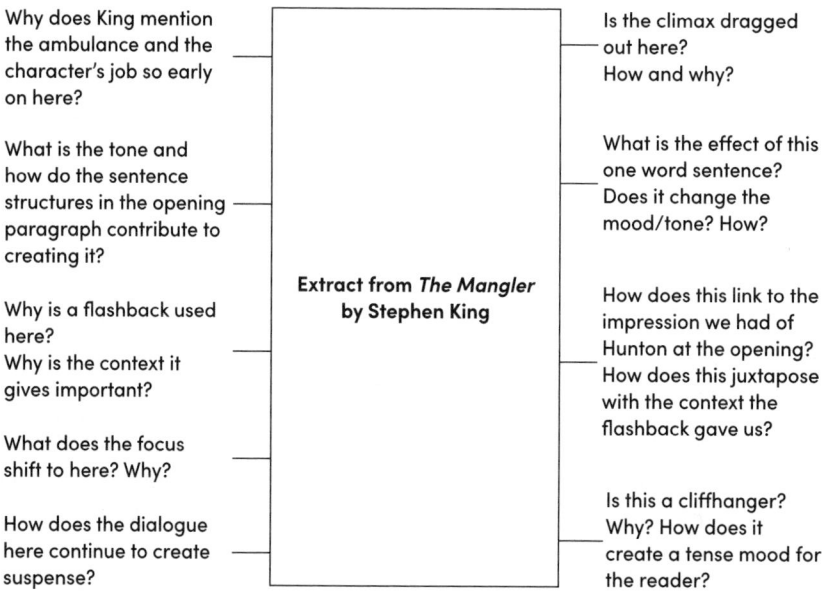

Figure 3.9 Stephen King's *The Mangler* worksheet

However, this is just one text you could look at. It is useful to give students the opportunity to annotate and analyse how writers open, develop and conclude their pieces with a wide range of different text types, alongside a wider discussion of how tone, sentence variety and paragraph organisation contribute to the overall structure.

Over our careers we have been guilty of providing writing frames, so we are not going to proclaim that they are terrible. There is a place for them as a scaffold but, like all scaffolds, they should be taken away at some point. As Ball and Fairlamb (2025) recently wrote in their book on scaffolding, scaffolds that are never taken away are not scaffolds – they are just lesson plans. Writing frames like 'drop/shift/zoom in/zoom out/link' can be useful, especially in the planning stages but often you can see a mile off when students are led by structure rather than content and what is written becomes slave to a flashback and cyclical structure. It is often ideas in more transactional writing that students struggle with, so if frames are helpful, an acronym like MESI (see Figure 3.10) may help students come up with more coherent arguments, while not limiting them to a specific structure.

	Use the MESI acronym to organise your ideas	
• Write less and craft more. • Make a plan and sequence your ideas. • Link paragraphs using discourse markers. • Avoid over-using linguistic devices. • Vary your sentence openings to create effects. • Use a wide range of different punctuation. • Be ambitious in using interesting vocabulary. • Proofread what you have written.	MORAL	Is the behaviour/issue right or wrong? Why? What is the right thing to think/behave? Why?
	ECONOMIC	Is there a cost? Is the cost fair? Does everyone benefit? Is there a waste of money? Does it support anyone/anything financially?
	SOCIAL	What are the effects on society? Which communities does it affect? Who benefits from it? Does it educate? Does it send a message? Will it help anyone/anything in the future?
	INDIVIDUAL	How does it affect individual people? How would they feel/act? Are there any examples (generic) to show this? Does it empower individuals? Does it discriminate against individuals?

Figure 3.10 MESI answer frame

Another way to stress that both writers and readers use similar strategies, knowledge and skills to create meaning is looking at what famous authors say about their processes of writing. Stephen King for example, has spoken widely about the craft of writing. He emphasises that in creative writing, content naturally dictates structure, rather than adhering to rigid, pre-planned frameworks. In his memoir *On Writing: A Memoir of the Craft*, King likens stories to fossils:

> 'Stories are found things, like fossils in the ground ... The writer's job is to use the tools in his or her toolbox to get as much of each one out of the ground intact as possible.' (King, 2000)

This metaphor suggests that a writer's role is to uncover the story's inherent form, allowing the content, characters, situations and themes to shape its structure organically. King often begins with a compelling 'what if' scenario and allows the narrative to evolve from there. He notes:

> 'The situation comes first. The characters—always flat and unfeatured, to begin with—come next. Once these things are fixed in my mind, I begin to narrate.' (King, 2000)

He avoids imposing predetermined plots, believing that doing so can constrain the natural development of the story. Instead, he trusts that the story will create its own patterns naturally and organically if he follows it faithfully. This is a great lesson for students that the structure is driven by the plot and that it can be used to emphasise the mood or tone the plot creates.

Once the plot is secure, visual aids can help students to structure their writing effectively at the planning stage. Storyboards, flowcharts or essay maps for transactional writing can help students to visualise structure before drafting. Having students explain why they are using that focus to a peer can also help them craft their writing.

Use assessments of student writing to inform instruction and feedback

Few people could disagree that it is essential for teachers to use assessments of student writing to inform instruction and feedback. Doing so makes teaching responsive, targeted and effective because well-informed assessment practice leads directly to improved student outcomes. This is because assessment provides teachers with a clear picture of what students have understood and where they need further guidance. By closely analysing student writing, teachers can pinpoint specific skills which need reinforcement and celebrate strengths to boost student confidence and motivation. Dylan Wiliam (2011) also highlights that effective teachers adapt their instruction based on ongoing assessment insights. So, assessments allow teachers to deliver targeted instruction which helps students really improve the structure of their writing, as it meets them where they are.

John Hattie's research (2009) identifies feedback as one of the most powerful factors influencing student achievement, with formative assessment integral to effective feedback. However, this feedback needs to be precise and actionable, clarifying exactly where and how students can improve. Therefore, effective feedback from writing assessments should be:

- **Focused**, targeting specific, achievable writing skills or strategies.
- **Clear and actionable**, indicating precisely how students can improve, rather than vague encouragement. (EEF, 2021a)

This feedback can take many forms, whether verbal while the teacher is circulating or written comments after assessments. Whatever the modality, the key is that students are then given the time to action the feedback on their writing structure and redraft based on your comments. Giving them this time also encourages students to view writing as a dynamic, iterative process involving drafting, revising and refining. For teachers, assessments are used here to guide students through multiple revisions. So, feedback becomes integral to the drafting and revision stages rather than just a final judgement.

HACK #3.7: VISUALISER

Whole-class feedback using the visualiser may be a quick and effective way to help develop students' use of structural techniques in their writing. Dr Andrew Atherton wrote a detailed blog (Atherton, 2021) about how he uses it, where he shows how he uses a template to outline what excellence looks like, with a list of success criteria and a model as well as a space for any misconceptions he has seen across the class. He also has codes that match to a piece of feedback; these codes correspond to a code that has been written on student's work, with bespoke comments for students who have a different target. This means that students know exactly what they need to do to improve. This is then scaffolded even further by a 'Together Task' which the class all complete together based on whatever he thinks will have maximum impact across the class. This task is often connected to the 'excellence is ... and here's what it looks like' section of the feedback lesson, which is done live with a visualiser, so he can articulate his thought processes while completing. He generously shared his template and, inspired by this, we have created a structure specific one (Figure 3.11).

TASK:		Your next steps	
Excellent structure for a suspense story		1	
		2	
And it looks like this	And it looks like this	3	
		4	
Our Together Task		5	

Figure 3.11 Together task writing scaffold

ORACY

What?

There are two factors at play when we consider what structure means when seen through an oracy lens. The first is how *students* can structure their talk and communicate more effectively and the second is how *teachers* can structure talk to ensure that it is a meaningful part of the lesson.

The Ofsted Subject Report refers to oracy as 'spoken language' and stresses that:

> 'the secondary curriculum should continue to teach them the [spoken language] components explicitly, including the vocabulary, register, tone and body language that they can use to communicate their ideas effectively. This teaching allows pupils to make choices about the language and grammatical structures they use.' (Ofsted, 2024)

Through the inclusion of 'grammatical structures' here, it makes it clear that structure is not just a key consideration in reading and writing, it is also important when we are developing our students' oracy skills.

The Oracy Education Commission *We need to talk* report (2024) also stresses the importance of this. The report emphasises that oracy is fundamentally important because it equips young people to articulate ideas clearly, listen actively and engage constructively and critically with others. Specifically, teaching students how to structure talk is vital because structured speech enables them to effectively communicate ideas, reason through arguments and clarify their thinking. Structured oracy supports deeper understanding and cognitive engagement. Approaches like dialogic teaching encourage students to build their knowledge actively through well-organised conversations, questioning and reasoning aloud. By explicitly teaching structured speech, teachers can help students confidently express their ideas and evaluate arguments. Structuring talk also helps students develop essential interpersonal and academic skills, ultimately enabling them to thrive as engaged, reflective citizens even after they leave our care.

There are also some compelling links between cognitive science and helping our students structure their talk. For example, structured talk may help manage cognitive load by breaking down information into manageable segments. Cognitive Load Theory highlights how limited working memory capacity makes it challenging for learners to process new information if presented chaotically. So, structured speech provides frameworks that reduce extraneous cognitive load, enabling students to articulate and comprehend ideas more effectively (Sweller, van Merriënboer and Paas, 2019). Schema theory also highlights that structured talk supports the organisation of knowledge into meaningful patterns or schemas, which can aid comprehension and recall. Anderson's work on schema theory underlines that clear speech structures help students organise and integrate new information with existing mental schemas, improving overall understanding and recall (Anderson, 1984).

Structuring talk to clearly articulate concepts might also act as a form of retrieval practice, which strengthens long-term memory. Cognitive science research by Roediger and Karpicke (2006) demonstrates how actively recalling information (such as in structured oral presentations) promotes deeper learning than passive review. Perhaps, explicitly structuring oral tasks to require retrieval can then reinforce retention. Structured talk may also help students explicitly manage and monitor their thinking processes. Research shows that structured opportunities to verbalise thought processes can enhance metacognitive awareness and self-regulation skills (Flavell, 1979; Schraw and Dennison, 1994).

Creating the right climate for learning is the key to using structured talk and helping students structure their own talk. Let's explore how we can do this.

How?

Believe it or not, well-structured direct instruction and oracy are not in opposition to one another ... even though tribal spats may sometimes make us think they are. As Barbara Bleiman (2021) states: 'A balance between classroom dialogue and teacher input is essential.' Robin Alexander adds:

> 'There is a danger ... that we consign all but [... discussion and dialogue] to the despised archive of 'traditional methods'. In fact, exposition and recitation have an important role in teaching, for facts need to be imparted, information needs to be memorised, and explanations need to be provided, and even the deeply unfashionable rote has a place (memorising tables, rules, spellings and so on).' (Alexander, 2001)

This is sensible. We are sure you have all made the mistake of asking students to turn and talk to their partner or a group about their opinion to find that they do this for ten seconds before getting distracted and discussing the latest episode of *Love Island*. As the EEF highlights, the use of structured questioning to develop reading comprehension and the use of purposeful, curriculum-focused, dialogue and interaction, can make a tangible difference to student outcomes – particularly for our most disadvantaged students (EEF, 2025a). Yet, the classroom culture needed to be able to structure dialogic activities well does not just appear by osmosis; it needs to be crafted. Neil Mercer (2003) terms this the 'dialogic climate.'

HACK #3.8: REFLECT ON ORACY USE

Where opportunities for oracy take place in terms of the structure and sequencing of the lesson is also another consideration. In the *Class Teaching* blog, Fran Haynes (2019) outlines a useful set of questions that teachers can reflect on to ensure that talk is a meaningful part of the learning in the classroom.

- What types of talk are likely to be most beneficial for learning? This might include thinking individually about teacher talk and student talk, and then how the two work together.
- How can we structure talk so that it supports learning rather than being a disparate activity?
- How can we ensure that all students benefit from the talk (teacher's or students') used in the classroom?

Helping students to structure their own talk is also helpful. David Didau (2018) has shared his strategy for this that he calls 'structured discussion.' The teacher asks a question and directs it at a student. After the student gives an answer, the teacher then asks the student to elevate their response, rather than just accepting it, by asking them to 'speak like an essay.' This may be more difficult for some students, which is where the teaching skill of scaffolding comes into play. Didau then recommends that students repeat this answer, with the teacher mediating to make sure students are supported to speak in more academic language.

HACK #3.9: SENTENCE STEMS

Other strategies might be to provide sentence stems for talk as you would for writing. Zwiers (2019) suggests that explicitly teaching three features of enhanced conversation and the language or 'talk moves' that are associated with them can help students more effectively structure their talk.

- **Building ideas:** 'I agree/disagree with ___ because ...', 'I'd like to add onto what ___ said ...', 'What do you think ...?', 'I wonder why ...', 'What if ...'
- **Clarifying ideas:** 'Can you say your answer in a different way?', 'I don't understand why you ...', 'How do you know that's the right answer?', 'Can you explain why?'
- **Supporting ideas:** 'Where did you read (or get) that?', 'Can you give an example?', 'How do you know?', 'On page 'X' it says ...'

Students can also practise creating coherent structures in their talk using the ABCQ strategy: Agree, Build, Challenge or Question. Figure 3.12 is a table with these sentence stems included.

Giving a new opinion I think that ... My opinion is ... I believe that ... In my view ...	Agreeing I agree with ... because ... I would argue the same thing because ... The reason I agree with ...is ... That is an interesting point because ...
Building I would like to build on ...'s point because ... I agree with ... but I need to add ... In addition to ...'s point ... Building on what ... said ... That is a good argument however it needs ...	Challenge or Question I don't think ... is right because ... I would like to challenge this because ... I disagree with ...because ... My own view is different because ... What do you think about this counter argument?

Figure 3.12 Agree, Build, Challenge or Question table scaffold

HACK #3.10: DISCIPLINED DISCUSSION

Teachers can also explicitly teach students how to structure their speeches and oracy work through modelling and demonstrating clear speech structures, such as the classic introduction–body–conclusion framework, so students see how speeches flow logically. Analysing exemplary speeches together to identify clear transitions, openings and conclusions can also help students see structural choices in action. This might include exploring and practising how to craft engaging introductions, through using rhetorical questions, anecdotes or powerful statements. It could also involve demonstrating how to construct impactful conclusions, reinforcing key points and leaving a memorable impression.

Once students possess a well-developed mental model that is underpinned by a strong knowledge of what effective structure in speech looks like, they can take part in paired or group planning sessions which include peer feedback on the logical flow and clarity of ideas. Checklists and rubrics focused specifically on speech structure and delivery can be used to support this peer and self-assessment.

Doug Lemov (2024) calls this kind of work 'disciplined discussion'. This is not the enemy of the spontaneous exploration we love about English; it is a way of carefully constructing and scaffolding student talk with high-quality feedback that is essential to their success, both academically and as a member of society.

Why?

Aside from preparing students for one of the trickiest questions on the exam, teaching students about text structures enables them to better comprehend and retain information. Meyer and Ray (2011) reviewed studies demonstrating that teaching students to recognise and use text structures significantly improves their reading comprehension, especially with expository texts. The EEF (2021b) also emphasises the importance of teaching reading comprehension strategies, including understanding text structures, to support literacy development.

In addition, explicit instruction in writing structures helps students organise their thoughts and communicate effectively. Hebert *et al.* (2021) found that teaching students to use specific text structures in informational writing led to significant improvements in the quality of their writing. Furthermore, the International Literacy Association (2020) highlights that teaching writing not only enhances students' writing skills but also supports reading development, as students learn to analyse text structures and apply them in their own writing.

Teaching structure in reading, writing and oracy provides students with tools to organise and express their ideas effectively. By understanding and applying structural conventions, students become more proficient and confident communicators.

CHAPTER 4: INFERENCE AND MAKING MEANING

Inference is more than a natural response to storytelling. It is a cognitive skill that we, as teachers, must explicitly teach and nurture. When students are shown how to both identify and interpret subtle clues left by a writer, they begin to move beyond surface-level comprehension towards the deeper and more nuanced understanding of meaning that we want them to achieve. We have a responsibility to guide students in recognising and constructing implied meaning, ideas that are not stated outright but essential to a significant and relevant interpretation. Students make inferences daily, even if they are not conscious of this; our role, then, is to bring this process into focus for them, for once they understand what inference is and how to deliberately use it, they will gain a skill set that extends far beyond our classrooms. Equally, it is important to clarify a distinction between inference and analysis, two processes that are related but also distinct. Alongside this, teaching students to recognise and identify use of symbolism and recurring motifs will enrich their ability to interpret literature with greater independence. As teachers, we can position inference as both a reading strategy and a tool for creative writing. By doing so, we can engage students with a more interpretive relationship when it comes to language, one that encourages them to find meaning both at surface level, and deeper, plumbing depths to consider an author's intent, or when it comes to creative writing, their own.

READING

What?

Let's begin by considering how one might define inference. I include here a student-friendly definition:

Inference is a conclusion or prediction drawn from clues in the text or image combined with prior knowledge.

Inference is far more complex than it might appear initially. It is not just about writing down what something suggests. Teaching inference effectively requires careful and intentional instruction because it is a core comprehension skill, one that can enable readers to move beyond the literal meaning of a text and access the deeper levels of meaning such as metaphor, symbolism, characters as conscious constructs, and authorial intent.

Perhaps inference presents us with a particular challenge because it relies heavily on not only a student's understanding of the text itself, but also on the way in which that understanding is amalgamated with their own experiences, background knowledge and cultural context. In order to make an inference in the first place, students need to draw on a wide spectrum of knowledge, something that we cannot assume, especially if we work in contexts where students have limited exposure to diverse perspectives or literary traditions. This, then, presents a rallying call to action for us educators. We must provide students with access to a rich and varied literary landscape, introducing them to voices, cultures and ideas they might not be in a position to encounter. In doing this, we can help foster the cultural capital necessary for more sophisticated and interpretive work, allowing students to engage with confidence when it comes to unfamiliar texts.

> 'Ofsted added the term "cultural capital" to its school inspection handbook in 2019, which describes "... the essential knowledge that pupils need to be educated citizens, introducing them to the best that has been thought and said and helping to engender an appreciation of human creativity and achievement."' (Rees, 2024)

Through the lens of teaching inference, one can see how this might work. We cannot fully appreciate ideas centred around 'human creativity and achievement' if we cannot access a text. If we cannot access a text, we cannot infer.

As a side note, it should be noted that 'improving a pupil's cultural capital is not ... just a matter of giving them a book or sending them to see a play. We must ensure that, along with teaching the knowledge content of the curriculum, we enable pupils to function as well-informed individuals now and after they leave school.' (Rees, 2024)

With this in mind:

> 'Research has found that students' inferencing skills are associated with their reading comprehension skills, meaning that children with poor inference generation skills often have comprehension difficulties. Less skilled readers do not generate as many inferences as more capable readers, and some evidence suggests that their difficulties with inference generation may cause their comprehension difficulties.' (Rice et al., 2024)

Students engage in inferences every day, meaning we have the opportunity to spotlight this process and guide students in refining it. What must be noted is how dynamic inference is, shifting not only with the type of text that is being studied, but also with the reader's own background knowledge, lived experiences and context. Each student brings a unique perspective and lens through which meaning is made. These individual differences and ideas are assets for us to use, helping us to shape the way students infer while offering us valuable ideas as to how we might approach the teaching of inference. What a text suggests to one reader may differ significantly from what it suggests to another, yet if both ideas are rooted in the text, neither is more valid than the other. In this sense, inference becomes a gateway for student voice and student agency when it comes to approaching a text.

What must also be noted is the fact that inference develops over time. Through collaboration and classroom discussion, creating space for dialogue is vital, allowing students to rehearse the expression of their ideas in a safe space where they can share their understandings of literature.

Teaching inference, however, goes far beyond a shared understanding of literature. In an age where students have seemingly unlimited access to misinformation, unverified content and algorithm-driven social media timelines, we have a moral imperative to equip students with critical thinking skills to enable them to question, evaluate and interpret information. We need to think about how we can get students asking the right questions so they can independently sense-check the things they read on Instagram or watch on TikTok, posts that will often go unchecked for accuracy or bias. We are in a unique position as English teachers, where we *can* discuss the manipulation of language, to be able to do this.

Inference is essential to understanding text passages, because authors don't always explicitly explain their thoughts, their ideas, their motivations for writing in the first place. Of course, it is our job to teach students how they can comprehend this: 'Comprehending while reading is sometimes explained as the construction of a mental model that requires readers to integrate information from the text with their own experiences and background knowledge to make full sense of what they read' (Sedita, 2024). Perhaps this is why inference and prediction is a part of the EEF's strategies for their 'Improving literacy in secondary schools' report. As part of 'Develop pupils' ability to read and access academic texts', the EEF says: 'Students predict what might happen as a text is read. This causes them to pay close attention to the text, which means they can closely monitor their own comprehension.' (Quigley and Coleman, 2018). This, running alongside strategies such as activating prior knowledge, questioning, clarifying and summarising, can allow students to access more complex texts: 'Additionally, students need to make inferences that go beyond the literal words in the sentence and draw upon their knowledge of their subject.' (Quigley and Coleman, 2018)

This echoes 'research by Andersen and Pearson [who found that] those who are proficient in reading use their prior knowledge as well as textual information to draw conclusions, make critical judgements and form interpretations from the text read. They found that inferences can take the form of conclusions, predictions or new ideas.' (Casey, 2022)

In conclusion, inference lies at the heart of reading comprehension and making meaning. It requires more than a simple statement about what a text suggests, demanding integration of textual clues from our own background knowledge and experiences. This means we also have a duty to build cultural capital (thinking carefully about what this might look like, for I'm well aware that is a sentence that is easier said than done!) and expose students to a range of texts from different perspectives. By explicitly teaching inference skills, we can equip students to unlock complexities within literary meaning and critically engage with rapid flows of information encountered daily.

In short, inference allows our students to become thoughtful, discerning readers, a skill essential for studying texts in school and in the wider world.

How?

HACK #4.1: ESTABLISHING PRIOR KNOWLEDGE OF A TOPIC

A simple yet important strategy when guiding students to make inferences is to first establish their prior knowledge. This serves as a valuable foundation for introducing new ideas and deepening understanding. This might be completed through a quick baseline assessment, open discussion, or mind or concept mapping. However it is completed, looking at what students already know allows us to tailor our instruction more intentionally.

CHAPTER 4: INFERENCE AND MAKING MEANING

Careful attention, however, needs to be paid to where in the lesson this recall of prior knowledge is being asked to take place. Too often I have seen teachers ask students to get down what they already know about a topic, perhaps as a 'Do Now' task, only for that knowledge to then be acknowledged, but remain unused as the lesson moves on. A lack of structure to retrieving prior knowledge can mean we miss crucial opportunities to scaffold student thinking when it comes to using that knowledge later on in a lesson.

If inference relies on an ability to connect new information to existing knowledge, then we need to understand first what that existing knowledge is. We need to assess prior knowledge so that it allows us to *plan* accordingly. However that prior knowledge is assessed, we need to ask if we're giving ourselves enough time to review that data and plan in a way that means new inferences are going to be stronger. If we allow ourselves this time, instruction becomes more responsive and we can look at how we help students integrate what they read with what they already know, an essential and important step in developing critical readers in our classrooms.

HACK #4.2: MAKING BASIC INFERENCES THROUGH IMAGES

Images are an extremely effective way of helping students to make inferences; these images can be used as an impactful pre-reading strategy when it comes to predicting what might happen in a text. This approach, based on an idea by Chris Curtis, allows students to think and discuss a text before they even read it. For example, if one was about to read Ted Hughes' *Bayonet Charge,* one might place the image in Figure 4.1 in front of students with a set of questions that guide student thinking about the contents of the poem.

Questions to help generate simple inferences might include the following.

1. What do you think is happening in this scene? What makes you think this?
2. What emotions do you think the soldier in the image is experiencing? How can you tell?
3. What does the facial expression and body language suggest about the character's experience?

Figure 4.1 A bayonet charge

Questions like these, based on the images, are great at directing students to infer, because students then immediately root their ideas in the evidence. If they

87

don't do this when sharing, we can easily ask 'What makes you say that?' to force them to refer back to the original sources and explain their thoughts.

Based on these general questions, one might then want to highlight specifics.

1. What might this image be saying about war?
2. What clues suggest the soldier is not fully in control of his actions?
3. What do you think is more dangerous to the soldier: the enemy, or something else? Explain your thinking.
4. If this image were the climax of a story, what do you think happened before it? What might happen after?
5. Based on these images, do you think the poem we are reading today will be pro-war or anti-war? Why?

One of the most important aspects of teaching inference, to me, is ensuring students are aware of when they are doing it, how they are doing it and, finally, why this matters. Students can make inferences instinctively, but they need to be aware of the interpretive process they are engaging with. Our role is to help them develop a conscious awareness of this skill so they can apply it deliberately and effectively across different contexts.

But how can we tell when students are truly making inferences? Typically, they will begin to refer to specific clues or evidence. They fill in what has been left unsaid. They might ask or answer 'why' questions. ('Why is the hare in pain?' or 'Why might this reflect the soldier's own fear or trauma?'). As they gather more information, students may revise their initial interpretations: 'At first I thought the soldier was brave, but now I think he's actually terrified and confused because ....' These shifts in thinking reveal that inference is taking place.

This process provides a scaffold between visual and textual analysis. After working through an image, I might then introduce the poem or text it relates to. We can assess whether our initial inferences align with the writer's work and even return to the original image to 'attach' quotations to certain visual elements that by now we are familiar with. In this way, students can see how inference works across different mediums: moving from visual interpretations to a close reading of language, which many will find more challenging.

HACK #4.3: INFERENCE VS ANALYSIS

One thing I think students tend to misunderstand is the idea of inference as analysis and analysis as inference. Students often believe the two are interchangeable and that if they are inferring then they are analysing too. While it is true that analysis does include an element of inference, I find that separating the two, so students can really appreciate the differences, is vital. When students make this mistake, I will begin by defining the two for them. For example.

- **Inference** is a conclusion or prediction drawn from clues in the text or image, combined with prior knowledge.
- **Analysis** is the close examination of a text's structure, language, techniques or elements to explain how they contribute to its overall meaning, purpose or effect.

Students benefit from knowing the basic building blocks of both to avoid them slipping into pure inference when actually they've been tasked with analysis, believing them both to be the same thing.

To combat this, a simple resource that uses film shots before then moving these skills and ideas to the written word can be useful. I use (any) film shots to ask basic-level inference questions. For example, based on what students can see I might ask the following questions.

- What can we infer (predict) about the setting of this film?
- What can we infer about this man's life from the clothes he is wearing?
- What can we infer about how the man and the woman in the shot are feeling?

From this, I then ask students, 'If we were analysing, what questions should we be asking instead?' After hearing contributions from the class, I then ask the analysis questions.

- Why does the director use a camera angle that is slightly tilted upwards? How is he hoping to present the house to his audience?
- Why has the director chosen to make the weather dreary? What atmosphere is he trying to create?
- Why is the man closer to the screen? What does the director want to draw the reader's attention to?

Once we've answered these, I'll then ask students to think about the differences between the two sets of questions. The first set centres on interpreting clues within the scene to make inferences about context, character or emotion. The second set of questions is based more around the intentions and choices of a director. Students are looking at and evaluating reasons as to why purposeful creative decisions have been made.

With these observations we can then transfer this way of thinking to a text and consider what we can infer and what we need to analyse in terms of purposeful decisions that have been made by a writer. To bridge this gap, I might provide students with a resource like Figure 4.2, where I get them to rehearse responses to both kinds of questions.

TEACHER HACKS ENGLISH

INFERENCE

What can we infer about this particular night?

What can we infer about how Levison Wood is feeling when he first hears the gunfire?

What can we infer about Levison Wood's experiences in the army based on this paragraph?

What can we infer about Levison Wood's state of mind and thoughts on his trip based on this paragraph?

ANALYSIS

What language device has Levison Wood used to describe the darkness? What is the effect? Why has he used this particular language device?

What language device is this? What is the effect? Why use this particular device to describe what is happening?

Why has Levison Wood decided to place these sentences on a line by themselves? What is the effect of this structure?

Why is there a high concentration of verbs in this paragraphs? What is Levison Wood trying to do here? What effect do they have on the reader?

Levison Wood is thinking about a swamp called the Sudd that he will have to pass in the future. This swamp is hugely difficult to get through. Why describe it as a 'spectre'? What device is this?

No sooner had I settled into my room than the **darkness smothered the hotel**. Lying in the comforting blackness, I tried not to think of what tomorrow had in store. My plan was to go back to the local commander and talk about leaving Bor for the north – but, the more I thought about it, the less real it felt. Bor was only the front line of the ongoing war; whatever the north had in store, it would be much, much worse.

In that moment, the night came alive. Gunshots punctured the silence, machine-gun fire rattling perilously close to the hotel. I sat up. Through the shuttered windows, I saw the darkness illuminated in flashes of brilliant red, tracers lighting up the skies above Bor.

I scrambled out of bed, stumbling onto the veranda. In the room alongside me, Siraje, my Ugandan porter, was already awake. As the thud of heavy weapons played in bursts outside the hotel, we hurried to pack our rucksacks. "Where to?" Siraje asked. Outside the room, I looked across the courtyard. Soldiers and armed civilians were already gathering among the shadows. Who were they?

There was only one way to go. "Up," I said, and started to run.

Across the courtyard, close to the river's edge a half-finished five-storey building stood as a reminder of better times. We **burst** through the shattered door and **swept** away the hanging wires that blocked the stairwell. **Running** up the concrete stairs, we didn't **stop** until reaching the open rooftop. If the hotel was to be **stormed** again, I judged this would be the safest place.

From here, we could see the street fight being played out in snatches of light, machine-gun fire in the thoroughfares, fires erupting in buildings a few streets away. The night was warm, and the sounds and smells put me in mind of my tour in Afghanistan, which seemed such a long time ago.

The fire-fight lasted for forty-five minutes, finally slowing down to a succession of sporadic bursts. As the worst abated, I looked to the north. All that I could see, by the light of the waning moon reflected in the shimmering waters of the Nile, were the rooftops of Bor, stretching on into an indistinguishable horizon. But I knew what was waiting for me up there. Beyond the boundaries of the town, the marshes seemed to go on forever. Miles away to the north, the key towns of Bentiu, Malakal and Renk were being contested by rebels. Escaping villagers were following the river south, searching for sanctuary in hastily erected camps – and, always, **there was the spectre of the impenetrable Sudd.**

In that moment, it seemed I had a decision to make. Four hundred miles of war-torn swampland lay ahead of me on my journey, but the question was – was this stretch of the Nile going to deny me, as it had so many others?

Why end the extract on a rhetorical question? What is the effect? What tone/atmosphere does it create?

Figure 4.2 Inference and analysis example

In this example, taken from *Walking the Nile* by Levison Wood, we can see how inferences can be made about the focaliser of the extract. The analysis, then, comes in the form of Wood's choices and the creative decisions he has made in order to present his recounting of events to a reader.

If students are struggling with analysis because they're mistaking inference for it, try using tasks like this, tasks that clearly highlight the distinction between the two skills while recognising how they also correspond with one another.

HACK #4.4: LAYERS OF MEANING

One way to consider a text is through the layers of meaning. This also helps with inference, because it allows students to think about both what a text means on a literal surface level and also the hidden, deeper symbolic meaning of what a writer is trying to express.

Let's take the following passage of text from *Of Mice and Men* as an example. Although many schools have moved away from this text now, it serves the point I am trying to make here.

> The wooden latch raised. The door opened and a tall, stoop-shouldered old man came in. He was dressed in blue jeans and he carried a big push-broom in his left hand. Behind him came George, and behind George, Lennie.
>
> "The boss was expectin' you last night," the old man said. "He was sore as hell when you wasn't here to go out this morning." He pointed with his right arm, and out of the sleeve came a round stick-like wrist, but no hand. "You can have them two beds there," he said, indicating two bunks near the stove.
>
> George stepped over and threw his blankets down on the burlap sack of straw that was a mattress. He looked into his box shelf and then picked a small yellow can from it.
>
> "Say. What the hell's this?"
>
> "I don't know," said the old man.
>
> "Says 'positively kills lice, roaches and other scourges.' What the hell kind of bed you giving us, anyways. We don't want no pants rabbits."

At this point, you might ask students the following question.

1. What is happening in this text on a **literal** level?

This initial question checks whether students understand the basic 'goings on' of the text. At this moment, George and Lennie have arrived late at the ranch where they are due to work and are met by Candy, an old man who shows them to their bunks. George inspects the sleeping area, only to find a can of insect killer, which clearly alarms him, prompting him to question the cleanliness of the place. To summarise, on a surface level, characters are simply being shown where they will sleep and George is concerned about the conditions.

Establishing this baseline understanding is important; understanding needs to be secure in order to go deeper. At this point, you might ask the next question.

2. What is happening in this passage on a **symbolic** level?

This is where the rich interpretation begins. The can of bug spray, for instance, symbolises more than just the poor hygiene that George is worried about. In this moment, Steinbeck alludes to broader themes of dehumanisation, suggesting even the most basic human needs, a clean place to stay and a suitable room to sleep in, are neglected. The spray itself implies infestation and filth, along with a nomadic lifestyle that mirrors the disposability of migrant workers who are disregarded and seemingly shunned through the set of circumstances in which they have found themselves.

Candy, as a construct, consolidates this idea of disposability through his very presence. His missing hand marks him out as weak, and in this harsh world Steinbeck has created, the weak are discarded and forgotten about. He is a manifestation of the fate of those who have nothing left to contribute physically. Even the bunkhouse, through its stark, utilitarian description reflects the impermanence of the workers who stay there. The lack of comfort or personal connection in Steinbeck's constructed setting is another way of highlighting the emotional detachment of the characters.

In short, this passage reflects themes of isolation, mistrust and how poverty results in dehumanising conditions for those who are just trying to survive day by day. By guiding students to move from literal events to symbolic meaning, new meanings and new interpretations are unlocked. Students can access a whole new world of ideas, allowing them to engage in a more analytical and empathetic level.

But how do we do this? We know what Steinbeck's passage is really getting at here because we're the experts in the classroom. How do we get students to recognise this symbolic level independently? The key to helping students with this is through the questions we ask. With any given passage, we might pose a selection of the following.

- What objects stand out?
- What feels odd or out of place?
- What words or images are repeated?
- Are there any details that seem oddly specific?

CHAPTER 4: INFERENCE AND MAKING MEANING

We are sometimes too quick to get students interpreting, when actually what we should be doing is getting them noticing.

Once students have established the 'what', then we can move them to the 'why' and their inferences, by asking open, but more specific questions. The aim here is to encourage interpretive thinking within our students. Questions you might ask here include:

- Why might Steinbeck mention lice and roaches?
- Why tell us Candy has no hand?
- Why are the bunks described as they are?

Train students to also look for unusual or unnecessary details, for repeated imagery or themes, or even physical objects that carry some emotional weight. Alongside this, think about zooming out. What larger idea does this detail connect to that is present in the text? How might this reflect the character's situation or world view? Could this represent something beyond itself?

Another variation of this activity lies in layers of meaning within a character: looking at them physically, emotionally and psychologically.

> '[Looking at a character] physically presents the character's current state, their surface layer as such, emotionally reveals how they are feeling in this moment, and psychologically allows us to consider the underlying reasons for the character's behaviour and mood at the moment. It also lends itself quite nicely to tentative language, as it is (almost) impossible to refer to someone's psychological state with any sense of certainty, as we're not inside their head, with a detail documented history of their previous experiences.' Howard (2019a)

Characters are created as conscious constructs, but that doesn't mean they are two dimensional. Writers will craft multi-layered characters to reflect the complexity of real people, people with histories, desires, wants, needs and fears. By examining characters through a physical, emotional and psychological lens, we can move students beyond surface-level interpretation and begin to unpick how authors embed nuance in their creations and why.

Let's consider what this might look like taking one of Sheila Birling's lines from *An Inspector Calls* as an example. At this moment, Sheila is confronting her father, Mr. Birling, over the treatment of his workers in his factory.

> **Sheila:** But these girls aren't cheap labour – they're people.

TEACHER HACKS ENGLISH

Physically, Sheila might be imagined as tense or animated in this moment, perhaps standing, with a sharpness in her tone or a gesture that shows urgency. Her physical presence likely reflects a shift because she is no longer the passive, light-hearted girl we saw earlier, but someone taking a moral stand.

Emotionally, Sheila is clearly moved. She is feeling a sense of compassion, frustration and perhaps guilt. She's no longer detached from the consequences of her privilege. The emotional weight in her words suggests she's beginning to feel responsible and disturbed by the treatment of the working-class women, especially Eva.

Psychologically, this moment marks a turning point. Sheila is starting to internalise the inspector's message and confront uncomfortable truths about class, power and her own complicity. Her language humanises the girls which is at odds with what her parents think and feel.

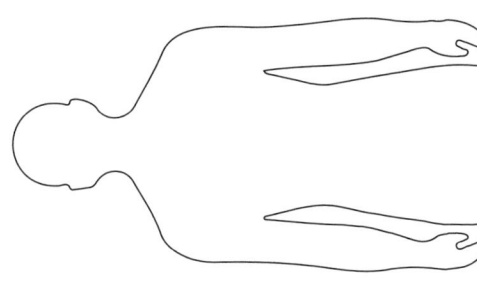

Sheila: But these girls aren't cheap labour – they're people.

1. **Consider what the character might be doing physically at this point. What can we infer based on what she is saying?**

2. **Based on the line, consider what the character may be feeling emotionally at this point. Explain the reason behind your thinking.**

3. **What about psychologically? Why is the character behaving in this way?**

Figure 4.3 Character thinking task

As you can see in Figure 4.3, through layers of meaning and looking at characters using these different lenses, students can make much stronger inferences to ensure every aspect of the character is covered. You can repeat this activity at various points through your reading of a novel or play too, in order to track how a character is changing over time and what might be the catalyst for such a change.

HACK #4.5: SYMBOLISM AND MOTIFS

Symbolism and motifs are deeply connected to inference; it is important we consider how to teach these literary tools in a way that supports interpretive skills. A symbol is an object, action or detail that represents a deeper idea, while a motif is a recurring element that draws attention to a particular theme or concept. Crucially, these devices are rarely explained explicitly within a text. Instead, their significance must be inferred by the reader.

When students engage with symbols and/or motifs, they are rehearsing the very skill of drawing meaning from what is implied rather than stated. It is therefore required for them to look at how these elements appear, when they recur, where they recur and what thematic or emotional importance they carry within the story. Teaching students to interpret symbols and motifs, then, is not separate from teaching inference. Instead, it is inference in action.

That's why this strategy belongs here: helping students recognise and interpret symbols and motifs is a powerful way to strengthen their inferential thinking.

If students are struggling with the concept of symbolism, get them to start with what they already know. Students may have an understanding of common symbols without even knowing that they do. Figure 4.4 shows some common symbols.

Symbols	Meaning
Red rose	Love or romance
White flag	Surrender or peace
Snake	Evil or betrayal
Storm	Anger or doom
Fog or mist	Isolation or confusion
Season of spring	New beginning or birth
Skull	Death

Figure 4.4 Common symbols

Start by discussing why these symbols might mean what they do. Students will tend to know the majority of these symbols, so it is a good plan to start here and use their background knowledge to help increase confidence and establish a baseline. These are universal symbols, symbols that everyone tends to understand. For example, 'the colour green is a symbol for new life and that natural world.' (Webb, 2022)

Yet as teachers, this can be challenging to teach, not because students don't know the meaning, but because they cannot identify these symbols independently in the first place. Students tend to be fine if we as teachers explain to them why something is a symbol. They can often regurgitate the symbolic significance of a particular idea if it's been taught to them previously. However, they are never quite confident to find these in the first place. This tends to be the case with 'obscure symbols', symbols 'that are understood more narrowly, so their meaning might be limited to the context of that text, genre or writer' (Webb, 2022). In this case, the following is what I explain to students when we are looking at the idea of symbolism.

1. **Look for repetition.**
   If an object, image or colour appears (or is mentioned) multiple times throughout a story, it's worth paying close attention to. Repetition often signals some sort of deeper significance. For example, in *A Christmas Carol*, fire and sources of light appear frequently. They're not just sources of warmth, but representations of hope, transformation and emotional and moral awakening. In *The Great Gatsby*, the recurring green light is not merely a beacon on Daisy's dock; it symbolises Gatsby's longing and the elusive nature of the American Dream. Even if students aren't sure what the repetition *means* at first, noticing that it exists is the first step toward interpretation.

2. **Consider how characters react.**
   Pay attention to how characters respond to specific objects or images. Do they fear it? Reflect on it? Obsess over it or even treasure it? For example, Marley's ghost in *A Christmas Carol* reflects on the chains he 'forged in life', which represent his moral transgressions and missed opportunities to help others, while mirroring how he is metaphorically imprisoned by his eternal damnation to simply observe those whom he could have helped. Scrooge's fear of those chains connects to his own potential fate. In *The Great Gatsby*, Gatsby's emotional fixation on the green light reveals his yearning for an idealised future. The more emotionally charged or personal a character's reaction, the more likely it is that the object holds some sort of importance.

3. **Connect symbols to big ideas.**
   Symbols usually tie into the larger themes or messages of a story. We need to ask what a story is really about. Then consider how the object or image relates to those ideas. For example, in *A Christmas Carol*, the chains, ghosts

and coldness all relate to themes of redemption, isolation and compassion. Understanding the story's core ideas helps clarify why a writer has suffused an object or idea with a symbolic meaning.

4. **Pay attention to when and where symbols appear.**
   Timing and placement often offer a lot when it comes to identifying a symbol or decoding its meaning. Does the object appear during a turning point in the story? Is it connected to a major event or shift in character development? Placement matters and symbols will often show up during key moments.

These ideas can work particularly well with 'cold reads' (reading an entire text through in its entirety, pausing to check for understanding at various intervals before moving on, as opposed to stopping to analyse bit by bit), because students are more likely to have a holistic overview of the entire text and so can therefore pick up easily on these patterns and recurring objects and images.

So where does inference come into play here? Inference makes itself known when we ask students to consider what the symbol might mean, why the writer may have chosen that particular symbol, and how it helps writers to convey their message and ideas to a reader. To what extent is the symbol a vehicle through which the writer's ideas are presented?

You could combine this idea with Teacher Hack 4.2, by giving students an image that shows a particular symbol or motif in it and ask students to consider what it might represent based on what they can see in the picture. For example, the image in Figure 4.5, based on Shakespeare's *Macbeth*, could generate rich discussion based on its inclusion of the skull, daggers and blood. Conversation could be directed to consider how these elements connect to one another and how, together, they create an understanding regarding themes of violence, betrayal and the destructive consequences of moral failings and unchecked power.

Figure 4.5 Macbeth image

HACK #4.6: HOW DID YOU ARRIVE AT THAT INFERENCE?

A simple probing question to ask when students have made an inference is 'How did you arrive at that inference?'. This helps us as teachers to consider the thought processes of our students. You could use this question to unpick a really strong answer, or to unpick where an inference has gone slightly wrong, an answer that is perhaps not rooted in the text. Either way, it is a good means of getting a student to evaluate their thinking.

WRITING

What?

Inference operates on two levels in our classrooms, through reading and writing, both of which are important when it comes to development of literacy. When reading, inferences involve recognising and unpacking layers of meaning, moving from what is clearly stated to the implied. Students learn to spot and explain these suggestions, developing an awareness of what lies beneath the surface of a text.

In creative writing, inference takes on a different purpose. Here, students are not merely interpreting meaning, but are deliberately constructing it by learning how to embed suggestions and subtext, crafting work and keeping in mind what a reader might interpret from it that isn't directly stated. In short, to read with inference is to decode implied meaning, to write is to encode meaning for others to realise. Writing, of course, has two strands that demand our attention. Students must not only encode meaning as authors themselves, but also need to learn how to articulate their understanding of meaning in another text, as readers. This section of the chapter explores both, and presents ideas on how students can write creatively with inference in mind and how they can write analytically about the inferences they have identified in texts independently.

Students need to recognise that these strands, of inference, creative and analytical, reinforce one another. Students who understand how inference is constructed in writing can become more adept at recognising it in reading, although this transfer does not always happen naturally. We must encourage them to see readers as writers and writers as readers. When they read like writers, they begin to notice the deliberate choices an author makes to suggest meaning, just as they have done in their own pieces. When they write like readers, they can consider how their audience will interpret the choices they have made.

CHAPTER 4: INFERENCE AND MAKING MEANING

Effective teaching nurtures both sides. By developing these capacities, students have the opportunity to grow into thoughtful, skilled communicators, capable of both crafting meaning and uncovering it in another's work.

How?

 HACK #4.7: PHRASES FOR INFERENCE

In an academic sense, providing sentence stems for inference is really important, alongside modelling their use and giving students extended time to rehearse their ideas. Different sentence stems have different purposes, so explain to students what these are. Figure 4.6 shows some sentence stem examples.

Evidence-based inference phrases	Observation-based phrases
• It could be implied that ___ because ___. • This may suggest that ___. • Based on ___, it could be argued ___. • The author's implication here is that ___ because of ___. • It seems as if ___ due to ___.	• From this line alone, it is reasonable to infer that ___. • The character's actions show that ___.
Cause and effect style phrases	**Uncertainty and reasoning phrases**
• Since it is clear that ___, it's likely that ___. • If ___ is true, then ___ might be the case.	• It is possible that ___ because ___. • It's likely/unlikely that___ due to ___. • Perhaps ___.

Figure 4.6 Sentence stem examples

These sentence starters may seem straightforward, but they are essential for teaching students how to develop and hone an academic voice. Introducing them explicitly allows students to mirror the tone and structure of typical literary criticism in their own writing, while also serving as an effective means of teaching tentative language. Given that inferences, by nature, are predictions and therefore inherently tentative, this way of writing is an absolute must.

When modelling an inference to students using this scaffolded support, ensure that the rationale behind your choice of sentence is verbalised – why is this particular sentence appropriate in context? Not only will this reinforce the concept of inference but it will also help students to avoid common pitfalls that simplify the inference, especially when they use phrases like 'From this I can infer ...'. Our goal is to guide students towards adopting the conventions of literary criticism as closely as possible, seamlessly integrating our inferences into a wider answer.

Explicit teaching of the sentence frames in this way can also help clarify common misconceptions. For example, I've frequently encountered students writing, 'From

99

this, the text infers ...'. Phrasing like this reflects a fundamental misunderstanding. Texts *imply*, readers *infer*. Teaching this distinction through modelling and verbal explanations will help with the development of a critical voice.

HACK #4.8: SHOW, DON'T TELL/REFLECT AND REVISE FOR INFERENCE

From a creative standpoint, I tell my students not to give everything away at once, but this is harder than it first appears. I suppose the first step here is to really train students in the idea of 'show, don't tell', an old phrase, one that I remember learning when I was at school, but one that still resonates. We've all heard the adage, commonly attributed to Anton Chekhov: 'Don't tell me the moon is shining; show me the glint of light on broken glass.'

When students simply tell us everything in their writing, they leave no room for inference. Their writing can lack depth if every detail is presented plainly, without suggestion or subtext. Everything becomes surface level, offering little beyond the literal for their reader to engage with. Effective writing should always make a reader think, and should always get the reader to *do* something. After all, if students are not actively constructing meaning then they become rather passive observers of events. To support this, model the principle of 'show, don't tell' in your teaching. Think aloud as you write in front of students. Make the invisible process of thinking visible. Explain your choices and how you aim to convey meaning through description, action or dialogue for students to use as a guide for their own creative pieces.

After the initial drafting phase, encourage students to revisit their work, not just to proofread, but to review with inference in mind. Ask questions to help with this.

- What should the reader be able to infer here?
- Have I said too much? Too little? Is the writing too abstract to follow?
- Where might I use action or detail to suggest something, rather than explicitly stating it?

Mini whiteboards are an appropriate resource to help with these quick revision tasks. Ask students to identify one or two lines in their work where they think they have given too much away or where their meaning is too explicit. Ask them to rewrite these lines while thinking about what they want their reader to be inferring. Ask students to turn and talk to the person sitting next to them to invite challenge and suggestions before asking them to hold up their boards, narrating the changes you see. Invite selected students to verbalise what they changed and why. Encourage reflection: How does this new, revised version better engage the reader by allowing them to infer?

A teacher script for this scenario might look something like this.

Teacher: Okay, we've finished our first drafts. Now I want us to revise our work, and we're going to focus on how we can make meaning for a reader. Let me show you what I mean.

Firstly, let's consider what I wrote in my first draft. I wrote the following line about my setting: 'The small town was boring and quiet'. What might be wrong with this sentence?

Student 1: It's a bit boring. It needs more detail.

Student 2: It's quite a short sentence.

Teacher: Both good suggestions. Well done. There's nothing wrong with a short sentence. The sentence itself is fine. It's getting my point across that I want to make. But there's a problem here in that I've told the reader everything. There's no space for you as a reader to figure anything out. But good writing lets the reader do a bit of work.

So...now we're going to look at showing you the town is boring instead of just telling you. Let me think out loud here. I need to consider what makes a town boring.

I'm thinking of a place where there's nothing to do. Maybe all of the shops are closed. One person might be walking a dog but the rest is quite quiet because there's nowhere really to go. So instead of telling you it's boring, I'm going to show it instead.

[Teacher writes the revision aloud on board as students watch.]

'A stray dog barked feebly somewhere down the road, dust drifting across the deserted street. Swinging in the breeze, a small squeak could be heard at various intervals from the 'For sale' sign outside the old butchers, boarded up, forgotten, in a town that, in the absence of people, had fallen mostly quiet, like a silent yawn.'

Notice in this script how the teacher really breaks the task down in order to model the thinking process. They take individual ideas about what they could write in their 'show, don't tell' description before putting them together to create the final piece. For me, 'show, don't tell' is all about the drafting and redrafting, working and manipulating a piece of writing to a point where it doesn't give everything away at once, where the reader has to figure things out for themselves and infer, where the reader can fill in the gaps rather than just being simply told.

'Show, don't tell' is an old hack, but still pertinent. The focus, however, needs to be brought back to the teacher's modelling of it.

HACK #4.9: THINKING ABOUT SUBTEXT THROUGH DIALOGUE

Subtext refers to the meaning that lies beneath the surface of words on the page, the implicit or unspoken ideas that, while not directly stated, are understood by the reader or audience. In short, it is the idea of 'reading between the lines'. This concept, I think, is easier to grasp when analysing literature. Teaching students to write with subtext is much more challenging!

One of the most effective ways to introduce subtext in writing is through dialogue. Yet in my experience, creating realistic dialogue is something I think students struggle with the most. Too often, I've seen creative pieces completely overwhelmed by long passages of dialogue with little to no narrative context and these are often at the expense of descriptive detail that would allow readers to anchor the conversation in a time or place. This kind of writing often falls flat, because it fails to create anything vivid or immersive for a reader. While some may vehemently disagree with this direction, I often encourage students to limit their use of dialogue in favour of more varied narrative techniques. However, when used purposefully and successfully, dialogue can be an effective driver for subtext.

To help students grasp the concept of subtext through dialogue, I break it down simply for them.

- **Text:** What the character *says*.
- **Subtext:** What the character *means*.

Subtext must be present if students are wanting to emulate realistic and engaging dialogue because in reality people very rarely say exactly what they mean. Our conversations are full of suggestions, tinged with implications and packed with emotional undercurrents, which is perhaps why we are so taken aback when someone is blunt with us. Helping students to understand this then opens up exciting opportunities for more sophisticated writing, where they can begin to experiment with language and making meaning, all by considering what is left *unsaid*.

This hack is about supporting students in crafting dialogue that hints at meaning beyond the literal. By focusing on what their characters really mean, students can write with greater subtlety, and we can also draw attention to how other authors do this in their writing when approaching a text from an analytical standpoint.

1. **Start with personal experience.**
   Begin by grounding the idea of subtext in students' own lives. For example, you could ask, 'Do you always say exactly what you're thinking?' Encourage them to think of a time when they said one thing but meant another, saying

'I'm fine' even if they weren't, for example. This helps students immediately connect to the idea that people will speak in coded ways, because they themselves will have done it at some point in their lives.

2. **Practise writing.**
Next, ask students to write a brief exchange between two people on their mini whiteboards. One character is saying something while clearly meaning something else. This offers students a low stakes, low threat way of experimenting with subtext. At this point, if the concept is new, students might be a bit 'on the nose' with their exchanges, or even, when verbalising their ideas if they're sharing, explain the subtext they're going for, but not quite managing to create it. If this is the case, be honest with them. Intervene and allow them to draft. (e.g. 'I'm not quite sure that subtext comes through in what you've written there. How could we make that character's thoughts more obvious without sacrificing subtext?')

3. **Explore subtext through authentic texts.**
Share a dialogue-rich extract from a short play or novel where characters conceal their true feelings. Have students identify the literal meaning of what is being said. Then ask them to discuss what they think the characters are really thinking or feeling before giving them the chance to justify their inferences. What clues are supporting their interpretations? This is a reading activity, yes, but the idea is that students can emulate this model when rehearsing and drafting their own pieces.

4. **Explicitly teach the methods.**
After discussion, introduce specific common methods writers employ to convey subtext in character interactions. These might include:

- Pauses, hesitations or interruptions.
- Details about body language or details about setting.
- Changing the subject or avoiding the question.
- A disconnect between the words and actions of a character.
- Tone and delivery (e.g. '"Nice glasses," she said, smirking').

A useful follow-up task to this would be to give students a neutral line of dialogue and ask them to rewrite it in multiple different ways, each time with a different intention when it comes to subtext, reinforcing how a small change can make a great impact on meaning.

5. **Construct dialogue with subtext.**
Present students with a scenario where they must write dialogue that includes hidden meaning. Give students the subtext they are trying to achieve or get them to think of their own. Afterwards, students can swap their work and try to

infer in each other's writing what the goal around the subtext was, reinforcing the connection between reading and writing inferences.

6. **Explore conflict.**
Provide a new prompt, this time centred around conflict. Ask students to write a 'polite argument', a scene where two characters disagree with one another but remain civil. The challenge is to convey tension through what is not said, relying on implied meaning rather than explicit confrontation.

7. **Reflect and consolidate.**
After these activities, ask students to define the term 'subtext' in their own words, ideally on mini whiteboards or through class discussion, allowing you to complete a quick, formative check and intervene as necessary.

ORACY

What?

> 'In English, high-quality dialogue supports students' comprehension and interpretation of texts (including inference, deduction and the use of evidence) as well as being a vital part of their development as writers.' (Oracy Education Commission, 2024)

Mary Myatt (2022b) argues that 'while much classroom talk focuses on checking comprehension, which is a good thing, it doesn't go far enough to develop pupils' thinking.' She says talk is vital because 'it promotes the conditions for inference':

> 'Too often pupils are asked to infer something from a text, but they do not have enough practice at doing this. The skill of inference is to tease out what has not been said explicitly. We need to pose the question 'What conclusions might we draw from this?' For example, 'the girl is wearing a fancy dress and carrying a bouquet of flowers.' We might infer from this that she is a flower girl at a wedding. This takes it beyond a statement of the obvious, to a possible scenario. And finally, talk is an entitlement for every pupil. Having one's voice heard is at the heart of confidence, that an individual's ideas matter, that they can be respectfully challenged and affirmed.' (Myatt, 2022b)

Learning about inference, and learning to *talk* about inference, is needed because it transforms a complex, often abstract, process into something more concrete and accessible. When students verbalise their inferences, and when teachers prompt them to explain the steps they took to arrive at their conclusions, we move closer to making the invisible visible. This gives us powerful insight and data into students' interpretive thinking, something that is not always evident through a written response. By encouraging students to not just explain what they inferred, but also how they inferred it, we invite them into metacognitive territory: they begin to reflect on their own thinking. Metacognition is essential for academic growth, yet for it to be truly effective, it must be embedded as part of a consistent, whole-school strategy, rather than relegated to individual classrooms and teachers.

The benefits of inference-centred discussion extend further than simply pushing students to consider meaning beyond the literal. Inference-based talk requires students to listen carefully, consider alternative viewpoints and engage with perspectives they may not have previously encountered. Lots of attention is often paid to the speaking part of discussion, but not necessarily the listening. To infer from what a partner is saying, close attention needs to be paid and active listening needs to happen. Inference is a life skill. We use it to read social cues, to interpret news, to make decisions and navigate relationships, and so rehearsing it through structured conversation in the classroom not only deepens comprehension, but also acts as a bridge between thinking, language and learning.

Learning about inference through talk is not about trying to find a right answer. It's about giving students the chance and opportunity to learn about how we understand the world, building curious and inquisitive learners as a result.

How?

HACK #4.10: INFERENCE DEBATES AND UNPICKING IMPLIED MEANING

Debates are an excellent way of helping students engage with a text. Start by giving the class a debate motion that requires them to infer. This is really important to get right because you need to ensure the statement elicits interpretation and not just recall. The goal is for students to draw conclusions from the text and support them with inference. This is also a really good way for students to consider rehearsing their ideas before they commit them to paper. For example:

'Romeo and Juliet's fate is determined by their own choices, not destiny.' To what extent do you agree?'

Have students find textual evidence to support their opinion on the statement. Have them practise their inference by deliberately constructing a set of questions that will allow for this.

- What does the behaviour of these characters imply to back up or argue against this statement?
- What does a symbol or event suggest about the theme?
- What can be inferred from what the characters *don't* say or do?
- How do repeated patterns (like imagery, language or plot events) suggest a position on the debate topic?
- How does the writer's tone suggest a judgment or bias about the events or characters?

Allow the debate to happen. Ask students to consider what things suggest to them or what they imply so that we know they are making these inferences. The next step is to draw verbal attention to the inference and to allow students to be able to unpack them. We are asking students here to explain their reasoning, to verbalise the journey of their thinking from evidence, to inference and finally to their overall claim. This way, not only have students verbalised during the debate itself but also continue to do so in the aftermath when they are required to discuss their rationale. Questions like the following will help with this.

- What in the text has led you to that conclusion?
- Can you walk us through how you got from X to Y?

One thing oracy is particularly good for is testing the strength of the inference. Through probing questions, we can show students that inference is not the same as opinion. It must be backed up and challenged in order to build critical thinking. Questions to help with this might be similar to the following.

- Could there be another way to interpret that action or line?
- What might someone who disagrees with you say?

In a debate, focus too on the 'how', not just the 'what'. We often ask students to focus on what they can infer and what a text suggests but we rarely go beyond that. Students can give their inferences but how powerful would it be if we then followed this up with 'How does that inference support your argument?' Sometimes students can make a valid inference but it might not always connect clearly to the debate. Students need encouragement to help tighten the link between analysis and claim.

During a debate, draw attention to strong inferences. Say to students, 'That's an excellent inference because you've used Capulet's words and then discussed the consequences of his actions to back up your claims.' This sets a precedent for other inferences and acts as a model for which other students can emulate the responses.

Inference debates offer a powerful and practical strategy for deepening students' engagement with literature. If we push students to move beyond the surface level recall and into interpretation, we're helping them to develop the skills that underpin strong reading, writing and thinking. As an oracy task, it allows us to comment on student responses immediately as an observer. Debates don't just help students understand what happens in a text, they help them to explore why it matters. The act of verbalising allows students to test and refine their thinking before committing it to paper and, through this, we can get to a place where inference becomes a habit of thought.

Why?

Inference is far more than a reading comprehension strategy. It is a way of thinking, a bridge between what is explicit, and what is suggested. When students infer, rooting their answers in a text, they demonstrate deep engagement. They are not simply decoding words on a page, they are actively making meaning by piecing together what is said and how it relates to what is left unsaid. This ability to interpret, question and read between the lines is what lies at the heart of English.

Crucially, inference is where the roles of reader and writer meet. When we frame students as both readers and writers, and help them see how one role informs the other, we draw attention to the ways in which knowledge around English connects. Students should not be passive recipients of information; instead, they are active meaning-makers.

So why is inference particularly important in English, even though it appears in other subjects, like History? From my perspective, inference deserves special consideration when thinking about English as a discipline because it underpins all strands of our subject: reading, writing, and speaking and listening. When students articulate an inference verbally, they practise reasoning and interpretation. When they write creatively, they can look at embedding layers of meaning for themselves. When they're reading, they're uncovering subtext, thinking about choices a writer has made to influence a reader's thoughts and interpretations.

Inference, then, is a thread that weaves itself through the very tapestry of English education. Indeed, it surfaces repeatedly throughout the hacks explored in this very book, and not by coincidence but by design. It is a skill we continually foster, which perhaps means we sometimes just assume that students can do it. Such an assumption is dangerous. We need to be clear that students can infer and read in-between the lines. To do this is to think critically and creatively. To think critically and creatively is to truly understand and to communicate with purpose and insight.

CHAPTER 5: CONTEXT

Teaching context in English language and literature is necessary because it helps students understand that texts are not isolated objects but acts of communication shaped by particular times, places, audiences and purposes. When students learn to read with context in mind, the text becomes more intelligible and more meaningful: they can see not only what is happening, but why an author makes certain choices, what an original audience might have assumed, and how ideas, values and conventions influence meaning. In literature, this deepens interpretation by making themes, characterisation, tone and viewpoint easier to grasp and easier to support with evidence from the text.

Importantly, context strengthens analysis rather than replacing it. Effective teaching does not turn English into a history lesson; instead, it equips students to explain how contextual knowledge helps them interpret language, form and structure. It supports them in moving beyond spotting features to articulating significance: why a metaphor lands a certain way, why a narrative voice feels credible or unsettling, why particular representations might reflect (or challenge) the norms of a time.

Context teaching is also an issue of equity. Students arrive with different levels of cultural knowledge and different access to the experiences that often sit behind canonical texts and wider reading. If contextual understanding is treated as something students should 'just know' or pick up outside school, then success in English becomes partly a test of background rather than learning. Making context explicit helps ensure that all students, not only those with greater cultural capital, can access complex texts and develop powerful interpretations.

READING

What?

Context can be one of the trickiest things to teach in English...it is so easy to get carried away and turn English into a history lesson. We have already discussed how great literature teaching involves students being able to engage with the text they are studying as a living, breathing thing, that they can situate in terms of literary movements and schools of thought. We have also explored ideas of the text as a vehicle or construct, which writers use to impart a message. Therefore helping students understand the historical events or public attitudes that may have shaped and inspired the writer's big ideas in a text seems a logical step. However, like many approaches in the English teaching community, the explicit teaching of context as a tool for analysis has not been without its criticisms. Barbara Bleiman recently wrote a passionate article for *TES*, where she argued that this approach is causing many students to fall out of love with English. She highlighted that in classrooms where knowledge about context is not frontloaded, students are 'encouraged to think for themselves, explore, generate their own ideas and express them in varied ways,' whereas in others, 'literary analysis is a fixed academic format to be learned and followed.' (Bleiman, 2025) She believes that the latter approach is too mechanistic, that it does not encourage students to develop the individual voice that is so important in the discipline. We can certainly see where Bleiman is coming from. However, having worked in tough schools, in areas of high deprivation in the last twenty years, we have also seen the lack of equity, as those students who have high levels of cultural capital consistently possess the background knowledge to be able to engage with texts in a more thoughtful and developed way. Teachers have a duty to help level this playing field and if that means explicit teaching of the gaps they have in knowledge that are acting as barriers to analysis, then this seems like a no-brainer. If not now, when? If not us, who?

For teachers, keeping abreast of the depth of subject knowledge needed to teach context well can be challenging. Christine Counsell (2018a) emphasises the importance of both breadth and depth in teachers' subject knowledge, particularly through her concepts of 'core' and 'hinterland' knowledge. Core knowledge refers to the essential facts, concepts and principles that students are expected to retain in their long-term memory. It's the foundational content that underpins a subject (Counsell, 2018b). Hinterland knowledge encompasses the broader context that enriches and gives meaning to the core knowledge. It's not merely supplementary; it's integral to deepening students' understanding (Parker, 2022). Counsell argues that without hinterland knowledge, teaching can become a mere transmission of isolated facts, leading to superficial understanding. By integrating hinterland content, teachers provide students with a richer, more connected grasp of the subject matter (Parker, 2022).

Relating Christine Counsell's concepts of core and hinterland knowledge to English literature teaching involves seeing literature not just as texts to be dissected for exams, but as cultural artifacts rooted in richer, broader contexts. For literature teaching, the core knowledge is the foundational knowledge teachers want students to deeply internalise. This might include the texts themselves, including the plot, characters, themes, structure, language and form. Then there is the literary terminology and the knowledge of the analytical skills and techniques students can use for closely reading texts and articulating interpretations clearly. Hinterland knowledge is particularly compelling for English literature as it provides essential context that brings texts alive. That may be the historical and cultural context; for example, knowing about the Victorian era deeply enhances understanding of Dickens or understanding post-colonial contexts enriches comprehension of Achebe's poetry. It may also be biographical knowledge, such as insights into authors' lives, influences and intentions; for example, that Orwell's experiences in colonial Burma shaped his views in *Animal Farm* and *1984*. These two understandings of context are fairly common in schools and have certainly fed into teacher input when studying texts at every school we have worked at. There are four other less common approaches to context which do not seem to be as prevalent in schools and which can also be useful for students.

- **Intertextuality and literary tradition:** Recognising allusions to classical literature, mythology or earlier works, which deepen a reader's appreciation and insight into authors' choices. This might include biblical allusions in *A Christmas Carol*.
- **Broader thematic explorations:** Ideas about human psychology, philosophy, ethics or politics that inform why literature matters, enabling students to make meaningful connections between texts and their own experiences. For example, ideas about evolution and physiognomy in *Jekyll and Hyde*.
- **Links to modern context:** Relating the broader themes, messages and big ideas of the text to modern ideas, events and beliefs. For example, connecting the #MeToo movement to Eric's behaviour in *An Inspector Calls*.
- **The context of the extract:** In Paper 1, where students are given an extract, context can also include the situation of the extract itself within the wider context of the play/novel.

Incorporating hinterland knowledge well can transform how students engage with literature. Rather than simply noting themes in Shakespeare's *Macbeth*, students might explore the historical anxieties around regicide and the divine right of kings, enhancing their grasp of why the play's messages resonated deeply with contemporary audiences. Studying Mary Shelley's *Frankenstein* alongside hinterland knowledge about Romanticism, Enlightenment philosophy and emerging scientific debates, profoundly enriches students' engagement and analysis as they are able to situate the text and see literature as reflective of and responsive to its time. Older texts can sometimes seem stuffy and abstract to students, so by understanding the relevance, it is much easier to imagine them as breathing entities.

Yet, due to the sometimes limited view teachers can have of what context actually is, it can mean that context can be taught badly, often as a bolt on, where responses include vague comments about beliefs, prefaced with 'back in those days.' These statements are usually broad and sweeping, such as 'Back in Shakespeare's time, all women were controlled by their husbands,' when of course it was much more nuanced than that. Even worse, are the random pub-quiz style historical comments about authors, such as that Duffy is a 'lesbian' and that Plath 'stuck her head in the oven and killed herself.' Who can blame our students for wanting to show off their knowledge? But the mark scheme is clear that these types of context will not propel students into a top band.

Context would come under AO3, which states: 'Show understanding of the relationships between texts and the contexts in which they were written.' It is the word 'relationships' that is key. This indicates that simple comments and pub quiz-style facts are not going to cut the mustard. Instead, it is how that context has shaped what has been written and how it has contributed to the author's intentions. It needs to be embedded and move analysis forward, rather than stall it. This is something which comes up again and again in AQA's Examiner's Reports, as demonstrated by the table in Figure 5.1, collating comments on context since 2017.

As the comments from the Examiner's Reports demonstrate, AO3 is still one of the assessment objectives both teachers and students can have difficulties with. It is clear that students need explicit teaching and modelling on how to embed context properly in their responses, so that it is relevant and moves their analysis and thinking along. Students need to take the big themes and ideas of the play identified in the question as a starting point and show their understanding and appreciation by developing their interpretation of the play and its message for them. The context should be used alongside the text to lead them to discussion of relevant ideas, in relation to the focus of the question and an exploration as to why the writer has presented their ideas in this particular way: why the characters behave in the way they do, why the scene is set in this particular place and why this theme is significant in the text.

Exam Series	Comments on context
2017	The mark scheme recognises a broad interpretation of context, meaning that the text does not exist in isolation, but the context within which it can be understood and interpreted is wide and varied. For example, the context of the text itself – placing the extract within the larger context of the play, of a literary form or genre, of the student's own contemporary context as well as historical context. Sweeping assertions did little to improve answers, whereas reasoned responses to specific details showed understanding and careful thought. Statements of historical detail 'bolted on' to a response did little to demonstrate any real understanding of the text in relation to a context. So claiming 'All Elizabethan women were …' was vague. On the other hand suggesting that 'Lady Macbeth is a disturbing example of womankind because she denies her gender' indicated a willingness to move outwards from the text and place the text in a wider context
2018	Many responses offered historical detail on James 1 and Daemonologie and the divine right of kings in an attempt to address the context, which was used with varying degrees of success. As basic factual information, it doesn't contribute very effectively to an explanation of the character's attitudes which is the focus of the question. Students were more effective when they tried to use this information to explain the rationale for the characters' choices and the import of Macbeth's ability to even contemplate killing Duncan. Students were just as able to access marks for context by exploring ideas about superstition, moral choices and moral disintegration which showed they were engaging with the situation Macbeth and Banquo found themselves in and the different ways in which they responded to it.
2019	As has been noted, it seems that 'bolt on' statements of historical context are being replaced by similarly 'bolted on' statements of critical theory, which show that a student has been told something, but which is not fully understood or explained or integrated into an interpretation of the text being discussed.
2020	Students who have engaged with the focus of the question have done well as this directs them towards certain ideas and themes in the text and implicitly relates to this descriptor in the mark scheme have done well. Context can be historical context, but only where it is directly relevant to the focus of the question. So a consideration of Poor Laws is relevant to a question about poverty on A Christmas Carol; less relevant are chunks of biographical information, random historical facts or sweeping generalisations, along the lines of 'All women in Elizabethan England were …'
2021	AO3 tends to be more bolted-on and less integrated into a view of ideas about power and control at a wider level. However, it was noted that students seem to be getting better at integrating such contextual information into their responses and tailoring it to the demands of the task. This approach is to be encouraged as it enables students to talk more widely about the text's universal ideas.
2022	There continued to be evidence of the issues that have been addressed in reports from previous series', the most obvious of these being the use of unnecessary historical detail and sweeping generalisation as a means of trying to address AO3 context. There continues to be evidence of a 'model' paragraph which ends with a random or repeated sentence containing explicit contextual information: 'In Jacobean England …', and then gives some generalised information about the era. This seldom adds to the quality of the preceding paragraph, because it does not link to the focus of the paragraph. When students tie context into the themes and ideas of the play, the focus of the question or ground it in specific details, they do much better.

Exam Series	Comments on context
2023	The understanding that if the student clearly addresses the question, then they will be writing about the ideas of the text, is becoming increasing embedded in responses, leading to better, more fluent answers to the question that engage more thoughtfully with the writer's ideas and the student's interpretation of these. So, for example, there might be the acknowledgement that Scrooge, at the start of the novella, embodies Malthusian values, rather than a lengthy paragraph about Thomas Malthus and his theories about population growth. The student can then explore why Dickens has done this, and what he is suggesting about society's attitudes, which demonstrates their thinking about the novella's ideas far more effectively.
2024	Light and shade can be given to an interpretation by making wider connections, but this is an English Literature exam rather than a History exam and the focus is the text itself, therefore references to the historical context should be succinct. Interestingly, far more pertinent to an appreciation of context, were students who linked the character or ideas of the text to their own situation – one student wrote hugely perceptively about how the Elizabeth Bennet is an inspirational role model today because she refuses to be judged, not just by class but also by gender.

Figure 5.1 AQA Examiner Reports summary on AO3

How?

One thing I think that is key is to demystify and explain the choices we make as teachers and the evidence that underpins it. This has worked well with things like sharing research on metacognition and the most effective ways to revise, using Dunlosky's Toolkit (Dunlosky *et al.*, 2013). Therefore, it might be effective to start with explaining Counsell's idea of core (text details, literary techniques) and hinterland (broader historical, cultural and social contexts) knowledge explicitly. We might then show students how hinterland knowledge adds depth to their interpretations, rather than simply stating disconnected facts.

We might then model paragraph writing, explicitly demonstrating how context can inform interpretations. We could provide a step-by-step example, clearly showing the integration of relevant context with specific textual analysis. This might then lead to some guided practice, where we give students targeted prompts that encourage them to consider specific contextual details directly relevant to the text's themes or characters, for example, 'How might Jacobean views on kingship affect Macbeth's guilt?'

HACK #5.1: CONTEXT CAROUSEL

One way of helping them make their own judgements on the relevance of context might be to do a context carousel. Don't worry, this doesn't involve loads of cutting up, getting out of seats or guillotine use – it can be done on one A3 sheet or a simple PowerPoint slide on the board. You could have some different types of context (historical, social, biographical, literary). Then give students a question focus and ask them to make brief notes on how each context might inform their analysis with the question focus. Afterward, students might discuss and select the most relevant points to integrate into a paragraph. The example for *A Taste of Honey* in Figure 5.2 could be replicated for any text.

Post-war working-class poverty (1950s Britain) *A Taste of Honey* was written during the late 1950s, a period marked by post-war austerity and widespread poverty in Britain. Many working-class communities, like Jo and Helen's, lived in substandard housing and faced limited economic opportunities.	Delaney Shelagh Delaney was born in Salford in 1938 and attended local schools before working briefly in retail.
Limited roles and expectations for women During the 1950s, societal expectations for women were predominantly restrictive: women often faced stigma for being unmarried mothers or for deviating from traditional roles.	Cultural movement of 'kitchen sink realism' *A Taste of Honey* fits within the 'kitchen sink drama' movement, which aimed to depict ordinary, everyday experiences of working-class life with brutal honesty.

Figure 5.2 Context carousel example

They could also create mind maps linking key themes or characters to relevant contextual ideas. The key is to ensure that each context element is clearly connected back to a specific interpretation or textual detail, or to the focus of the question.

HACK #5.2: INTEGRATE OR ELIMINATE?

Provide sample paragraphs with context either bolted-on or well-integrated. Students can then discuss which paragraphs integrate context effectively and rewrite ineffective examples, such as in the example from *Julius Caesar* in Figure 5.3.

HACK #5.3: CHECKLIST FOR STUDENTS

It is also important to remove scaffolds and encourage students to ask themselves 'so what?' after including context. This pushes students to explain clearly why the context is relevant and how it illuminates their analysis. I produced a metacognitive bookmark for students with three questions to help scaffold this process, shown in Figure 5.4.

CHAPTER 5: CONTEXT

In Shakespeare's *Julius Caesar*, the line, 'Cowards die many times before their deaths; the valiant never taste of death but once' encapsulates the complex Roman ideal of bravery and honour. Spoken by Caesar in Act 2, Scene 2, this assertion highlights Caesar's stoicism and courage, crucial attributes valued within Roman society. During Shakespeare's own Elizabethan era, this concept resonated deeply with contemporary audiences living under a monarchy that, like ancient Rome, prized strength, leadership, and a willingness to confront mortality without fear. Caesar's dismissal of Calpurnia's warnings subtly critiques the precarious balance between bravery and hubris, posing broader philosophical questions about fate, ambition, and the tragic consequences of pride. While Caesar perceives courage as noble and straightforward, Shakespeare problematises this belief, exposing how unchecked bravery can tip into destructive arrogance – a nuanced exploration of power that warns Shakespeare's audience of the perils facing their own ambitious rulers.

Rewrite this second ineffective example
In Julius Caesar, the line, 'Et tu, Brute?—Then fall, Caesar!' shows Caesar's surprise that Brutus betrays him. Caesar trusted Brutus completely and did not expect betrayal from him. Shakespeare wrote during the reign of Elizabeth I, who became queen in 1558 and ruled for 45 years. Her reign was known as the Golden Age and she supported arts and culture, which allowed playwrights like Shakespeare to flourish. Caesar's death scene highlights betrayal and dramatic tension. Shakespeare's plays were performed at the Globe Theatre, and audiences attended regularly, enjoying themes like betrayal and revenge in the plays.

In Shakespeare's Julius Caesar, the line, 'Cowards die many times before their deaths; the valiant never taste of death but once' shows Caesar's bravery. Caesar clearly believes he is fearless and will not back down in the face of danger. Shakespeare wrote during Elizabethan England, a time when Queen Elizabeth ruled and there were lots of battles and people were concerned about bravery and honour. Caesar ignores Calpurnia's warnings about the Ides of March, demonstrating his courage and his belief that he should not fear death. Shakespeare's plays were popular during his lifetime, and Julius Caesar is based on historical events from ancient Rome.

Rewrite

Figure 5.3 Example of rewriting an ineffective answer

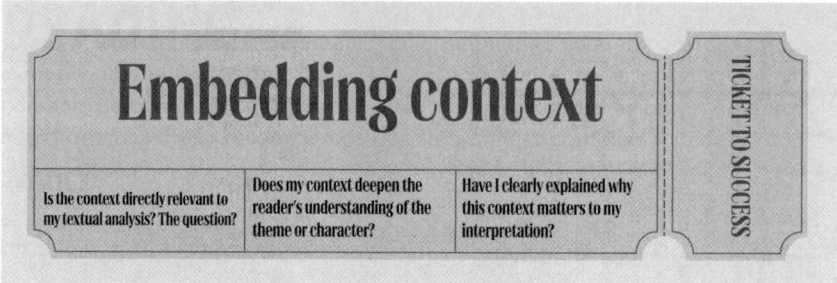

Figure 5.4 Metacognitive bookmark

WRITING

What?

Teaching context within creative and transactional writing can refer to many things but in this case we are focusing on guiding students to consider the particular circumstances, audience, purpose and background that shape how a piece of writing is produced and received. Unlike context in literature which, as we have considered, often emphasises historical or cultural influences, context in creative and transactional writing involves understanding how writers can effectively tailor their message based on specific real-world or imagined situations.

For creative writing, such as the 'narrate/describe' task in the English Language papers, this might include the following.

- **Audience awareness:** Students considering who the intended readers are and then shaping the tone, style and vocabulary accordingly.
- **Purpose and intention:** Understanding the goal, mood and tone and how that shapes decisions about character, setting, vocabulary and plot.
- **Setting and situation:** Knowing how to embed narratives in believable social, cultural, historical or imagined environments to enhance authenticity.
- **Character voice and perspective:** Writing authentically from characters' viewpoints involves understanding their personal context, background and motivations and how this impacts their thoughts and actions.

For example, a student writing a narrative set in wartime Britain might include subtle details about rationing or social attitudes, shaping dialogue and descriptions to build authenticity rather than explicitly stating historical facts.

In transactional writing the list is similar but different.

- **Purpose and intent:** Students must clearly understand why they're writing, whether to inform, persuade, instruct or argue. This then directly influences content, tone and structure.
- **Audience and reader expectations:** Tailoring language, formality, detail and approach to engage the reader.
- **Medium and form:** Students need awareness of conventions associated with different text types (letters, articles, reports, speeches) and need to then adapt their style and structure accordingly.

Therefore, a student crafting a persuasive speech about environmental issues may use emotive language, relevant contemporary examples and rhetorical techniques, knowing the audience's likely values and current concerns.

The AQA mark scheme references some of these considerations in the mark schemes for the writing tasks in both language papers. At the top end, it states that candidates' tone, style and register will be assuredly matched to purpose and audience. This means that in order for students to do well in their written tasks, they must ensure that what they write and how they write it must take into account the purpose, audience and format of the task; writing must then be crafted to match this.

How?

🔒 HACK #5.4: AUDIENCE PROFILES

As we have discussed, it is useful for students to be able to explicitly define their readers, as it sharpens their focus and helps them to develop tailored language and content choices. It also encourages students to imagine the reader's perspectives and reactions, which can help their writing seem more authentic, so that they become more self-aware about how their choices influence reader engagement and response. This is also a crossover with considerations about authorial intent in literature!

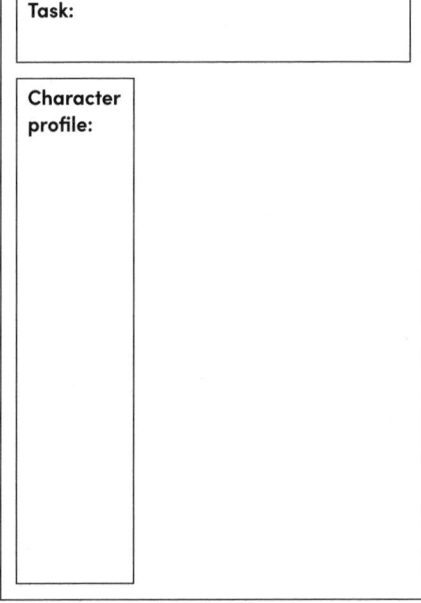

Figure 5.5 Template for character profile task

For this activity, students should be given varied scenarios such as a formal letter, a narrative for children or an article for teenagers and then be asked to create a detailed profile of their intended audience. This might include their age, interests, beliefs or concerns. They can then write a short piece explicitly tailored to their created audience profiles, with space around the outside for them to annotate why they made the choices based on the reader profile. The reflection part of this activity could also be peer assessment, where peers judge how they effectively adjusted their tone, style and language. Figure 5.5 is a template for this activity.

HACK #5.5: IN THEIR SHOES

Students often think that if they are doing the describe question in Language Paper 1 that they cannot include some work on characterisation. This may be due to the fact that when we practise this question, we often give students pictures of landscapes and scenes, which may not have people in it. It could also be due to some of the scaffolds teachers use to help students structure a description, such as splitting the image into squares and asking them to zoom in, or drop-shift-zoom type scaffolds which might not lend themselves to characterisation. It is important to remind students that the description or narrative is inspired by the image – it does not need to be exact. Therefore, they might include things outside the frame that realistically link.

To help with this, provide students with an image such as a marketplace and character role cards to describe their context, e.g. background, motivations, historical/social environment. Students should then be prompted to write short monologues or diary entries from their character's viewpoint based on their innermost thoughts and feelings in the scene.

HACK #5.6: SHAPING PURPOSE

Give students one broad topic, for example, climate change, and assign different purposes, including to persuade, inform, argue or entertain to different groups. Each group is then asked to write a paragraph tailored explicitly to their assigned purpose. The groups can then share and analyse how the content, language and tone changes according to the purpose. This activity ensures students consciously shape their writing according to a clearly defined goal. It also encourages precision, as students select vocabulary, rhetorical devices and structures more deliberately and consciously matched to their writing's purpose. Regular practice also helps them adapt to varied purposes and makes students versatile and confident writers across different contexts.

HACK #5.7: MATCH THE MEDIUM

It is really helpful to work with students to enhance their structural awareness; if they can explicitly recognise features that are unique to each text type, it will help them adjust their writing fluidly across formats. Evaluating different text types may also foster deeper analytical skills, which can help them to justify and rationalise their own writing choices.

For this hack, introduce students to a selection of different text types, like speeches, articles, blog posts and formal letters. In pairs, they can then analyse these mentor texts to identify their conventions. These can be broadly grouped into three headings: format, language and style.

Individually, they can then rewrite one text type into another form, adapting style and content to match the new medium. This might be an informal blog post into a persuasive formal letter, for example.

HACK #5.8: THE DEVIL IS IN THE DETAIL

This is one of my favourite things to do as I love a bit of historical fiction! Provide students with a historical or contemporary setting, such as the Swinging Sixties or a dystopian future. Ask them to research or brainstorm small contextual details such as clothing, technology and social norms and then to write a narrative scene embedding these subtle details naturally. These can then be shared with the rest of the class under the visualiser, while the student explains their choices. This hack encourages thoughtful embedding because it helps students avoid common pitfalls, such as forced or obvious inclusion of irrelevant contextual information.

ORACY

What?

In a similar way, teaching context in oracy involves guiding students to understand and respond to the particular circumstances, audiences, purposes and backgrounds that shape spoken communication. However, unlike in written forms, context in oracy requires students to dynamically adapt their language, tone, style and approach in real-time conversations, discussions, debates and presentations. This can be tricky.

The Ofsted English Subject Report (2024) states that schools should 'understand the different components of written and spoken language and how to sequence, explicitly teach and assess them. For example … how to identify the grammar and vocabulary that pupils need to be taught, and to consider how tone, register and syntax differ, depending on the form chosen.' The report also highlighted that many students are not being given the opportunity to develop this skill and that this is becoming clear when students complete their Spoken Language endorsement at GCSE.

Other research also consistently underscores the critical role of context in oracy, highlighting that effective communication is deeply influenced by factors such as audience, purpose, setting and cultural norms. One of the things I struggled with most when I went away to university as a first generation undergraduate with limited cultural capital was the ability to adjust the way I spoke depending on context. It set me apart from those with more affluent backgrounds right from the outset.

Studies in educational settings, particularly those focusing on content and language integrated learning (CLIL) and disciplinary literacy, have demonstrated that oracy cannot be separated from content knowledge and cultural context. This emphasises the importance of integrating language development with subject-specific learning to foster genuine comprehension and effective communication (Wellington and Osborne, 2001). Indeed, linguist Dell Hymes (1974) developed the SPEAKING model, which outlines components of effective communication: Setting, Participants, Ends (purposes), Act sequence, Key (tone), Instrumentalities (channels), Norms, and Genre. This illustrates that understanding the context, such as who is speaking, to whom and for what purpose, is essential for meaningful interaction.

Context in oracy might include the following.

- Audience awareness, where students recognise who they're speaking to and tailor their vocabulary, register and content accordingly, as well as being sensitive to audience reactions and adjusting their speech in response.
- Clarifying their spoken goals (to persuade, inform, entertain, discuss, debate or instruct) and then in turn ensuring their tone, emphasis and rhetorical choices match their intended purpose.
- Understanding how formal or informal a situation is, which then influences word choice, body language and delivery. Part of this is recognising contextual cues such as social norms, expected behaviours or conventions specific to particular speaking scenarios.
- Considering their role (as a peer, leader, negotiator, presenter) and shaping their speech accordingly.

This really matters as teaching context in oracy helps students to develop effective and adaptable speaking skills, meaning that they can engage meaningfully and empathetically with diverse audiences. This will then lead to the building of confidence in varying communicative situations, as well as enhanced listening and responsiveness to others' ideas.

How?

These ideas for hacks can be effective as they explicitly teach students how to consciously consider and respond to various speaking contexts, encouraging them to actively adapt their language in real-time. They also build key oracy skills including listening, adaptability, critical thinking and reflective practice.

HACK #5.9: AUDIENCE SWITCH

Ask students to prepare a brief speech on a topic that is similar to a task they may get for the writing task on Language Paper 2. After some planning time, they can initially deliver the speech informally to peers. They can then adapt the same speech for a formal audience, such as an assembly or school governors. Students can even film the two different speeches and then discuss the differences in language, tone and style used, focusing on how they match the purpose, tone and format.

HACK #5.10: ORACY PLAYBACK

Again, this involves listening to recordings of speeches and debates – these could be by your own students or others. There are some from YouTube which have been used as exemplars from AQA and other exam boards. As a class, you would listen back and identify how well the speakers adapted to the audience, purpose and situation and codify how they did this. The students can then try using these active ingredients in their own oracy work with varying different tasks.

Why?

As we have outlined, Christine Counsell distinguishes between core knowledge (essential facts and concepts students must retain) and hinterland knowledge, which enriches and gives meaning to the core. In literature, this means that while students need to understand the plot and characters, their appreciation deepens when they grasp the historical, cultural or philosophical contexts (hinterland) that inform the text. This approach prevents superficial learning and fosters a more profound engagement with the material (Parker, 2022). Students who are able to interpret texts in an original way often have a wide general knowledge, which helps them make sense of what they are reading. This also links to Cognitive Load Theory, which posits that learners have limited working memory capacity (Sweller, Ayres and Kalyuga, 2011). By integrating context into teaching, we can help students to build schemas. These organised knowledge structures facilitate understanding and memory retention. For instance, understanding the social norms of Elizabethan England can help students make sense of character motivations in Shakespeare's plays.

Teaching students to reflect on their learning processes through metacognition also enables them to plan, monitor and evaluate their understanding and performance (EEF, 2025b). Therefore, when students consider questions like 'Why is this context important?' or 'How does this information influence my interpretation?' they engage in deeper learning and develop the ability to use this skill independently when facing a new extract or essay question.

Finally, developing oracy skills is crucial for students' academic success and social mobility. Research indicates that students from diverse backgrounds benefit from explicit instruction in adapting language to different contexts, audiences and purposes. This not only improves their communication skills but also builds cultural capital, empowering them to navigate various social and academic settings confidently (Mercer and Littleton, 2007).

CHAPTER 6: COMPARING TEXTS

Teaching comparison in English matters because it develops the habit of reading, writing and speaking with alertness and judgement. When students compare, they learn to look for patterns, such as recurring ideas or repeated techniques and to also notice when a writer follows those patterns or deliberately break them. That process sharpens their interpretative confidence: instead of simply spotting features or paraphrasing content, students begin to weigh significance. They can explain not only *what* is happening in a text, but *why* it has been crafted that way, what alternatives were available and what difference those choices make for meaning and effect.

Comparison also moves students beyond treating texts as self-contained artefacts. In English, meaning is shaped by relationships: between a text and its genre, between a speaker and their audience, between a writer's purpose and the methods they select, between a text and the cultural moment that produced it. Relational thinking helps students make these links deliberately. They learn to connect ideas, methods and meanings across different texts and to recognise that language behaves differently depending on context.

Crucially, comparison turns observation into argument. It gives students a disciplined way of thinking that supports clearer analytical writing and more coherent discussion. Rather than listing techniques, students learn to group evidence, prioritise what matters and build lines of reasoning: '*this* choice creates this effect here, whereas *that* choice creates a different effect there, and the contrast matters because it reveals something about viewpoint, purpose or values.' Over time, students also become more flexible learners. What they understand about tone in one text, structure in another, or register in a third becomes transferable knowledge they can apply to new reading, unfamiliar unseen texts and their own writing and speaking.

READING

What?

Comparison sits at the heart of English as a discipline. Whether students are comparing poems, novels, extracts, non-fiction texts, spoken viewpoints, or writers' methods, they are being asked to engage in a distinctly disciplinary way of thinking. Comparison is not simply about identifying what is similar or different; it is about understanding how writers respond to shared ideas, contexts and purposes.

Yet for many students, comparison is one of the hardest skills to master. We have all read responses where students write about one text, then the other, with only a cursory 'both writers show ...' tacked on at the end. Others resort to feature-spotting, listing techniques without explaining their comparative significance. Of course, one of the challenges with teaching comparison is that it places a heavy demand on working memory. In AQA Language Paper 2, Question 4 for example, students must:

- Understand two (or more) texts securely.
- Identify the viewpoints of the writers.
- Decide what is similar or different about the viewpoints.
- Analyse how those viewpoints are portrayed through the methods the writers use.
- Articulate this clearly using subject-specific vocabulary.

It is no wonder then, that without careful scaffolding, this can easily overload students, particularly those with less secure background knowledge or weaker literacy skills. As with context, comparison can become an invisible curriculum expectation – something teachers assume students will pick up through exposure, rather than a skill to be taught deliberately.

From an equity perspective, this matters enormously. Students with high levels of cultural capital often arrive already familiar with comparative thinking: they can draw parallels, synthesise ideas, and generalise with confidence. Others need to be shown how comparison works, step by step. If we want all students to succeed, comparison must be demystified.

Bourdieu's theory of cultural capital argues that schools implicitly reward ways of thinking, speaking, and reasoning that mirror middle-class social practices. Comparative thinking – drawing analogies, abstracting patterns, synthesising ideas – is one of these practices (Bourdieu, 1977). Research building on Bourdieu shows that middle-class students are more likely to encounter comparison, classification and generalisation in family talk, reading and cultural experiences. Working-class students are more likely to experience context-bound, descriptive talk, unless schools explicitly teach abstract reasoning. This is supported by classroom discourse studies such as by Basil Bernstein, who distinguished between:

- Elaborated codes (abstract, comparative, generalising language).
- Restricted codes (context-specific, descriptive language).

Comparative writing and talk rely heavily on elaborated codes (Bernstein, 2000). When schools assume students already possess these, inequity is reproduced rather than challenged. Essentially, students with higher cultural capital often recognise comparison as a familiar way of thinking, while others require explicit modelling and rehearsal to access the same academic moves.

As with context, Christine Counsell's distinction between core and hinterland knowledge is particularly useful here. Core knowledge in comparison includes:

- Secure understanding of each text (plot, themes, methods, viewpoints).
- Knowledge of comparative vocabulary (whereas, similarly, in contrast, more significantly).
- Familiarity with comparative structures and paragraph models.

Hinterland knowledge, however, is what allows comparison to become insightful rather than mechanical. This might include knowledge of shared literary traditions or genres, awareness of different historical, social or ideological contexts and understanding of how writers respond to one another, directly or indirectly (Counsell, 2018b). For example, comparing war poems without understanding differing conflicts, purposes or genres limits students to surface-level comments. Hinterland knowledge allows them to explore why writers treat similar subject matter in different ways, and what those choices reveal.

It is also worth noting that comparison is explicitly rewarded in assessment of literature. In AQA GCSE Literature, comparison is embedded within AO3 and AO4. Mark schemes consistently reward students who make conceptual, integrated comparisons, rather than separate comments on each text. This tells us something important: comparison is not an add-on; it is the thinking itself.

How?

As with context, the first step is explicit explanation. Students benefit from understanding what comparison actually is and what it is not. Comparison is not:

- Listing similarities.
- Writing about texts separately.
- Forcing links that are irrelevant.

Instead, comparison is about placing texts in dialogue with one another. Modelling is crucial here. Teachers should regularly think aloud, showing how they select a meaningful point of comparison and how they use one text to illuminate the other. A useful starting point is to frame comparison around ideas, not texts. Rather than asking 'How are these poems similar?', we might ask 'How do these writers present power?' or 'How do these perspectives on conflict differ?' This shifts students away from surface features and towards conceptual thinking.

HACK #6.1: THE COMPARISON SPINE

Provide students with a simple comparative sentence stem that forces integration, such as:

While Writer A presents ..., Writer B ..., suggesting that ...

Students can then build outward from this spine, adding:

- Evidence from both texts.
- Analysis of methods.
- Contextual or conceptual insight.

This helps prevent the common 'Text A paragraph/Text B paragraph' structure and instead encourages genuinely comparative writing.

HACK #6.2: SAME, DIFFERENT, SO WHAT?

After identifying a similarity or difference, students must answer the question 'So what?' For example:

Same: Both writers explore isolation

Different: One presents it as emotional, the other as physical

So what? This reflects ... because ...

This mirrors metacognitive approaches by helping students move beyond description into interpretation.

 HACK #6.3: COMPARATIVE SORTING

Give students a bank of statements, quotations and ideas from two texts. Ask them to sort these into:

- Similar.
- Different.
- Connected but contrasting.

The crucial step is the discussion afterwards: why have they grouped them this way? This makes comparative thinking visible and collaborative.

WRITING

What?

After students have spent time reading and comparing the texts, they then need to write up their response. In AQA GCSE English Language Paper 2, students are explicitly required to compare writers' ideas and perspectives (Question 2) and to evaluate how viewpoints are presented across two texts (Question 4). Similarly, unseen poetry comparison demands that students identify connections, contrasts and conceptual patterns between unfamiliar texts under time pressure. These tasks require far more than surface-level reading: students must synthesise information, prioritise ideas and shape responses with precision. Crucially, as with the reading section of this chapter, research suggests that these forms of comparative thinking are not intuitive and must be explicitly taught.

In AQA Language Paper 2 Question 2, students are asked to compare writers' ideas or perspectives on a given topic across two non-fiction texts. This requires them to identify points of similarity or difference, select relevant evidence from both sources, and articulate connections using comparative language. Question 4 raises the cognitive demand further by asking students to evaluate how effectively writers convey their viewpoints, requiring comparison not only of ideas but of methods, tone and rhetorical choices. Examiner reports repeatedly note that weaker responses treat the texts separately, while stronger responses integrate them conceptually, moving fluidly between sources. This distinction aligns with research on novice–expert differences, which shows that novices tend to process information sequentially, while experts organise knowledge relationally and conceptually (Chi, Feltovich and Glaser, 1981).

From a cognitive perspective, as previously discussed, these tasks place significant demands on working memory. Students must hold two texts in mind simultaneously, track similarities and differences, and make evaluative judgements. Cognitive Load Theory explains why this is particularly challenging for learners with less secure background knowledge: when intrinsic load is high, students are more likely to revert to simplistic strategies, such as summarising first one text and then the other (Sweller, Ayres and Kalyuga, 2011). Research consistently shows that explicit instructional supports, such as comparative sentence stems, worked examples and model paragraphs, help to reduce extraneous cognitive load and enable students to engage in higher-order thinking (Kirschner, Sweller and Clark, 2006).

The same principles apply to unseen poetry comparison. When students encounter two unfamiliar poems, they are required to identify thematic connections, contrasts in tone or perspective, and differences in writerly method, often within a single extended response. Studies in disciplinary literacy demonstrate that synthesis across texts is one of the most demanding literacy practices and does not develop through exposure alone (Shanahan and Shanahan, 2008). Expert readers are able to compare texts by abstracting ideas and recognising patterns, while less experienced readers focus on surface features unless guided otherwise. This explains why some students appear immediately comfortable with unseen comparison, while others struggle to move beyond basic feature-spotting.

Writing research further reinforces the need for explicit teaching. Graham and Hebert's (2011) meta-analysis shows that writing tasks requiring students to integrate and synthesise ideas significantly improve comprehension, but only when students are taught how to organise their thinking. Without explicit modelling, weaker writers often know what they want to say about individual texts but struggle to structure ideas relationally rather than sequentially. In the context of AQA Language Paper 2, this can result in responses that identify techniques accurately but fail to compare their effects meaningfully.

In transactional writing tasks, comparison may be less explicit but is no less important. Students are often required to weigh arguments, acknowledge alternative viewpoints or adapt content for different audiences and purposes. These processes involve evaluative comparison: deciding which ideas to foreground, which to challenge and how to shape tone and register accordingly.

Across both language and literature papers, the pedagogical implication is clear: writing up a comparison must also be demystified. When the writing up of a comparison is deliberately taught, structured and practised, it becomes a powerful lever for improving outcomes in AQA Language Paper 2 and unseen poetry alike.

How?

HACK #6.4: COMPARATIVE PLANNING GRIDS

Before writing, students complete a grid with:

- Viewpoint A.
- Viewpoint B.
- Points of agreement.
- Points of tension.

Only then do students plan their response. This ensures comparison happens before writing, not as an afterthought.

HACK #6.5: REWRITE WITH A SHIFT

Give students a strong paragraph written from one perspective. Ask them to rewrite it from a contrasting viewpoint, then reflect on:

- What changed.
- Why those changes were necessary.
- What this reveals about purpose and audience.

This builds flexibility and comparative awareness simultaneously.

ORACY

What?

Comparison is central to effective spoken communication. Whether students are participating in debates, structured discussions, presentations or exploratory talk, they are routinely required to acknowledge alternative viewpoints, compare evidence or ideas, and respond dynamically to others in real time. These are not peripheral speaking skills; they sit at the heart of what it means to communicate thoughtfully and persuasively. Yet for many students, comparative oracy remains one of the most challenging aspects of spoken language, particularly under the cognitive and social pressure of live interaction.

Research in educational linguistics and classroom discourse consistently shows that spoken comparison is cognitively demanding. Unlike written comparison when done well, which allows for planning, drafting and revision, oracy requires students to hold multiple ideas in working memory while simultaneously monitoring audience response, selecting appropriate language and shaping their contribution on the spot. This places a heavy load on working memory, particularly for students with less secure background knowledge or limited experience of formal academic talk (Sweller, Ayres and Kalyuga, 2011).

Classroom studies of dialogic teaching suggest that without explicit instruction, comparative talk tends to be dominated by a small number of confident students. Alexander's research on classroom dialogue demonstrates that higher-order talk moves – such as building on, challenging or comparing ideas – rarely emerge spontaneously and must be deliberately scaffolded through teacher modelling and structured talk protocol (Alexander, 2017). When such structures are absent, classroom discussion can become either superficial or exclusionary, reinforcing existing participation gaps.

The Oracy Commission's report *We need to talk* (2024) highlights that oracy skills, particularly those involving reasoning, evaluation and comparison, are unevenly distributed across socioeconomic groups. Students from more advantaged backgrounds are more likely to have encountered comparative talk at home, while others rely almost entirely on school for access to these practices. The report argues that when schools fail to teach oracy explicitly, they inadvertently reproduce inequality, as the most academically valued forms of talk remain the preserve of a minority.

There is, however, strong evidence that explicit instruction can close this gap. Studies on exploratory talk show that when students are taught how to engage in structured comparison, through sentence stems, talk roles and explicit norms for responding to others, the quality of spoken reasoning improves significantly (Mercer and Littleton, 2007). Importantly, these gains are not limited to high-attaining students. Research indicates that structured dialogic approaches have a particularly positive impact on students who are less confident speakers, enabling them to participate more fully and develop academic voice (Howe *et al.*, 2019).

Comparative oracy is also closely linked to academic attainment beyond speaking itself. Oral comparison supports reading comprehension, writing quality and critical thinking by externalising reasoning processes. When students practise weighing ideas aloud, they rehearse the same cognitive moves required for evaluative writing and textual analysis. This aligns with research showing that talk is not merely a precursor to learning but a driver of it, particularly when it is structured around reasoning and comparison (Resnick, Asterhan and Clarke, 2015).

Teaching comparative oracy explicitly therefore serves multiple purposes. Pedagogically, it makes the hidden rules of academic talk visible. Cognitively, it reduces load by providing linguistic and structural scaffolds for complex thinking. Socially, it builds confidence and adaptability, enabling students to participate effectively in formal and informal speaking contexts. The Oracy Commission identifies these skills as foundational for social mobility, noting that employers consistently value the ability to compare options, justify decisions and respond thoughtfully to alternative perspectives.

In practical terms, this means that teachers should not assume students know how to compare ideas orally. Comparative sentence stems (e.g. 'In contrast to what X said ...', 'Both viewpoints suggest ...'), structured discussion formats and deliberate modelling of comparative responses are not crutches; they are equity tools.

How?

HACK #6.6: VERBAL COMPARE AND CONTRAST

Students are given two short viewpoints and must respond orally using comparative sentence stems only.

- In contrast ...
- Similarly ...
- More significantly ...

This constrains their language productively, helping them practise comparative structures fluently.

HACK #6.7: THE HOT SEAT COMPARISON

One student represents Text A, another Text B. The class asks comparative questions, forcing each student to respond in relation to the other. This is particularly effective for literature revision and builds confidence quickly.

Why?

Teaching comparison explicitly enables students to think more flexibly, more critically and more independently. By reducing cognitive load through clear models and repeated practice, we allow students to focus on meaning rather than mechanics.

From a curriculum perspective, comparison strengthens schema-building. When students link texts together, they create richer mental networks, improving retention and transfer. From an equity perspective, it levels the playing field, ensuring that all students, not just the most advantaged, can access high-level analytical thinking.

Ultimately, comparison is how English makes sense of the world: by placing voices, ideas and experiences alongside one another and asking what they reveal. Teaching students to do this well is one of the most powerful things we can do as English teachers.

CHAPTER 7: RHETORIC

Studying rhetoric in English matters because it shows students how language works as action, not just expression. Rhetoric is the craft of shaping words to achieve a purpose: to persuade, to inform, to build trust, to stir emotion, to challenge ideas, to prompt people to respond. When students understand this, they stop treating texts as neutral and begin to see them as deliberately constructed attempts to influence an audience.

It also develops critical literacy. In everyday life, students encounter persuasive language constantly – particularly on social media. Rhetorical awareness helps them evaluate what they are being asked to believe and why. Students learn to ask informed questions: who is speaking, what they want, what assumptions they rely on, and what has been left out. This reduces the risk of being swayed by emotional manipulation, or selective presentation – a vital skill in today's political climate.

Rhetoric improves students' own communication too. When students study how persuasion is built, they gain practical control over writing and speech: shaping ideas for a particular audience, for example, and making choices that match purpose. It helps students understand that language carries power and it equips them to use that power responsibly and effectively.

READING

What?

Research indicates that engaging students in the analysis of rhetorical texts can significantly enhance their writing abilities. This practice, known as rhetorical reading, involves examining how authors use language to persuade and convey meaning, thereby informing students' own writing strategies.

Martin Robinson (2013) takes this even further. He reimagines the classical trivium: grammar, dialectic and rhetoric, as a framework for modern education. He emphasises the importance of rhetoric, advocating for its integration into the curriculum to equip students with the skills to express ideas persuasively and participate actively in civic life. Indeed, Robinson argues that rhetoric is not merely about persuasive speech but encompasses the ability to communicate ideas effectively across various forms, fostering confidence and creativity in students, and emphasises that rhetoric should be a deliberate and integral part of the curriculum. He encourages educators to create opportunities for students to express their understanding through various mediums, such as speeches, debates and presentations. To bring rhetoric into the classroom, he suggests teaching its classical components.

- **Invention:** Developing arguments and ideas.
- **Arrangement:** Organising content logically.
- **Style:** Choosing appropriate language and tone.
- **Memory:** Internalising content for delivery.
- **Delivery:** Presenting ideas effectively.

He also highlights the importance of ethos (credibility), pathos (emotional connection) and logos (logical reasoning) in crafting compelling messages. A key art of learning how to do this well is of course reading a range of texts that are rhetorical in nature and analysing how they have created various effects so students can have a go themselves (Robinson, 2013).

There is a growing body of research to suggest that this might be a good idea. A meta-analysis on reading and writing by Graham *et al.* (2018), for example, reviewed 54 studies involving over 5000 students and found that reading interventions, including those focusing on rhetorical analysis, had a substantial positive effect on students' writing quality, with an effect size of 0.57. This suggests that reading and analysing texts can directly improve writing skills.

In addition, Hass and Flower (1988) emphasise that rhetorical reading enables students to construct meaning beyond the text itself. This deeper engagement with texts fosters critical thinking and enhances students' ability to craft persuasive arguments in their writing. Educational resources from institutions like Stanford University (2026) also advocate for teaching rhetorical analysis to help students become more aware of how audience and purpose shape writing. They state that this awareness is crucial for students to develop their own effective writing strategies.

Further research highlights that teaching rhetoric and the art of persuasive and purposeful communication significantly improves students' writing by enhancing their audience awareness, structural control and critical thinking. Rhetorical instruction helps students move beyond formulaic writing by teaching them to consider audience, purpose and context. Indeed, Fahnestock (2011) found that when students understand rhetorical concepts such as ethos, pathos and logos, they make more intentional language and structural choices in their writing.

How?

One of the things I always loved to teach was rhetorical analysis. I loved it because it's the moment when students start to see just how powerful and creative language can be. Instead of only asking *what* an author is saying, we dig into *how* they're saying it. We look at the tricks and techniques writers use and why they choose certain words, structures or tones, as well as talking about why those choices actually work. It's like pulling back the curtain on how persuasion really happens.

What I love even more is that these skills don't just stay in the classroom. Once students know how to spot the ways people, ads or companies try to persuade them, they can see the world differently. They start noticing how commercials get them to want things, how speeches can inspire action and how opinions are shaped online. It's a real-life superpower for making smarter, more thoughtful decisions. Once students realise that persuasion is everywhere (and that they can figure out exactly how it works) it's incredible to see the penny drop.

 HACK #7.1: INTRODUCTION TO RHETORICAL DEVICES

Of course, first students need to be taught about ethos, pathos and logos and how that might link to other rhetorical strategies they have previously learned, such as acronyms like AFOREST. To help students feel more confident with annotation and rhetorical analysis, we would always start simple and do it together. First, we annotate as a whole class so everyone can see the process in action. After that, students team up in pairs to try it themselves, comparing notes and bouncing ideas off each other. Then, they share their insights with another group and finally with the whole class. This step-by-step approach takes the pressure off and gives them lots of chances to practise. By the time they're annotating on their own, they've already seen examples, tested their ideas with a partner, and gotten feedback. It's a low-stress way to learn how to spot rhetorical devices and appeals and it really helps them build confidence along the way. There are a huge range of speeches you can use for this. Classic examples such as Martin Luther King Jr.'s 'I Have a Dream,' Abraham Lincoln's 'Gettysburg Address,' and Winston Churchill's speeches during World War II are always great ones to use. Other options include speeches by John F. Kennedy, Ronald Reagan and even some contemporary examples like Steve Jobs' commencement speech. My more recent favourite was Reese Witherspoon's 'Glamour Women of the Year' speech in 2015 and Emma Watson's speech to the United Nations for the HeForShe campaign. There are also film examples, such as speeches in *Gladiator, A Few Good Men, Braveheart, The Return of the King, Independence Day, Legally Blonde* and *Remember the Titans*, to name a few.

HACK #7.2: RHETORICAL TRIANGLE MAPPING

Rhetorical triangle mapping also helps students to see how a combination of appeals make a text more persuasive or effective. After they have been explicitly taught about ethos, pathos and logos, they would read a passage and highlight or label examples of each appeal and discuss how each one makes the other more effective. This gives students a concrete framework for understanding rhetorical strategies and helps them see the relationship between purpose, audience and technique.

HACK #7.3: RHETORICAL DEVICE SCAVENGER HUNT

For students who may need extra scaffolding, a rhetorical device scavenger hunt can also work well. Provide students with a short speech, article or advertisement. Then give them a checklist of rhetorical devices. Students can then hunt for examples in the text, highlight them and explain their effect. This helps students who may normally struggle to find the techniques in the text. Extra scaffolding can be given to help them analyse the effect, such as sentence starters or worked examples.

WRITING

What?

As well as equipping students with the skills necessary to deconstruct and evaluate arguments, rhetorical literacy enables them to build their own convincing arguments: a skill that will serve them well both in and beyond their time at school. As Kat Howard (2025) wrote in her blog, 'the ability to articulate ideas persuasively empowers students, fostering a sense of agency and confidence. By developing their knowledge of rhetoric as an overlay of the taught curriculum, a way to access and translate content, students gain the confidence to advocate for their beliefs, participate actively in civic discourse, and become influential and contributory members of their communities.' So our teaching of rhetoric definitely helps students feel empowered to give opinions in ways that make them heard.

In a recent paper, Richard Andrews also argued that rhetoric and argumentation should be central to the secondary school curriculum in England for its role in supporting democratic participation. He argued that effective communication requires understanding:

- Who is communicating.
- To whom.
- About what, why, where and how.

He also argues that students must learn to compose, interpret and recompose texts across different modes. He suggests that texts in the 21st century are often fluid, multimodal and interactive, blurring the line between fiction and non-fiction. So therefore, learning should emphasise both short forms (like social media arguments) and longer, structured texts necessary for democracy and higher education. Restoring rhetoric and argumentation to the curriculum in this way bridges the gap between language and literature, prepares students for critical engagement in society and ultimately supports the democratic mission of schools by empowering students to become active, reflective communicators (Andrews, 2019).

Teaching rhetoric well can also help students produce better writing. Research applying logos, ethos and pathos in academic writing found that students who use a balanced mix of appeals write more persuasive, engaging prose. Especially in argumentative or disciplinary writing, rhetorical variety improves impact and reader engagement (Mohamad, 2022).

How?

HACK #7.4: ANALYSING MENTOR TEXTS

Being able to use rhetoric well in writing relies of course on seeing and analysing lots of other examples before seeing some modelling by a teacher and then engaging in lots of deliberate practice with different stimulus. Analysing mentor texts for rhetorical moves is definitely an important first step as seeing rhetorical strategies in action helps students internalise how to apply them effectively themselves. So, to start, provide samples of strong essays, speeches or newspaper articles and guide students to annotate a particularly rhetorical strategy-rich section, such as a part that uses an analogy. Then provide a debate topic and ask them to imitate that rhetorical move in their own paragraph.

HACK #7.5: SOAPSTONE

Largely, I am not a huge fan of acronyms but have previously used SOAPSTone to create a rhetorical situation framework. I would ask students to break down a text using SOAPSTone (Speaker, Occasion, Audience, Purpose, Subject, Tone). Then, have them plan their writing by explicitly defining their own audience, purpose and tone. This helps students learn that rhetoric is situational, and writing choices must match purpose and audience. This judicious crafting of the use of rhetoric is something that students really struggle with, so it is well worth spending some time on it.

HACK #7.6: RHETORICAL REWRITE

Another idea is doing a rhetorical rewrite challenge. I would take a plain paragraph and challenge students to rewrite it three ways.

1. Logical (logos-focused, evidence-heavy)
2. Emotional (pathos-focused, vivid language)
3. Credible/authoritative (ethos-focused, expert voice)

They can discuss which version would work best for different audiences. This can be done in groups or using the visualiser as a class. It helps students practise flexible rhetorical thinking and understand how language shifts impact persuasion for different purposes and tones.

HACK #7.7: PEER REVIEW

Finally, peer review for rhetorical effectiveness can also work really well if students have been trained and are given focused prompts. During writing activities, assign peers to highlight rhetorical strategies in each other's drafts. Ask peers to give feedback on which strategies are effective and where the argument could be stronger using the prompts: 'this made me feel ...', 'this made me imagine ...', 'this made me think ...'. In this way, students learn to evaluate rhetoric critically and revise intentionally to strengthen their own writing.

ORACY

What?

According to Ofsted's English Review, for older pupils, the discipline of rhetoric can give an insight into how writers and orators use spoken language. 'Pupils can learn how spoken language is constructed and produced, and the connections between words, sentences and whole texts or in speech, from individual utterances to dialogues and speeches. Pupils can learn about the meanings and nuances of the spoken word, the craft of a writer or speaker, and the ways in which spoken language conveys, explores and manipulates meaning.' (Ofsted, 2022)

There is also much research across Australian and UK contexts emphasising the concept of rhetorical agency (the ability to speak intentionally and convincingly) as foundational to students becoming active, critically minded citizens, not passive information consumers (Green, Molyneux and Scull, 2022). Integrating rhetoric into oracy pedagogy is seen as vital to supporting participatory democracy; students learn not just to speak, but to shape public discourse (Jenkins, 2025).

The Oracy Education Commission's *We need to talk* report (2024) emphasised that effective speaking involves rhetorical understanding, beyond mere fluency, and is essential for holistic student development. Yet, research shows a gap: many secondary schools lack confidence in teaching spoken language and rhetoric, underscoring the need for intentional instruction in rhetorical skills as part of oracy teaching (RCSLT, 2021). This is important as in the Classics classroom, students exposed to rhetorical speaking tasks, such as debates and persuasive practice, developed greater rhetorical awareness, clarity in purpose and strategic communication skills that support critical thinking and argumentation across subjects (Tailor, 2016). In addition, higher education research on student presentations highlights the need for rhetorical structuring in speech assignments, indicating that rhetoric-informed preparation improves engagement and comprehension in public speaking contexts (Ducasse and Brown, 2022).

Essentially, research consistently points to the transformative effect of teaching rhetoric in spoken language.

- It builds students' agency, so they can shape arguments and make reasoned claims in public contexts.
- It strengthens oracy skills, making speaking both purposeful and persuasive.
- It bridges classroom learning with real-world communication needs, ensuring students are not just fluent speakers but strategic communicators.

How?

For some students, public speaking is one of their biggest fears and it has only worsened since the Covid-19 pandemic. A recent report from the Centre for Education and Youth (Millard, 2021) found that young people put oracy on a par with reading and writing. 75% think oracy is 'very important'; 78% say the same for literacy. However, less than a third (32%) of young people said their school/education prioritised oracy 'a lot.' 71% of teachers feel that online teaching negatively impacted on the development of pupils' oracy skills. However, teachers in state-funded settings were more than twice as likely to say the negative impact was 'significant'. One teacher in two said school closures negatively impacted the spoken language development of free school meal pupils – just one in five said the same of the most advantaged pupils. This is why it is so important to provide structured speech scaffolds to help students have the confidence to speak up.

HACK #7.8: TEMPLATES

It can be useful to provide students with templates for persuasive or informative speeches that highlight rhetorical techniques, as well as the structure, for example:

Hook → Thesis → Key points → Call to action
Include planned rhetorical questions, repetition, or parallelism.

You might then have students peer-review these speeches based on rhetorical effectiveness. This scaffolding makes rhetorical structures visible and repeatable, helping students plan their own speeches using the same templates.

HACK #7.9: ROLE PLAY

Role play can also be a great way of building confidence. You start by giving students real-world speaking scenarios, such as:

- Convincing the headteacher to allow a new club.
- Presenting a charity pitch.
- Explaining a complex concept to younger students.

Then assign each student a purpose and target audience to guide their rhetorical choices. This teaches students to adapt language, tone and structure for different audiences and goals.

After writing and planning, students can practise their speeches using peer rhetorical coaching. In pairs or small groups, students practise short speeches or presentations. Then peers provide feedback on their use of rhetorical devices, their clarity of purpose and argument and their audience engagement. Engaging the audience will need explicit teaching and there are great videos of real speeches on YouTube that demonstrate eye contact, hand gestures, intonation and pauses. You might even design a rubric for coaches to highlight. Students can then redraft their speech based on their target areas and perform it again. This can also be done as self-assessment using video. Not only does this encourage metacognition about rhetoric, but students also learn by both performing and analysing rhetorical moves, while the peer feedback reinforces authentic audience awareness.

Why?

Teaching rhetoric in reading, writing and oracy is really vital for many reasons. Essentially, exposure to diverse arguments helps students identify bias, assumptions and perspectives in texts – which in today's age of misinformation and fake news seems key. Encountering multiple rhetorical strategies (ethos, pathos, logos) enables students to also evaluate the effectiveness of communication. For example, comparing a political speech with an opinion piece from a newspaper helps students recognise tone, emotional appeals and logical reasoning. Reading rhetorical texts across media teaches them to discern credible sources, detect manipulation and understand persuasion in society. This skill is vital for responsible civic engagement, such as evaluating political messages, social campaigns or public debates. Exposing students to various rhetorical forms, such as editorials, speeches, advertisements, essays and even social media posts, broadens vocabulary, syntax and style awareness. Analysing rhetorical moves in professional texts then improves students' ability to construct coherent, evidence-based arguments themselves – a skill they need to develop beyond school.

Furthermore, rhetorical texts often represent different cultural, social and ideological viewpoints. Exposure to these perspectives helps students develop empathy, challenge their own assumptions and participate in respectful discourse. Again, something which is really critical in the modern age.

CHAPTER 8: GENERATING ORIGINAL INTERPRETATIONS AND THESIS STATEMENTS

Generating original interpretations is something we all want our students to be able to do upon reading a text. Barbara Bleiman (2020) expertly details how the teaching of a text allows those in our classrooms to 'develop the interpretative and critical "muscle" – allowing students to question, generate an interpretation, test it against others, hold complex and contradictory ideas in one's head, deal with ambiguity.' The ability to generate an interpretation is key; it is a way of expressing how one has not just understood what they are reading, but is able to critically evaluate it, forensically questioning and challenging a writer's intricacies when it comes to thinking about how a text has been constructed. Yet, time and again, we find students regurgitating the 'old favourites': safe ideas they latch onto in class, ideas that will appear in every essay up and down the country. If we want students to generate something original, and for their reading of the text to be more exploratory, we need to aid them in adding their unique voice to the wealth of literary criticism that is already out there. Offering students a range of critical voices can act as a first step to generating their own ideas. Students can struggle to form their own opinions, either because of limited reading experience or a lack of cultural capital. Starting by interrogating the interpretations of others is a way of scaffolding their own thinking when it comes to prompting their own original ideas.

READING

What?

Interpretation is a tricky beast, particularly when it comes to considering how we might explicitly teach it. Most of us will recognise the moment: a student tentatively raises their hand and asks, perhaps with a hint of incredulity, 'Did the author really mean that?' It is a fair question, one that is challenging to answer, or at least answer in a way that might be convincing to a fourteen year old on a Friday afternoon. After all, the author is not there to clarify their intent. Teachers would be forgiven, then, for leaning on Roland Barthes' seminal work on the 'Death of the Author' (1967) to help them with this. Barthes famously argues the act of reading decouples a text from its creator. The meaning of a text, from his perspective, does not reside in the author's intent but is instead born out of readers themselves. A text lives in its interpretation, not its origin.

Barthes argues that once a text enters the world, it becomes open-ended, detached from its author. It cannot possibly be pinned down to one interpretation. This is where students can often struggle. Many search for a definitive meaning, a singular raison d'être, yet as experts in our field, we know this is not doable. Texts, after all, are made up of myriad cultural references and linguistic and structural choices. To decode them completely and truncate them to one, overall meaning would be to participate in the impossible.

In practice, English teachers often fall into one of two camps: those who foreground the reader and those who prioritise the author. Barthes positions the reader as central, challenging the traditional notion of the author as the ultimate authority, arguing the modern idea of the author as an 'all powerful' figure is a relatively recent construct emerging from Western ideologies. Earlier societies, he says, tended to value the story over the storyteller, viewing narratives as collective cultural expressions rather than the product of an individual (Barthes, 1967).

This book does not aim to take a definitive side in this debate, but it does raise some important questions we need to think about when planning around the teaching of interpretations that emerge from reading.

- What happens if we only teach the basic interpretations, or 'our' interpretation? Do we risk infusing our own biases, consciously or not, when passing our interpretation on to students? How can this be avoided?

- How do we encourage students to engage with their own and existing interpretations, without them getting carried away with the (incorrect) assumption that 'anything goes'?
- Just because an interpretation is widely accepted (think the familiar reading of Scrooge described as being 'solitary as an oyster', for example), does that make it the most valid or the most useful?
- If texts are decoupled from the author, how do we approach the concept of authorial intent, integral to contextual points that must be made as a requirement of the GCSE? How can we strike a balance between the writer and reader as different stakeholders in a text?

And then we have to think about those who really struggle with generating their own thoughts and opinions on a text, regardless of the importance of a reader or writer. There is real value in explicitly teaching multiple interpretations. Not only does this challenge students to think critically and evaluate perspectives, but it also provides support for those who struggle to formulate their own ideas. The ideal scenario, of course, is that every student generates a unique insight about a text, but the reality is more complicated than that. Students enter the classroom with varied backgrounds, experiences and cultural capital. For those who have not had the opportunity to build this capital, an interpretation, often formed by exposure to different texts (or even the text that they are studying at that moment), can feel out of reach. We must ensure we are catering for every student.

By exposing students to a range of existing readings, and encouraging them to engage, evaluate and refine these ideas, we create a more inclusive space for literary analysis. Interpretation becomes less about finding the right answer and more about developing the knowledge and skills needed to engage with a text in a more effective and impactful way. The hacks described here centre a writer and a reader equally; all of them are low preparation but high impact ways of helping students consider existing interpretations as a frame for building their own.

How?

Students should have the prerequisite knowledge around plot, character and theme before this strategy is used. Once this has been established, we can move on to thinking about why a writer may have constructed the text in a particular way and students can begin considering how to interpret an author's ideas. The first 'non-negotiable' of such a strategy is that everyone must be participating, lending their voices to the conversation. 'Research with students between the ages of 6 and 14 shows that scaffolded classroom talk assists students to deepen their understanding of texts' (Mills, 2009), and this is exactly what this strategy aims to do.

CHAPTER 8: GENERATING ORIGINAL INTERPRETATIONS AND THESIS STATEMENTS

If one reflects on the ratio of students who contribute to conversations regarding the interpretations of a text, one may find that the same names are responsible for driving that talk forward. There are myriad reasons as to why students cannot enter the discussion: lack of effort, lack of concentration and lack of understanding. As teachers, we must model how to find the coveted 'original interpretation' through classroom talk, putting the right scaffolds in place to invite all students into the conversation. By doing this, we're promoting voice equity. We're telling our students their opinion matters and we want to hear what they have to say. If anything, that is where the power of this activity really lies.

The idea of a 'high thinking/high participation' classroom ratio is explored by Doug Lemov. When we think about what our classrooms look and sound like during discussion phases in our lesson, we will most likely find that we fall into one of the following categories (Busch, 2026b).

	Maximising cognitive engagement	
Thinking ratio	maximal learning	shallow land
	occasional learning	
	sparse participation	crickets
	Participation ratio	

Figure 8.1 Maximising cognitive engagement, or the 'ratio spectrum'

Lemov calls this the 'ratio spectrum' and sets out the differences between students who are actively thinking and those who are actively participating in the lesson. Students who do not have enough prerequisite knowledge are more likely to fall into the section labelled 'crickets', denoting the silence that follows a round of teacher questions that cannot be answered because of a lack of understanding of the basics.

A discussion of interpretations of a text can often fall into 'sparse participation', where a select few students will answer the deepest questions about the nature of English, with the vast majority unable to access and contribute to the profound conversations taking place. How can we move a class from minimal participation and learning to 'maximal learning', a phase where all students are responding to teacher instruction through writing, verbal probing questions and cold calling? For this to happen, we need to think carefully about how we scaffold students to get there.

HACK #8.1: EXPLICIT TEACHING OF INTERPRETATIONS

The following method models how to construct an interpretation through the discussion of thoughts and ideas that are already available, while also ensuring a high thinking, high participation ratio. Dissecting expert models allows students to think about the writer's intentions and ideas before they begin to ascribe their own ideas to what the teacher is presenting to them.

Rather than overwhelming students with a litany of interpretations, three at any given time gives teachers enough to instigate discussion and debate. For example, when studying *A Christmas Carol*, and analysing the characters of Ignorance and Want, students could be presented with the question and answers shown in Figure 8.2.

Consider the following question and the answers that follow:

Who are Ignorance and Want?

Answer A	Answer B	Answer C
Ignorance and Want are figures of fear. Through their feral appearance, they create fears of revolution, a generation that, if left unchecked, will rebel against their oppressors once they have grown into a life of criminality.	Ignorance and Want are figures of pathos. Through their feral appearance, they elicit sympathy from readers, who very quickly learn their actions have consequences which, if not addressed, can perpetuate into a cycle of misery.	Ignorance and Want are figures of obscurity. They are used by Dickens to expose the brutal realities of England's underclass to those who would deny their existence. The Spirit, in fierce condemnation, orders humanity to look at what it has done to the voiceless while it greedily fends for itself.

Figure 8.2 Ignorance and Want question and answers

Notice how short and chunked these interpretations are. This deliberate approach not only helps students to understand the responses to the question, but also gives space for them to add their own thoughts and musings to what they read. These three ideas, essentially, are the foundations for students to construct their own ideas.

The process that follows is a simple but effective one.

1. Present students with the question and multiple-choice answers. Ask them which they think is the correct answer. This can lead to some interesting debate, especially when they catch on to the fact that all the answers are valid because they are rooted within the text.

2. Ask students to write the letter of their chosen interpretation on a mini whiteboard. Ask students to hold up the boards and narrate what you see in terms of how many people have opted for particular interpretations. The purpose of said narration is to show students there are lots of differing opinions and one set way of approaching a text does not exist, while also ensuring a high thinking, high participation ratio, because everyone is having to make a decision.

3. Ask students to put down their boards and discuss their opinion with the person sitting next to them. If they are sitting next to someone who disagrees with them, ask the pair to debate who is correct and why. If they are sitting next to someone who has reached the same conclusion as they have, ask them to verbalise why the other two interpretations are incorrect or what reasoning someone else might have for choosing a different interpretation.

4. Give students the opportunity to change their mind. Ask them to hold their final decision up on the board, questioning those who have changed their minds and those who have stayed the same as to why they have made the decision they have.

At this point, we can really get students to interrogate their own thoughts and musings using probing questions (Sherrington 2013).

- What would someone who disagrees with you say?
- What is the theme that links all of these ideas together?
- What is the evidence that supports that suggestion?
- What makes you say that?

Approaching the scaffolding of generating interpretations in this way helps students who might struggle to enter the conversation. This isn't about asking them to learn prepared interpretations to regurgitate in an exam. It is about helping them to use existing thoughts or ideas they may not have encountered before to act as a basis for their own constructions. Through debate, interrogation and challenge, students quite often end up with something entirely new. The task and subsequent questions require students to think beyond their first response and, through asking them to argue for ideas they do not initially agree with, allowing teachers to distinguish between the separate variables of thinking and answering. As the Ofsted Subject Report for English (2024) states:

> 'Knowledge can be acquired through studying carefully chosen and sequenced texts that become increasingly complex in style and substantial in content and themes. This learning is best achieved with some explicit teaching and modelling, for example of different interpretations and ways to think and write critically.'

WRITING

What?

'If literary analysis is viewed as a key practice, it requires participants to habitually engage in the following practices: (a) read and reread texts to find cues that suggest new possibilities for interpretation, (b) participate in interpretive discussions of literary texts, (c) use writing both as a tool to support interpretive work and as a means to communicate interpretive arguments, and (d) maintain an openness to new interpretations and a willingness to revisit previous interpretive conclusions in the light of new evidence.' (Deane, 2020)

What's powerful about explicitly teaching students to explore different interpretations is that it allows us to guide them through most – if not all – of the practices listed above within a single lesson or sequence of lessons. When encouraging students to engage with multiple interpretations and to articulate their own ideas and responses, we're helping them move beyond verbal contributions and into structured, thoughtful written expression. This is vital, especially when we consider what students are required to do for GCSE, something we must not lose sight of, regardless of whether we agree or disagree with text choice or content that students need to cover in order to pass. The AQA mark scheme for literature says:

> 'At the top of the level, a candidate's response is likely to be a critical, exploratory, well-structured argument. It takes a conceptualised approach to the full task supported by a range of judicious references. There will be a fine grained and insightful analysis of language and form and structure supported by judicious use of subject terminology. Convincing exploration of one or more ideas/perspectives/contextual factors/interpretations.' (AQA, 2014)

Let's take the phrase, 'a critical, exploratory, well-structured argument.' This is what we're aiming for, yet students will often struggle to maintain a clear focus in their writing when 'communicat[ing] ... interpretive arguments' (Deane, 2020) – not because they lack ideas, but because they have not laid a stable groundwork for themselves before beginning to write.

Helping them plan and conceptualise an argument beforehand is essential to ensuring their analysis is both insightful and coherent. That's where thesis statements can help.

How?

Encouraging students to generate original interpretations is one of a number of key goals when it comes to English teaching. For many of our students, however, such interpretations remain elusive, enigmatic and ambiguous suppositions that are incredibly difficult to form let alone articulate in an essay under timed conditions. There is real value, then, in explicitly teaching interpretations too. As explored earlier, modelling how to construct insightful readings of a text is essential if we are to encourage students to develop and coherently present their own ideas.

Strong analytical responses should always begin with a clear, purposeful thesis statement. A thesis is the foundation of a student's argument; without it, the direction of their response can meander, resulting in an unfocused commentary that most likely drifts from the task at hand. The interpretations modelled in the 'Reading' section of this chapter serve as ideal starting points – these are, in essence, the germ of an idea when it comes to forming a full thesis statement. They will, of course, require refinement and expansion, but they contain the core insight that students can develop into a well-structured argument.

Before students can confidently write their own thesis statements, we need to demystify with them what makes a strong one. Understanding the purpose of a thesis is crucial; it is not simply an introduction, it is a 'roadmap' that guides the essay, that holds the ideas together and allows students to stay focused with what it is they are trying to argue. Without a clear sense of its function, students cannot hope to produce a thesis that supports the weight of a full argument. With this in mind, the following hack outlines a way to either introduce these statements in the classroom, or to 'polish' existing statements, considering the individual nature and the context of each of our curricula. This sequence is very much designed with exam preparation in mind, but a modified version could easily be adapted for KS3 in order to build the necessary skills when it comes to analytical writing.

HACK #8.2: THESIS STATEMENTS

1. Begin by showing students two definitions of a thesis statement. Ensure the similarities and shared features between the two are highlighted (like in the following example). Out of the two examples offered here, students often find the second definition more accessible; framing the thesis as a 'roadmap' for the essay is understandable metaphor that clearly promotes the idea that the thesis is central to an argument (and the completion of a cohesive essay), even when one has finished writing it. A thesis allows a student to consider their work holistically and decide whether it has achieved what they initially set out to do.

> *A thesis statement is a statement of **one's core argument**, the main idea, and/or **a concise summary of an essay**, research paper, etc. It is usually expressed in one or two sentences near the beginning of a paper, and may be reiterated elsewhere, such as in the conclusion.*
> (Miller and Pessoa, 2016)

> *The thesis statement is the announcement of **your analytical argument** that you intend to **make and prove** in the duration of your paper. **It is a road map for the paper**—it tells the reader what to expect from the rest of the paper. (Yothers, n.d.)*

After discussing these definitions, invite students to write their own, using the key features in bold from the examples to help them. This step encourages students to actively process what a thesis is, rather than simply memorising a given explanation.

2. Once students have attempted their own definitions, give them a set of high-quality thesis statements drawn from a variety of the set texts and their respective exam-style questions. Ask students to read through the examples, highlighting elements they have in common. This crucial exercise will help students identify the essential components of a strong thesis, the 'non-negotiables' we want them to emulate in their own statements when it comes to the deliberate practice phase of the lesson.

It is important to note that for the example thesis statements written in response to extract-based questions, students do not need to see the extracts at this point. The aim here is to isolate the thesis statement to analyse its components, its structure and purpose, rather than engage with the essay's main body. Here are three examples you might share in order for students to explore similarities.

Starting with this extract, write about how Shakespeare presents masculinity in the play.

> In the extract and throughout the play, Shakespeare presents masculinity as a complex force shaped by the social and historical context of the Jacobean era, where honour and power were highly valued. He highlights the struggles between aggressive masculinity and vulnerability, suggesting that true strength lies not just in physical dominance but in emotional depth and moral integrity. By exploring masculinity in this way, Shakespeare critiques societal expectations of men, encouraging the audience to reconsider what it means to be truly strong in a time when rigid notions of masculinity often led to tragedy and conflict.

How does Priestley present Gerald as a character who grapples with his sense of responsibility throughout *An Inspector Calls*?

In *An Inspector Calls*, Priestley presents Gerald as a character who initially resists taking responsibility for his actions, particularly in relation to his treatment of Eva Smith, reflecting his adherence to capitalist values. As the play progresses, however, Gerald begins to confront his role in her downfall, revealing his internal struggle between maintaining his privileged status and accepting moral accountability. Despite moments of self-awareness and potential growth, Gerald ultimately aligns himself with the older generation's views, demonstrating a lack of lasting change. Through Gerald's development, Priestley critiques the self-serving attitudes of the upper class and suggests that true responsibility requires acknowledging the consequences of one's actions, both personally and socially. Ultimately, Gerald's grappling with responsibility mirrors the broader theme of social responsibility that Priestley advocates for, urging the audience to reflect on their own roles within society.

Compare the ways poets present power in *Remains* and in one other poem from Power and Conflict.

In *Remains* by Simon Armitage and *My Last Duchess* by Robert Browning, the poets present power as a complex and destructive force to reveal its profound effects on individuals. Armitage explores the power of memory and trauma in the modern Iraq War, showing how violence haunts soldiers and shapes their identities. In contrast, Browning illustrates the oppressive power dynamics of the Renaissance, revealing the dark side of control in relationships to critique societal norms and expectations. By presenting power in these ways, both poets highlight to readers how it can lead to emotional conflict and tragic consequences, reflecting the deep human struggles that arise from its misuse.

The thesis statements here are lengthy, but this is not a concern. Clarity and precision will come with deliberate practice – at this stage, learning and consolidating the core components is what is important.

3. As students read and annotate the thesis samples, encourage them to identify the recurring ideas and features: the 'non-negotiables'. These are:

- Repeated references to key words from the question.
- Authorial intent: what the writer intends to achieve through the character or the theme.
- Authorial intent: why the writer presents a character or theme in the way they do.
- A very brief reference to the social/historical context.
- Reference to the reader or audience.

Once these have been established, instruct students to return to the sample statements and explicitly label each component of they have not done so already.

4. Now the focus needs to shift to the writing of a thesis statement. This should begin with planning, something which requires practice; students should be given regular opportunities for extended, deliberate rehearsal after having the planning process carefully modelled to them. The easiest, most effective way of doing this is to use the non-negotiables as prompts for notes. A simple planning table (see Figure 8.3) can support this, helping students to break down each element of the thesis before bringing them together into a cohesive argument.

Repeated reference to the key words in the question.	
Authorial intent – what the writer intends to achieve through the theme or character.	
Authorial intent – why the writer presents a character or theme in the way they do.	
Brief reference to social/historical context.	
Reference to the reader or audience.	

Figure 8.3 Planning table

Begin by completing the planning grid yourself, modelling the thought process behind how you are breaking down each step. For example, if you were writing a thesis statement for the question, 'How does Priestley present Gerald as a character who grapples with his sense of responsibility throughout *An Inspector Calls?*', you might begin as follows. Let's assume that the teacher at this point has gone through the command word for the question and is now focusing solely on how to construct the thesis:

> [Teacher places a copy of the question and the thesis statement plan under the visualiser.]
>
> **Teacher:** To begin with, I need to identify the key word or words from the question, because I'm going to use these throughout my thesis statement. This will show an examiner that I'm really staying focused on the question. I think I'm going to choose the key words here as 'grapples' and 'responsibility'.
>
> [Teacher circles the words 'grapples' and 'responsibility' on the exam question and then writes these onto the plan in key words row.]

CHAPTER 8: GENERATING ORIGINAL INTERPRETATIONS AND THESIS STATEMENTS

Teacher: Now write those down in the 'key words' box on your own blank copy of the plan.

[Teacher waits for students to complete this and checks that everyone has finished.]

Teacher: Now I'm going to explain why I chose 'grapples' and 'responsibility' as key words. I'm looking for words in the question that allow me to do or explore something. 'Responsibility', as we know, is a key theme, so I know already as someone who has studied the play that this is very important and will dominate a large part of the answer. The word 'grapples' shows that Gerald isn't straightforward – he is struggling or uncertain, so this will allow me to explore the journey he goes through. I can think about how Gerald deals with his own sense of responsibility. Let's now move on to the next box.

Once you have modelled to students the thought process for every non-negotiable, you might want to introduce a collaborative model. Pick another exam question for the same text or a different text and complete it together. A completed plan might look like Figure 8.4.

Starting with this extract, how does Dickens present the importance of family?

Repeated reference to the key words in the question.	Importance of family.
Authorial intent – what the writer intends to achieve through the theme or character.	Intends to show readers that family is the gateway to hope and love. Family serves as an escape from this harsh world.
Authorial intent – why the writer presents a character or theme in the way they do.	Through the characters of Fred and the Cratchits, Dickens presents family as important to highlight the dangers of ostracising oneself from others. Criticising those who place value on materialistic things instead of things that matter.
Brief reference to social/historical context.	Victorian period.
Reference to the reader or audience.	Readers are encouraged to see the value of family and our duty towards one another.

Figure 8.4 Completed exam plan

5. Once the plan is complete, model how to transform this into a full thesis statement. Draw the notes from the plan together to create a thesis that acts as a 'roadmap' for the rest of the essay. The thesis statement itself needs to be 'felt' through the paper, meaning it should answer the question and also indicate what a student will expand upon in the main body of the essay. A plan, transferred to a thesis statement, might look like Figure 8.5.

Starting with this extract, how does Dickens present the importance of family?

Importance of family	In 'A Christmas Carol,' Dickens profoundly illustrates that family is a vital source of hope and love, serving as a refuge from the harsh realities of his Victorian world. Through characters like Fred, Fezziwig and the Cratchits, Dickens highlights the dangers of ostracising oneself from others and critiques those who prioritise material wealth over meaningful relationships. By portraying the warmth and resilience found within important familial bonds, Dickens encourages readers to reflect on the importance of community and connection, ultimately urging them to recognise their moral duty to care for one
Intends to show readers that family is the gateway to hope and love. Family serves as an escape from this harsh world.	
Through the characters of Fred and the Cratchits, Dickens presents family as important to highlight the dangers of ostracising oneself from others. Criticising those who place value on materialistic things instead of things that matter.	
Victorian period	
Readers are encouraged to see the value of family and our duty towards one another.	

Figure 8.5 Thesis statement

Students will need repeated exposure and regular practice to hone their knowledge of what a thesis statement should do and their skill in writing them. To truly embed this, use every opportunity to highlight thesis statements in the classroom. For instance, when examining or modelling an analytical paragraph from the main body of an essay, it would be extremely useful to always show the accompanying thesis, even if that is not the main focus of the activity. Not only does it expose students to a wider range of examples but it allows them to consider the analytical paragraph more forensically. They can consider whether this paragraph fulfils its purpose in relation to the argument that was set up at the beginning.

If the thesis is the essay's 'roadmap', students need to use it to check if the rest of an essay is on the right path. Are the quotations, for example, judiciously chosen? Do they align with the argument that was established in the thesis? Is the single-word analysis adding to the points that are at the forefront of the initial statement? Is context woven seamlessly into the paragraph in relation to the argument, or is it an awkward bolt on with no real relevance?

Reinforcing this visually can be very useful; have students draw connections between the thesis and key ideas in the subsequent paragraphs in order to consolidate the idea that the argument established at the beginning should be felt throughout the remainder of the answer.

Modelling

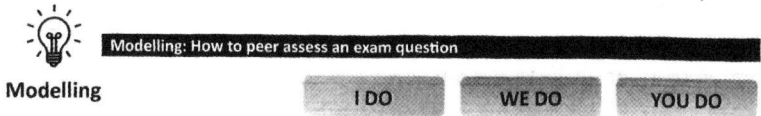

How does Priestley present Gerald as a character who grapples with his sense of responsibility throughout *An Inspector Calls*?

Thesis statement:

In 'An Inspector Calls', Priestley presents Gerald as a character who initially resists taking responsibility for his actions, particularly in relation to his treatment of Eva Smith, reflecting his adherence to capitalist values. As the play progresses, however, Gerald begins to confront his role in her downfall, revealing his internal struggle between maintaining his privileged status and accepting moral accountability. Despite moments of self-awareness and potential growth, Gerald ultimately aligns himself with the older generation's views, demonstrating a lack of lasting change. Through Gerald's development, Priestley critiques the self-serving attitudes of the upper class and suggests that true responsibility requires acknowledging the consequences of one's actions, both personally and socially. Ultimately, Gerald's grappling with responsibility mirrors the broader theme of social responsibility that Priestley advocates for, urging the audience to reflect on their own roles within society.

First argument:

At the start of *An Inspector Calls*, Priestley presents Gerald as a character who is reluctant to accept responsibility for his actions, as shown by his immediate defence of his conduct. This reluctance to acknowledge responsibility is clearly demonstrated when Gerald asserts to the Inspector, after his interrogation of Birling that, 'We're respectable citizens and not criminals.' Here, Gerald uses the word 'respectable' to distinguish himself and his class from the working class, emphasising his belief that status and wealth protect him from moral scrutiny. This not only highlights Gerald's initial denial of any wrongdoing but also reflects the wider attitude of the upper classes in 1912, who, Priestley argues, saw themselves as above reproach and immune to the consequences of their actions. The phrase 'not criminals' is telling because it shows how Gerald compartmentalises his actions, suggesting that as long as he doesn't commit an overtly illegal act, he sees no need for personal accountability. This reflects Priestley's critique of the capitalist society of the early 20th century, where those in power, like Gerald, often disregarded their moral obligations to those less fortunate. The use of 'respectable' is also important, as it links to the rigid social structures of the time, where social class determined one's ability to avoid responsibility. Gerald's initial refusal to engage with the notion of social responsibility in the play reflects Priestley's belief that the upper class's selfish attitudes needed to be challenged, particularly in the context of post-World War II Britain, where social reform was becoming more urgent.

Second argument:

A different aspect of Gerald's character that Priestley presents is his sense of emotional detachment and inconsistency, especially in his relationship with Sheila. Although Gerald appears to be in love with Sheila, his brief affair with Eva Smith reveals a level of disconnection and dishonesty in his personal relationships. When Sheila confronts him about his affair, Gerald's response is to rationalise his actions, saying, 'I've told you, I was awfully busy at the time.' This shows how Gerald attempts to deflect blame and avoid taking full responsibility for his emotional betrayal. By framing the affair as something that happened during a period

Figure 8.6 Student example thesis statement

HACK #8.3: TURNING INTERPRETATIONS INTO A THESIS

At this point, we can connect the act of writing a thesis statement back to the idea of original interpretations, as explored in the 'Reading' section of this Hack.

Consider the following three interpretations of the poem *War Photographer* by Carol Ann Duffy. These are interpretations that I used with a top set Year 11 class; they are quite dense, yet this was purposeful in order to really push students with their ideas and subsequent interpretations.

Considering the poem What is *War Photographer* about?		
A The ethical dilemma of documentation	B The conflict between objectivity and emotion	C Indifference in the face of suffering
War Photographer is primarily about the ethical dilemma faced by journalists and photographers, caught between their duty to document suffering and the emotional toll it takes on them. The poem questions whether witnessing and recording trauma is enough to spark meaningful change.	*War Photographer* is primarily about the tension between objectivity and humanity. The photographer's attempt to remain detached from the horrors they capture reveals the internal conflict between their professional role and the overwhelming emotional burden of documenting human suffering.	*War Photographer* is primarily about the gap between global suffering and local indifference. Duffy critiques the desensitisation of society, where people at home remain unaffected by the brutal realities of war, highlighting how distance creates emotional disengagement from human suffering.

Figure 8.7 Considering the poem *War Photographer*

After exploring the interpretations using the methods discussed previously, we can now consider how these ideas might be shaped into a thesis statement in response to a specific question. While these interpretations still need further development, the essential structure – the bare bones and main 'beats' – of a strong thesis are already in place. Let's consider this with the following question:

How is conflict presented in *War Photographer* by Carol Ann Duffy?

With this in mind, let's revisit the non-negotiables of a thesis statement.

- Repeated references to key words from the question.
- Authorial intent: what the writer intends to achieve through the character or the theme.
- Authorial intent: why the writer presents a character or theme in the way they do.

CHAPTER 8: GENERATING ORIGINAL INTERPRETATIONS AND THESIS STATEMENTS

- A very brief reference to the social/historical context.
- Reference to the reader or audience.

Interpretation B aligns well with the question and so can effectively be turned into a thesis statement: '*War Photographer* is primarily about the tension between objectivity and humanity. The photographer's attempt to remain detached from the horrors they capture reveals the internal conflict between their professional role and the overwhelming emotional burden of documenting human suffering.'

Therefore, a thesis statement for the question, containing all of the non-negotiables, could look like this. The bold part of the thesis shows the connection between the initial interpretation and how it has been integrated into an argument.

> In *War Photographer*, Carol Ann Duffy presents conflict through **the tension between objectivity and humanity, using the photographer's internal struggle to explore the emotional burden of documenting war. She portrays how the photographer must remain professionally detached while being deeply affected by the suffering he captures, reflecting the psychological cost of witnessing trauma**. Through this, Duffy highlights a broader social conflict – society's growing desensitisation to violence in the media. Set against the backdrop of late 20th-century global conflicts, the poem encourages readers to question their passive consumption of such images and consider the personal toll behind them. Duffy presents conflict in this way to provoke empathy and challenge the audience's moral responsibility as distant observers.

Transferring these interpretations into thesis statements will take time, but through slow, careful modelling of the process, and repeated opportunities for practice, students can gradually master the process in order to produce a strong start to a strong essay. Gradually phasing out the thesis statement plan is also important; we need to be at a place where students are planning their essays rather than just their first paragraphs. If students can get to a place where they master the writing of a thesis statement, the essay plan itself will act as a guide for what to include in the statement.

HACK #8.4: USING THE THESIS STATEMENT TO CREATE AN ARGUMENT

To support students in developing a fully written answer, begin by providing them with a thesis statement. Once they have identified the key, non-negotiables of the thesis statement, prompt them to think deeply with the following question:

'Based on this thesis statement, what would you expect the writer to explore or argue in their essay?'

Usually, we would want students to think about their argument for the essay before producing their thesis, but using the thesis as a starting point serves two important purposes: it consistently exposes students to high-quality examples, and it encourages them to actively consider content and structure while they work on mastering a cohesive statement. This is something they may not instinctively do; essay writing can often fall into a 'high participation, low thinking' ratio. All students are writing, but they're not necessarily thinking critically about what they're producing. Students will not be provided with a ready-made thesis in the exam, but regular practice with model statements can help them internalise the relationship between a thesis and the overall direction of an essay, aiding them in appreciating how a thesis will anchor their writing so they don't go off task.

1. Let's consider the following question and its respective thesis statement as an example.

Starting with this speech, explore how far Shakespeare presents Macbeth as a violent character. Write about:

- How Shakespeare presents Macbeth in this extract.
- How far Shakespeare presents Macbeth as a violent character in the play as a whole.

The extract provided for this question is the Captain's speech from *Macbeth*, Act 1, Scene 2 (see Figure 8.8).

> Throughout Macbeth, Shakespeare repeatedly presents Macbeth as a violent character in order to interrogate the devastating effects of unchecked ambition and the fragility of moral integrity when exposed to corrupting influences. By portraying Macbeth's descent into brutality—from valiant warrior to tyrannical murderer—Shakespeare intends to expose the psychological and political consequences of violating the natural order, a theme deeply relevant to his Jacobean audience, who feared the instability caused by regicide and divine punishment. In doing so, Shakespeare prompts the audience to reflect not only on the seductive nature of power but also on their own susceptibility to darkness when societal and moral constraints are removed.

2. Prompt students to consider what they might expect an essay using this thesis to include. Encourage them to provide specific moments from the text, drawn from both within and beyond the extract. Ideas should connect to the main theme of the question, in this case, violence.

CHAPTER 8: GENERATING ORIGINAL INTERPRETATIONS AND THESIS STATEMENTS

In the extract, Macbeth's acts of violence are celebrated because they are used to defend King and country. Macbeth is described as 'brave' for his acts of violence against Macdonald.

Corrupting influences could be referencing the witches or even Lady Macbeth herself. The essay might explore how and why these influences encourage Macbeth to be violent.

> Throughout Macbeth, Shakespeare repeatedly presents Macbeth as a violent character in order to interrogate the devastating effects of unchecked ambition and the fragility of moral integrity when exposed to corrupting influences. By portraying Macbeth's descent into brutality—from valiant warrior to tyrannical murderer—Shakespeare intends to expose the psychological and political consequences of violating the natural order, a theme deeply relevant to his Jacobean audience, who feared the instability caused by regicide and divine punishment. In doing so, Shakespeare prompts the audience to reflect not only on the seductive nature of power but also on their own susceptibility to darkness when societal and moral constraints are removed.

The essay is clearly going to talk about Macbeth's character arc. He is described as 'brave' in the extract, but the essay may track his status to 'butcher', as uttered by Malcolm in the final scene. This means the essay might discuss his murder of Duncan/ Banquo/ Macduff's family etc.

Contextually, the essay might discuss the effects that Macbeth's violence has on the Great Chain of Being and the Divine Right of Kings.

The essay might compare the violence of Macbeth's kingship to the piety of Edward the Confessor's, as alluded to in Act 4, Scene 3.

Figure 8.8 *Macbeth* answer with notes

It would be unrealistic to expect students to address every detail mined from the thesis statement, yet this offers a clear sense of the potential directions an essay could talk if this argument was established at the beginning, helping students to visualise the depth and breadth of possible interpretations and arguments.

Once students have shared and discussed their ideas, we can then consider how this might look in a simple plan format. An example of this is shown in Figure 8.9, with clear connections to the thesis statement included.

Starting with this speech, explore how far Shakespeare presents Macbeth as a violent character.

1. Extract:	2. Extract:
- Discuss word choice of 'brave' to describe Macbeth. Violence is something to be celebrated. - 'Smoked with bloody execution' – Macbeth is used to killing – has become desensitised to it, suggesting his reluctance to kill King Duncan later is because of his moral compass, not his inability to commit violence.	- 'Unseamed him from the nave to th'chaps' – compare violence here to the brutality directed towards Duncan's murder. ('his gash'd stabs look'd like a breach in nature/ For ruin's wasteful entrance') – Connect to Great Chain of Being - Imagery of blood throughout that begins to haunt the Macbeths. - Authorial intent – warning audiences as to the connections between violence and unchecked ambition.
3. Wider text	3. Wider text
- Violence becomes a psychological terror: 'Never shake/ Thy gory locks at me.' (Banquo's ghost) - Discuss violence as a perpetual, cyclical cycle ('I am in blood/ Stepp'd in so far that, should I wade no more,/ Returning were as tedious as go o'er.')	- Connections between Macbeth's brutal reign and Edward the Confessor's pious kingship. - Discussion around Macduff's act of regicide so as not to taint Malcolm's reign. By the end of the play, violence is celebrated once more.

Figure 8.9 Simple plan format example

ORACY

What?

James Britton says that 'reading and writing float on a sea of talk' (quoted in Mills, 2009). While this line is often quoted in isolation – as I have done here – it resonates because of the importance it places on oracy within a wider spectrum of knowledge and skills, particularly in the education of English as a subject. It serves as a reminder that oracy is not a segregated strand of literacy, but a vital part of it. Oracy acts as the foundations upon which reading and writing rest.

Oracy is especially vital when it comes to developing interpretations of a text. By allowing students to articulate their thoughts out loud, they can shape and refine their ideas, 'trying on' their interpretation before committing to paper. They can explore how it sounds, listen to challenges surrounding them and consider where their interpretations sit on the wider spectrum of discussion. Oracy in the classroom is a student's rehearsal space for thought.

Mary Myatt (2021b) speaks to this process in her own thoughts on classroom oracy: 'Approaches to support oral language include targeted reading aloud and book discussion with young children; explicitly extending pupils' spoken vocabulary; the use of structured questioning to develop reading comprehension; and the use of purposeful, curriculum-focused dialogue and interaction.' The hacks explored here reflect these ideas: purposeful classroom talk can unlock those meaningful interpretations that students hold but are sometimes reluctant to voice. Effective practice around oracy is not something that can happen naturally; careful planning of tasks is required in order to model and teach processes to students: 'Teachers often attribute pupils' weaknesses in speaking to a lack of confidence rather than realising that they have not been taught what they need to know about the topic under discussion to be able to form and articulate worthwhile contributions.' (Ofsted 2024) This means we as teachers need to ensure that students know a text well. Interpretation cannot happen in isolation. If we want students to voice meaningful ideas, they need meaningful foundations on which to comment.

How?

 HACK #8.5: ROOTING INTERPRETATIONS IN THE TEXT

When encouraging students to voice their own interpretations, it is crucial to emphasise that valid ideas must be grounded in the text. The well-worn adage, a misleading misconception that students tend to latch onto, that 'there is no right answer in English' is incorrect. While literature invites multiple readings, not all interpretations hold equal weight, and if we are suggesting that every idea is equally valid, we undermine a student's ability to guide themselves towards making more credible suggestions. For an interpretation to be considered valuable, it must be supported by textual evidence, rooted within the text itself to ensure that it is plausibly true.

With this in mind, it becomes essential to scaffold students' thinking so they understand exactly how to form plausible considerations of a text. One effective method – adapted from Hack 8.1, explored in the 'Reading' section of this chapter, involves the use of more oracy-based tasks, encouraging students to articulate their ideas, to 'try them out', before committing them to paper, allowing for evaluation and refinement. For example, in a recent Year 7 lesson on Alfred Tennyson's *The Lady of Shalott*, I noticed students were struggling to anchor their inferences and interpretations of characters in the poem. To address this, I displayed three AI-generated images of Sir Lancelot and asked students which one they believe best represented the character.

The impact was incredibly interesting; in order to respond accurately to the question, students had no choice but to return to the poem itself to check their ideas. Responses like 'I think B is the most accurate *because in the text it says* ...' were suddenly heard, and while one might argue that these are relatively straightforward justifications of ideas, they marked a significant shift in the way students were thinking about presenting their ideas. Using images to begin with, instead of written interpretations (as previously explored) is a low preparation but high impact way of instigating such discussion. The strategy is highly adaptation and can be used across any text. For example:

- Which of the following images best depicts Macbeth's character?
- Which of these images most accurately conveys Ozymandias' hubristic nature?

Once students are confident in rooting their ideas within a text, other discussions can take place, moving away from images as a stimulus. For example:

Which of the following is the most important thing that the ghost of Marley says?

1. 'I wear the chain I forged in life'.
2. 'Mankind was my business. The common welfare was my business; charity, mercy, forbearance, and benevolence, were, all, my business.'
3. 'Why did I walk through crowds of fellow-beings with my eyes turned down, and never raise them to that blessed Star which led the Wise Men to a poor abode!'

Oracy tasks like this seem like a natural progression from using images. Students are forced to consider other areas of the text that they know in order to present evidence for their opinion. Once students are confident in grounding their interpretations in the text, they can begin to explore more nuanced readings. This foundation skill, however, of linking ideas to the text to inform meaningful interpretations, is where literary analysis can begin.

HACK #8.6: USING PROBING QUESTIONS TO CREATE INTERPRETATIONS

This leads us to another simple, yet powerful teacher hack: asking the right questions to deepen interpretation. The types of question we ask in class matter greatly. Teachers ask hundreds of questions each day – some will be planned, but most are likely to be more spontaneous, shaped quickly in response to the context of a lesson. While questions will often check for understanding or prompt surface-level interpretations, the most effective are those that truly make students stop and think.

Questions that check for knowledge	What is Macbeth perhaps feeling here when he delivers his soliloquy?	'He's feeling conflicted. He's wondering whether he should kill Duncan.'	Why is he wondering whether he should kill Duncan?
Questions that push for extension	What is Macbeth perhaps feeling here when he delivers his soliloquy?	'He's feeling conflicted. He's wondering whether he should kill Duncan.'	Why is Macbeth's inner conflict potentially dangerous?
Questions that probe for interpretation	What is Macbeth perhaps feeling here when he delivers his soliloquy?	'He's feeling conflicted. He's wondering whether he should kill Duncan.'	And what would someone who disagrees with you say?

Figure 8.10 Probing questions to ask about *Macbeth*

Let's consider the questions that have been asked in Figure 8.10. Imagine students have been studying Act 1, Scene 7 of Shakespeare's *Macbeth*. A teacher may ask what Macbeth is feeling to elicit an indicator of understanding of the language. If a student responds 'He's feeling conflicted. He's wondering whether he should kill Duncan', a teacher might ask a follow-up question that checks for further knowledge: 'Why is he wondering whether he should kill Duncan?' A different question one could ask is one that maybe pushes for extension, giving space for students to further develop their original idea. A question that probes for interpretation, however is 'What would someone who disagrees with you say?' One might want to work through the previous follow-up questions first, yet 'probing questions', as Tom Sherrington (2013) calls them, are designed to challenge students to consider an alternative point of view or revisit their initial response. We all know those students who confidently share the first idea that pops into their head and then feel their work is done. A probing question will nudge them to return to the text, to reconsider and refine, inviting curiosity and reflection: What other ideas are out there that I have not yet explored?

Other examples of probing questions to generate original interpretations might include the following.

- What would be the opposite of that?
- Is there another explanation?
- Which of the ideas you have just shared has the biggest impact on the characters and events? Why?
- Is that always true or is that just the case in this example?
- What connects all of these ideas together? (Sherrington, 2013)

They are intense, powerful and rigorous, but a very effective way of bringing whole classes together to look at a text and ensure all are participating. These prompts to revisit initial ideas show students that interpretation is not about finding an answer, but about uncovering better ones.

HACK #8.7: SPEAKING FRAMES

As students become more confident with presenting their interpretations through oracy, we as teachers can begin to introduce the idea of producing ideas that contain the specificities of more nuanced readings. Speaking frames are a clear, easy to use, and helpful way of doing this.

Deeper meaning	Comparing to the other poems	Pick a word and explore
• I think the poem is really saying … • For me, the poem is teaching us … • On the surface, the poem is about … but under the surface it is about …	• This poem is a bit like … because … • The poem is the opposite of … because … • I think this poem shows an alternative perspective to … • This poem focuses more on … than …	• The word '…' makes me imagine … • The word '…' makes me think of … • The word '…' reminds me of … • The word '…' makes me feel …
Feelings	Symbols	Connections between aspects in the text
• To make us feel …, the writer shows us … • To make us feel …, the writer uses the image of … • To make us feel …, the writer uses the combination of … and …	• The writer uses … to be a symbol of … • … is usually a symbol of … but here it is used as a symbol of … • … is symbolic of the relationship between … and …	• The use of … and … makes u … • There is a pattern of … across the text. • The writer seems to be repeating …
An alternative way of looking at things	Developing / Increasing / Decreasing	Changes
• Another way to look at it is … • It could also suggest … • Someone else might think that …	• As the poem develops, the … increases because … • There's a marked decrease in … as the poem progresses. • I notice that … develops in the poem.	• The mood changes when … • The writer changes the tone of the voice when … • The turning point in the poem is when …

Figure 8.11 Speaking frame

This example, originally conceived and shared by English teacher, Chris Curtis, is easily adaptable to suit a variety of texts, although Curtis typically uses this frame when teaching poetry. Curtis presents one or two lines of a poem on the board at a time. Using the sentence starters in the grid, students are encouraged to comment on aspects such as language, structure, tone and implied meaning. This gives all students, regardless of confidence, a clear way into the text. Initial discussion may be slow, but eventually students will begin to share their thoughts, especially when use of the grid is modelled to them. When ideas have been shared, Curtis reveals another line or two prompting fresh conversation. (Curtis, 2019)

What is particularly effective about this approach is how it builds cumulative understanding. As more of the poem is revealed, students begin to make increasingly sophisticated interpretations. Student comments will gradually move from making meaning to meaning into making insights and perspectives. It is important to note that students are not confined to discussing only the most recent lines that have been revealed. If, for example, line 9 illuminates or exposes a new idea surrounding line 1, students can be encouraged to revisit and reinterpret earlier sections of the poem.

This cyclical process mirrors how readers engage with literature: revisiting earlier moments and using new information to prove or disprove inferences, ideas and interpretations.

 HACK #8.8 ASKING FOR OPINIONS

Possibly one of the simplest hacks in this book is a very simple question: Do you like the text? Why? Why not? So many times we delve straight into analysing, that we forget to ask students their own opinion about something.

While asking students if they like or dislike something may seem basic, its importance cannot be overstated. By inviting their own personal reflections, we are saying to students that their voices matter, that we want them to be heard. This in itself can be a spark that lights the fire of interpretation and generating original responses.

Of course, responses like 'It's boring' should always be gently challenged. Teacher modelling is key when it comes to how to frame an opinion; students need to be shown how to move beyond more generic comments and into text-based reasoning. Asking about likes or dislikes, however, can be a highly effective way of showing students how their thoughts can be used as the genesis for deep, meaningful classroom based talk.

Why?

Helping students with ways in which to express their own interpretations, and ways in which their interpretations can then be articulated into a cohesive and strong argument, is so important. Through the act of interpreting, students are not just showing us an understanding of a text, but *their* understanding of a text. Yet if we do not explicitly model how this can be done, we wrongfully exclude a large proportion of those we teach from accessing and engaging with the wider conversations that can be had about a text. Simply assuming students can think of original and/or multiple ideas about a text is not good enough, resulting, most likely in small fragments of knowledge wrongly amalgamated to suit needs catered to assessment objectives.

David Didau (2021b) argues:

> 'The goal here is "gapless instruction". Whenever we make assumption about what students might already know or be able to do, we create gaps. Some students have the wherewithal to fill those gaps themselves (or with the help of their extended networks) but others will fall into the gaps and be unable to progress. Whenever we try to teach a skill without breaking it into component knowledge we are almost certainly making it more difficult for the least advantaged students to succeed.'

Oracy plays a large part in the importance of generating interpretations too. Ideas and interpretations are borne out of dialogue where students are required to think hard through the ongoing conversation that is taking place. Rebekah Simon of Voice 21 states, 'Oracy is essential for the development of communication and argumentation skills, which are key to successful English learning.'

If anything, this shows how vital generating interpretations through oracy is, for an interpretation is a student's sense of argument. When a student interprets, they add their voice to a wealth of literary criticism. Classroom talk is an important way of helping students see themselves as legitimate critics of the texts they're presented with. Asking students to verbally justify their opinions and ideas allows them to develop such 'argumentation skills' and present their case for why they have understood the text in the way they have.

By finding ways to invite our students into the conversation, we promote voice equity. We're telling our students that their opinion matters; we want to hear what they have to say. If anything, that's where the power of such an activity truly lies (Pryke, 2022).

CHAPTER 9: CONSIDERING 'JUDICIOUS' QUOTATIONS

Quotations are a curious feature of literary analysis. While students must know them and use them, they can also be the bane of a teacher's life. 'Why this quotation?' 'How does it relate to the question?' 'This has nothing to do with what you're trying to say.' These frustrations are surely familiar to many of us.

The effective use of quotations goes far beyond simply sprinkling an essay with lines from a text. We need our students to see quotations as tools to hone their argument, not distract from it. When to use a quotation, why it should be used and how are crucial considerations. Yet too often, we encounter essays that are littered with unnecessarily lengthy passages of text that are regurgitated in some truncated form, included without clear purpose or understanding. In these cases, quotations can overwhelm a student's individual voice. Similarly, paraphrasing loses the nuance and beauty of the original language. It comes down to, then, the 'judicious' quotation: the considered selection of a short extract that is seamlessly embedded into a student's answer. This chapter explores how students can be guided to choose quotations purposefully, and how these choices can be examined for considerations around language and structure. Practical strategies outlined here can apply to both language and literature; they have been designed to ensure a writer's voice supports a student's thoughts rather than replacing them entirely.

READING

What?

Students are obsessed with quotations. They have, in a way, developed a quotation complex. This is, in no small part, something we as teachers have encouraged; perhaps, if we're being really honest with ourselves, entrenched. In a landscape dominated by closed-book exams, the memorisation of quotations has become a staple of classroom practice. As a result, we need to take some responsibility for the direction in which our teaching has evolved, and make a concerted effort to reconsider the ways in which we can look at quotations effectively and with impact.

A quick search reveals countless blogs and resources offering hints and techniques for helping students commit quotations to memory. But what if we reframed our approach entirely? What if quotations were not just lines to recite, to memorise, but a powerful window into a more nuanced and complex understanding of literature? Students need to know quotations, yes, but these small extracts of text should be more than a checklist to satisfy an exam rubric. The problem with memorising quotations is that students lose sight of what is appropriate and what is not. Various quotations will be shoehorned into a response regardless of their suitability and viability in relation to the question being asked. We've all had the student who dutifully includes that Scrooge is as 'solitary as an oyster' in an extended written response, regardless of whether the question concerns Scrooge, the ghosts or, dare I say it, a minor character like Martha Cratchit. Ultimately, this points to a surface-level engagement with the text, where quotations are deployed out of context and divorced from meaning.

David Didau, in his blog post 'Everyone values critical thinking' (2017), makes a compelling argument about the role of knowledge in thinking. He says:

> 'My position is summarised in these three propositions:
> 1. Knowledge is both what we think with and about.
> 2. We cannot think with or about something we don't know.
> 3. The more we know about something, the more sophisticated our thinking.'

There is so much to unpick here, but it is particularly striking when we consider this statement through the lens of quotation knowledge. We need to think about quotations, yes, but more importantly, we must think *with* them. They are tools, not ends in themselves. The more we know about a text, the more sophisticated our thinking around quotations and the way in which they allow us to consider a text holistically can be. They need to be active participants in our interpretation, becoming part of the fabric of analysis instead of 'items' to be ticked off. A historian would think with primary sources, a scientist with data. Literature students must think with the text – quotations aren't just included to prove they have revised and studied. It's what they do with them that counts. It's how quotations sharpen their insights.

Didau's comments also demand we reconsider the weight we also place on subject terminology when looking at quotations. Again, assessment criteria that demand the use of terminology has led many of us to emphasise the labelling of nouns and verbs and adjectives, often at the expense of deeper interpretation. Does recognising a noun, however, truly enhance a student's argument if they cannot explain why it matters?

Ultimately, it's time to re-evaluate our classroom culture around quotations. The hacks in this chapter are designed to help us move beyond memorisation and towards meaning. By encouraging students to engage with quotations as part of a broader interpretive process, we empower them to read more thoughtfully, write more insightfully, and think more critically.

How?

HACK #9.1: WORDS INSTEAD OF PHRASES

Students often becomes fixated on learning quotations. If we are honest with ourselves, this is something that can be easily reinforced by us as teachers. Reflecting on my own practice, it is clear that quotations dominate a significant portion of my teaching time. With the demands of the GCSE in mind, the focus is understandable. Quotations are, after all, a clear component of the many mark schemes we are forced to grapple with. However, there are risks that we must consider when looking at this approach, particularly when quotations are isolated from their broader context.

Too often, we pull out quotations and ask students to analyse them in isolation, treating them as standalone units of knowledge as opposed to an intricate part of a larger narrative or thematic structure. This can disjoint a student's understanding of the text. Instead of developing a holistic grasp of meaning, they are left juggling with 'pockets' of information.

One effective way to counter this is to shift the focus from entire quotations to individual words. As Chris Curtis (2019) argues, 'Looking at words changes how you teach because you begin to collect word banks and expand the students' repertoire of quotes.' Focusing on words encourages students to build connections across a text, noticing patterns and shifts in tone alongside the development of characters. It also means that a student's individual voice is not overwhelmed by a more dominant voice: that of the writer of the original text being studied. This is so important; we need a student's voice to shine through if they are to authoritatively share their thoughts on meaning with a reader.

With this in mind, let's take, as an example, the stage directions associated with the character of Sheila in *An Inspector Calls*, an often overlooked element of the text. A close look at just a few words can chart her journey across the play:

> Distressed (to the Inspector) – Scornfully (to Birling) – Reflectively (Howard 2019b)

Each term offers a window into her moral evolution. 'Distressed' reflects her immediate guilt and empathy upon learning of her role in Eva Smith's death. 'Scornfully' marks a growing disillusionment with the elder Birlings' attitudes, exposing the general divide that Priestley wants to draw his audience's attention to. Finally, 'reflectively' signals introspection, a self-awareness and openness to change.

A similar pattern can be seen in Shakespeare's *Macbeth*, where the titular character is described as 'brave' early on and ultimately as a 'butcher' by the end, these words framing the tragic arc of Macbeth's inevitable descent and helping students engage with characters as conscious constructs so that they can engage with a writer's purpose in a way that is conceptually rich.

This shift, then, from memorising lengthy quotations to carefully selecting a series of chosen words, has real value. Student retention increases and they are more likely to be able to make connections across the text because their ideas are rooted in strong connections that have not manifested themselves through rote learning but in a more thoughtful way that shows strong engagement with a text.

 ## HACK #9.2: CONNOTATION CHAINS

Let's stay focused on single-word analysis; quotations can be incredibly versatile when approached through a more strategic lens. One particularly effective method for deepening students' engagement with language is the use of connotation chains, a technique that allows students to unpack the layered implications of single words and develop them into more impressive interpretations. This strategy is most useful for students who struggle to work out what to say when analysing, and it complements Curtis' argument that focusing on individual words can expand a students' repertoire of tools.

This particular method was first introduced to me by Caroline Spalding and has since become a staple of my teaching practice. It works particularly well when paired with explicit modelling in the early stages of the strategy. Connotation chains require scaffolding and repeated practice, but they do aid students in generating ideas beyond the simple and basic, using minimal material. Let's illustrate the strategy using a previously discussed example: Malcolm's final judgement of Macbeth as a 'dead butcher'. Students will often be able to identify the key word within this phrase, 'butcher', but may not know how to begin plumbing its depths for analysis. Connotation chains offer a structured approach to starting this process.

Begin by writing the focal word, in this case 'butcher', and then ask students to generate a single-word connotation that might be associated with it. If this is the first time completing this method, model it yourself. For example:

> butcher → bloody

Ensure you verbalise the reasoning as to why you have chosen 'bloody'. For example, 'I've chosen 'bloody' because a butcher is someone who literally deals with blood. In this context, however, it suggests the violent nature of Macbeth's actions and the blood he has spilled.' The emphasis with your modelling needs to be on showing students the logical leap between the word taken from the text and its first association.

From here, continue the chain, with each new word a connotation of the previous word, rather than another connotation of the originally chosen quotation. For example, once one has found the connotation 'bloody', a connotation of that might be 'violence.' A connotation of 'violence' might then be 'chaos' and so on.

> butcher → bloody → violence → chaos

By the time four or five connotations have been found, students have a set of interconnected ideas that act as a scaffold for constructing an analytical argument. This next step will also need modelling, but these ideas might turn into something like this:

> By calling Macbeth a 'dead **butcher**,' Malcolm strips him of any former honour, reducing him to a mere killer. The noun 'butcher' implies senseless, **bloody** slaughter, emphasising the **violent** nature of Macbeth's actions. His murders are not noble but savage, driven by ambition. This excessive bloodshed leads to widespread violence, infecting Scotland with fear. Ultimately, Macbeth's rule descends into **chaos**, showing how ambition unchecked by morality results in destruction, disorder, and a complete loss of humanity.

By arming students with this strategy, we can encourage them to write a lot about a little, something that can aid them in constructing a more exploratory response.

HACK #9.3: QUOTATION DRILLS

Of course, there are moments where longer quotations are both necessary and needed. Figure 9.1 shows a variation on a more traditional quotation explosion.

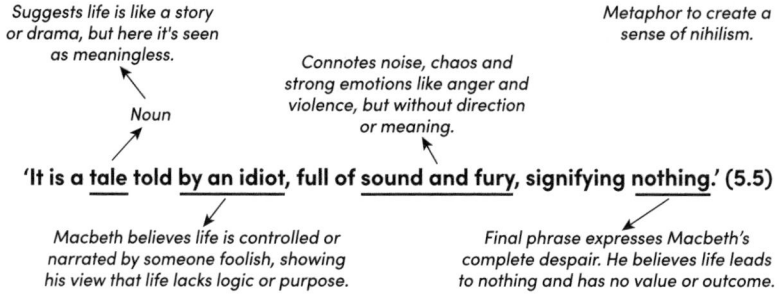

Figure 9.1 Quotation explosion example

A quotation drill is a little more structured. I wanted to use something with my class that allowed students to consider what they should be looking out for when picking and using quotations, although I do still annotate them using collective ideas too. A drill gives us the safety that students are picking up and discussing things that they need to discuss. When considering quotations, we want them to consider how they can be read in relation to their context within the wider text as a whole. We need students to be able to make connections between this moment and other moments in the text. Quotations have a rippled effect. What a writer constructs is not necessarily only relevant at the exact moment it appears in a text. Quotations have consequences. They affect the immediate presence, but ripple through the rest of a text too and can often be felt much later than their initial appearance. It is important students come to this realisation so the connections they can make are made obvious.

Quotation drills I originally envisaged looked like Figure 9.2.

You will notice how there is a heavy emphasis on subject terminology here. This is something students spend too much time on. It actually doesn't matter if Shakespeare has used a noun or an adjective at some point in a sentence or phrase. Students should be concentrating on making meaning from a text, nothing else. What matters is the ability for students to say something about these quotations that contributes to the thesis statement, alongside a main argument that connects to the text's big ideas. Therefore, a redesigned quotation drill may look something like Figure 9.3.

CHAPTER 9: CONSIDERING 'JUDICIOUS' QUOTATIONS

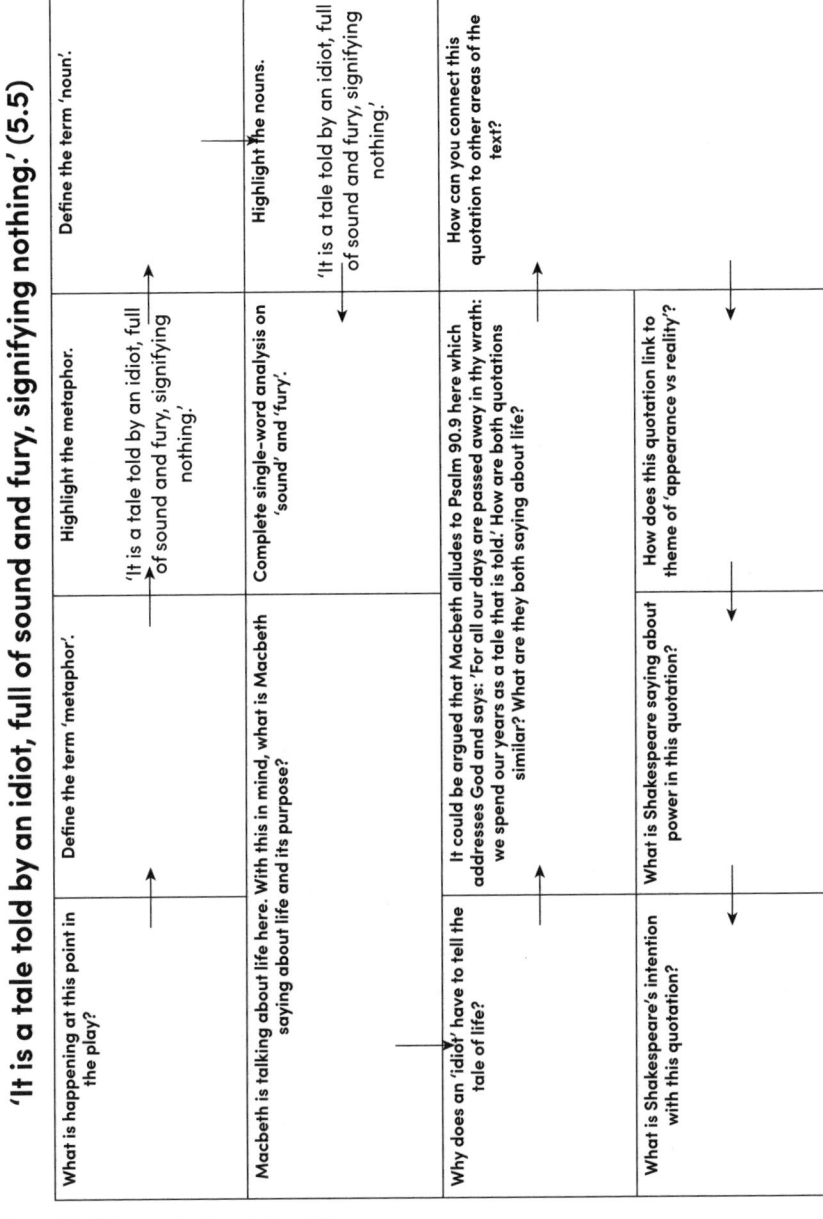

Figure 9.2 Old example of quotation drill

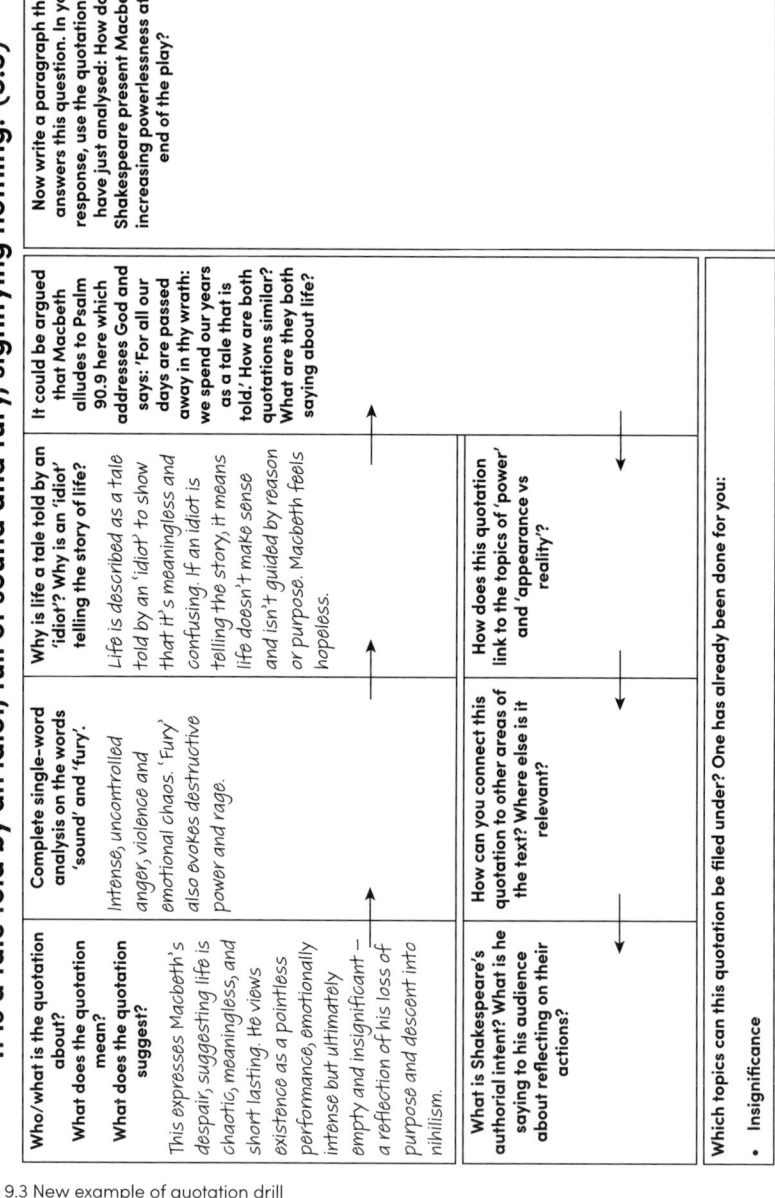

Figure 9.3 New example of quotation drill

As you can see, the emphasis shifts to connecting the quotation to other areas of the text, moving students' attention away from things that dominate their attention but shouldn't. Greater encouragement needs to be placed on subject terminology like 'stage', 'character' or 'act' rather than 'noun' or 'adjective', otherwise our analysis can all become very superficial.

WRITING

What?

When it comes to writing about quotations, the key is not just identifying or presenting them, but weaving them seamlessly into analysis. Quotations must be seen as part of the narrative of an argument, instead of isolated pieces of evidence where connections between them are not made explicit. Once students have understood and engaged with this idea, they can move beyond the simple act of repeating words, to exploring the significance of those words within a broader context. This can help develop more cohesive and sophisticated arguments, showing a clear understanding of how the author's language shapes meaning.

Moreover, the process of selecting the right quotation is a vital skill students must develop. How many times have we seen students write about a quotation where they can only say one strong point about it before their analysis begins to die out? In high-pressure situations like exams, students need to confidently consider which quotation is going to allow them to unlock the crucial meaning of the question by helping them to consider multiple layers of meaning. When students are confident in selecting appropriate quotations, they gain more control over their writing, allowing them to construct responses that are both informed and thoughtful, focused and purposeful.

How?

HACK #9.4: STOP MENTIONING THE QUOTATION!

A quick hack that is always worth mentioning when it comes to writing is teaching students how to avoid using the word 'quote' or 'quotation' in their written responses. Embedding a quotation properly means students should avoid this lazy way of leading them into using a line from a text in their answer. For example, let's consider the following quotation from George Orwell's *1984:*

'Winston Smith, his chin nuzzled into his breast in an effort to escape the vile wind, slipped quickly through the glass doors of Victory Mansions, though not quickly enough to prevent a swirl of gritty dust from entering along with him.'

If students were answering a question such as 'How does George Orwell use language to portray a dystopian setting?', we might find that students answer in one of two ways.

> The setting in the opening of Orwell's *1984* is clearly bleak and cold. The quotation 'an effort to escape the vile wind' shows this because the word 'vile' has connotations of something that is foul or holding a deep dislike.

> The setting at the beginning of Orwell's *1984* is clearly bleak and cold. Early in the novel, as Winston walks home through the streets of London, he struggles against 'the vile wind', 'vile' suggesting something foul and deeply unpleasant, emphasising the harsh, oppressive environment that reflects the grim atmosphere of this dystopian world.

The second clearly sounds better and more mature than the first. Teach students to place their quotation in context to where it appears in the text. This allows students to better demonstrate an understanding of the passage as a whole. It sounds more sophisticated and the quotation is integrated onto the fabric of the analysis rather than drawing the reader's attention to the fact it is there in the first place.

HACK #9.5: THE BIG 5 FOR LANGUAGE AND STRUCTURE

When it comes to teaching quotations, there is a clear, significant distinction between literature and language. For literature, quotations can be pre-taught, rehearsed and memorised. As teachers, we guide students to understand their meanings and significance within the broader themes of the text. However, this approach, while useful, presents us with a dilemma, for it deskills students in their ability to independently select meaningful content – especially when it comes to unseen texts, such as from the language paper. Overemphasis on predetermined quotations in literature can hinder a student's ability to engage with texts critically and independently – this, of course, leads to regurgitation of class ideas, with little thought as to what a student thinks as an individual.

In contrast, the English Language paper – regardless of any criticisms we might have regarding its efficacy and suitability, requires students to make real-time decisions about what is significant in a given extract. Therefore, it is vital to teach them independence when it comes to quotations, to make their selection a tangible process that allows them to succeed.

This hack is especially helpful for students who need that extra support in identifying key moments from the text that needs to be analysed to meet the requirements of the language questions. Originally developed by English teacher, Sarah Burt (who has kindly allowed us to share the strategy within this book), this hack provides students with a concrete method for approaching unseen extracts. It helps them focus on what to look for, offering a framework for selecting quotations, based on features that are likely to be present. This approach will remain effective, even with the adjustments to the language paper, first sat in 2026.

When looking at trends across previous AQA Language exam extracts, Burt, who has amalgamated a series of ideas from a range of sources to construct this approach, has identified a recurring pattern. From this, we can select a Big 5 for both language and structure, a set of key methods and/or features that frequently appear in the extracts (see Figure 9.4). These five areas are key in providing students with a reliable starting point when analysing language and structure. While not every extract will contain all five, it is highly likely that at least three will be present in any given source. Teaching students to recognise and discuss these recurring features, can increase their confidence, independence and the quality of their analysis. This is not about 'feature spotting'. While students do need to be able to say something about the things they're looking out for, this is about making the process of selection of quotations easier.

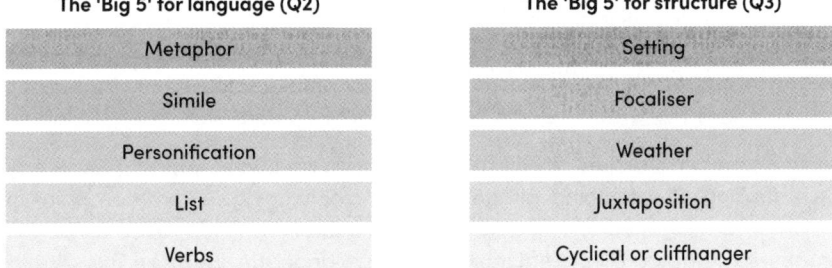

Figure 9.4 Burt's Big 5 for language and structure

These are what students should be looking out for; they are the most common ideas that are found within the extracts that are given for students to analyse. Let's consider the extract that was given for the *Brighton Rock* paper to see what this might look like in practice. Figure 9.5 is an example of how each of these Big 5 appear in the extract.

In this example, each of the Big 5 appears in the extract, helping students to identify the kinds of quotations they might select. Burt's strategy goes beyond simple feature spotting – it gives students a focused way of engaging with a text. While they are not expected to write about every feature they identify, this approach can help students to consider a more thoughtful and developed response. Crucially, it directs their attention to what is worth discussing. One practical tip I regularly use with my classes is this: 'If in doubt, seek the verbs out.' Verbs are often rich with meaning and function, and there's almost always something valuable to say about how they are used. This simple mantra sticks with students, and if they're very stuck, they have a starting point to get their answer going.

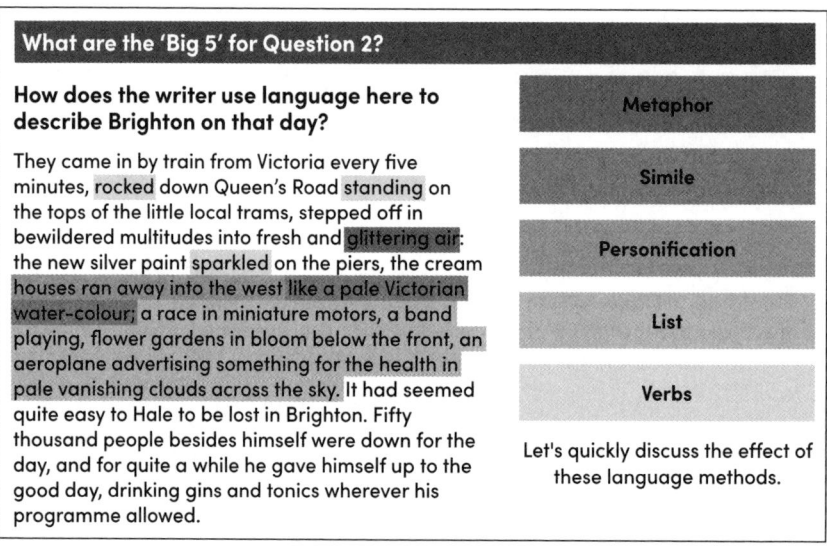

Figure 9.5 Big 5 for Question 2

When it comes to structure, specifically AQA English Language Paper 1, Question 3, we're looking at something altogether more challenging. A common point of confusion among students when it comes to quotations is the role they play in an answer if they are not required to analyse language. To make this clearer and more accessible, the Big 5 for structure can be put to use. Again, this gives students a clear framework for approaching structural features and identifying quotations that reflect key shifts or patterns in the text. Figure 9.6 shows how I introduce the Big 5 for structure.

CHAPTER 9: CONSIDERING 'JUDICIOUS' QUOTATIONS

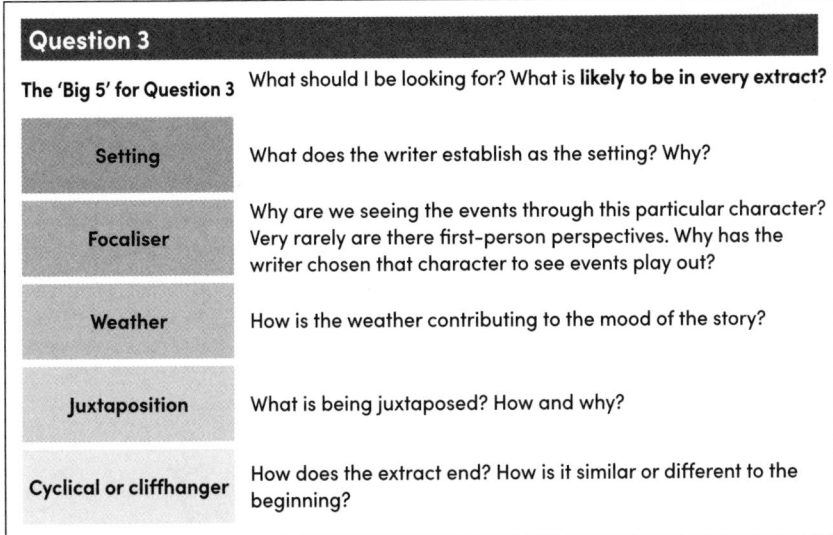

Figure 9.6 Big 5 for Question 3

When approaching this question, it is essential for students to consider what the writer is establishing at the beginning of the text, and then to track how things shift or develop as the extract progresses. Burt highlights that the first three elements of the Big 5 for structure are often introduced in the opening of the extract. If students can identify and reflect on these early on, they are better equipped to consider and explore how the writer's structural choices evolve through the text.

Let's look at this in practice, this time with an extract from *The Silent Land* by Graham Joyce (2010). In this extract, a young married couple, Zoe and Jake, are skiing when they are caught in an avalanche:

> It was snowing again. Gentle six-pointed flakes from a picture book were settling on her jacket sleeve. The mountain air prickled with ice and the smell of pine resin. Several hundred metres below lay the dark outline of Saint-Bernard-en-Haut, their Pyrenean resort village; across to the west, the irregular peaks of the mountain range.
>
> Zoe pulled the air into her lungs, feeling the cracking cold of it before letting go. And when the mountain seemed to nod and sigh back at her, she almost thought she could die in that place, and happily.

As you can see, the setting, weather and focaliser are definitely established here. If students know to identify these, they are more likely to select the quotations we need them to select in order to answer the question in the way the mark scheme requires. With this in mind, a student might come up with something like this as their first paragraph:

> The writer begins the extract by zooming in on the setting; the description of the 'dark outline of Saint-Bernard-en-Haut' far below establishes a sense of isolation, emphasising both the physical distance and the quiet remoteness of the location. It is important the reader is made aware of this isolation early on, as it increases the sense of vulnerability and danger once the avalanche begins later in the extract. The weather, 'snowing again' with 'six-pointed flakes from a picture book', introduces a serene and almost magical atmosphere, contrasting sharply with the 'prickling' cold of the mountain air. Through Zoe as the focaliser, the reader experiences the environment through her heightened senses, from the raw sensation of 'cracking cold' as she breathes to her deep emotional response, where she 'almost thought she could die in that place, and happily.' This is structurally significant because it establishes a reflective, internal tone early in the text, encouraging the reader to focus not just on the external environment, but on Zoe's inner state and emotional connection to the setting. This careful layering of detail draws the reader deeper into her experience and sets the tone for what may follow.
>
> As the extract progresses, the writer moves from ... to ...

Notice how, by focusing on the Big 5, the quotations that are chosen are judicious, because the student is considering the needs of the question. This, of course, might be written by a student who is aiming for higher marks, but let's consider what a student further down the mark scheme might come up with:

> At the start of the extract, the writer focuses on the setting by describing the 'dark outline of Saint-Bernard-en-Haut' in the distance. This makes the place feel quiet and far away, which helps create a feeling of isolation. This is important because it makes the reader feel like something dangerous could happen later, like the avalanche. The weather is described as 'snowing again' with 'six-pointed flakes from a picture book', which makes the scene seem peaceful at first. The writer uses Zoe's point of view to show how she feels, especially when she says she 'almost thought she could die in that place, and happily.' This shows she feels something strong and emotional about the setting. Overall, this beginning sets up the calm before the storm and makes us focus on how Zoe is feeling.

While there are improvements to be made here, the quotations selected allow the student to consider what is established, in order to track how the extract changes through the answer. While talking about what the writer 'zooms in' on, or how the extract 'changes focus', students can then consider the other two of the Big 5 to guide their selection of quotations through the text.

Burt extends the concept further by proposing that the Big 5 for language and the Big 5 for structure can amalgamate to form a Big 10 for Question 4 in AQA English Language Paper 1. This is where both elements can be considered in tandem. If certain techniques from the respective Big 5 lists do not feature prominently in earlier questions, it is likely they will emerge in responses to Question 4. This is not to promote the idea that students must address every element within the Big 10, nor is there a requirement for an even balance between language and structure.

This approach has been genuinely transformative for my students. It provides them with a tangible, strategic framework that anchors their responses within an effective selection of quotations – particularly in a question that is often approached hastily (or left out altogether!) by students so they can progress to later sections of the paper. Perhaps more importantly, this hack does not restrict students from exploring other analytical avenues. Rather, it encourages the use of precise, purposeful quotations that enhance the quality of their analysis.

Perhaps an unforeseen benefit of integrating the Big 5 into these earlier questions is its influence on students' approach to the creative writing component of the exam. With a clearer understanding of key structural methods, and having considered how extracts change throughout because of writers' decisions, students can move beyond generic checklists that we are keen for them to avoid and engage with (and use) a refined set of methods. Application of these methods is reinforced through the source, which provides contextual examples and acts as a model for how these techniques can function effectively within a text.

HACK #9.6: TRIM, EMBED, EXPAND

One highly effective method for helping students to engage critically with textual evidence is the 'trim, embed, expand' hack. Students can often struggle to identify which parts of a quotation are essential for their writing and so will often 'dump' an entire sentence (or in some cases, sentences) in their answer to be on the safe side. While an entire quotation may be necessary for full comprehension during reading, not all of it is required, or even appropriate, when it comes to incorporation in their own response. This strategy breaks down the process into three clear stages. Begin with modelling this hack and offer students repeated exposure to it in order to help them commit the process to memory.

Stage 1 – Trim the quotation

Begin by providing students with a lengthy but relevant quotation from a text. This might be a passage that tempts students to include in its entirety in their responses. For example, a class studying Chimamanda Ngozi Adichie's *Purple Hibiscus* might use the opening line when analysing the character of Papa:

> Things started to fall apart at home when my brother, Jaja, did not go to communion and Papa flung his heavy missal across the room and broke figurines on the étagère.

The quotation is in need of trimming. We need to select a concise, impactful fragment that offers enough to analyse while also allowing space for a student's own voice. Potential trims might include the following.

- 'Papa flung his heavy missal'
- 'broke the figurines on the étagère'
- 'things started to fall apart'

Each 'trim' is valid because they offer a focused idea ripe for analysis. For this example, let's consider 'Papa flung his heavy missal'. Verbalise for students why your selected fragment has been chosen. For example:

> I've selected this fragment because it reveals a powerful juxtaposition that I think I could discuss in detail when it comes to my written response. Firstly, I'm always looking for verbs because there's always lots you can say about them. You can tell a lot about a situation based on the verbs that are used. Notice how this quotation contains a verb which suggests ideas of violence but that violence is entwined with religion. That's really going to help me write a lot about a small fragment.

Explicit articulation of the selection process helps to model critical thinking, aiding students to understand not only what to pick but why.

Stage 2 – Embed the quotation

Embedding quotations smoothly is often the greatest challenge for students. Many insert quotations as if they are standalone snippets rather than integrated parts of their argument. Teaching embedding isn't just about fluency. It's about maintaining the student's own individual voice while letting the quotation support and not overshadow their ideas. Quotations must fit grammatically and stylistically within sentences, ensuring they reinforce the point. A useful teaching approach is to contrast a non-example with an example.

Non-example:

> 'Papa flung his heavy missal.' This shows he is angry at the opening of the novel because …

Make explicit here how the quotation feels isolated and disrupts the fluency of the point.

Improved example:

> Adichie uses a moment when Papa 'flung his heavy missal' to expose a disturbing link between religion and violence in the household.

This sentence integrates the quotation as part of a cohesive thought. The student's voice leads, and the quotation serves to support the analysis. Ask students to consider the differences between the two before articulating them yourself.

Encourage students to practise embedding by starting with their own ideas and weaving in the quotation. Use mini whiteboards to foster a high-thinking, high-participation ratio and to be sure the process of embedding is fully understood.

Stage 3 – Expand on your idea

Once students can trim and embed their quotations effectively, the next step is to expand their analysis, allowing their interpretations to deepen. For example, an expanded analysis of the quotation fragment explored previously might be:

> This violent act, committed with a sacred object, highlights the hypocrisy in Papa's character. His strict religious faith is twisted into a justification for abuse. The 'heavy missal' symbolises how religion weighs down the family, not with comfort, but with fear and control. Through this moment, Adichie critiques how religious devotion can be manipulated to mask and enable cruelty within a home.

Of course, we need to help students to get to this point of expansion. Exemplars like this are necessary, but we cannot expect students to be able to produce this first time round. Guide students behind your examples of expansion, explaining clearly what you're writing and why you're writing it in this way. Make the following prompts explicit to students and explain how they have influenced your model response, whether this is pre-prepared or demonstrated live.

- Don't assume the meaning is obvious.
- Clarify any important words or images.
- Why does this moment matter in the context of the story?
- How does this moment connect to broader themes, conflicts or relationships?
- In what way does the quotation support the central argument or thesis?
- What does the author's use of symbolism, tone or literary devices reveal here?

'Trim, embed, expand' can help guide students to use quotations with precision and purpose, and also allows for a clear, three steps in terms of how to teach this area of extended written responses. By selecting the most judicious fragments and integrating them smoothly into their writing, students gain control over their evidence and strengthen their arguments. When all is said and done, this hack helps students move beyond simply stating what a text says, enabling them to explain why it matters.

ORACY

What?

Students are often expected to leap straight from reading to writing when analysing quotations, ignoring the fundamental process of thought. One could argue that structured talk, the skill of speaking and listening effectively, provides a crucial bridge between the two. Through discussion, students can trial ideas aloud, test interpretation with peers, dig deeper together to avoid surface level analysis, and clarify their own thinking. Verbal rehearsal helps students make more informed and deliberate choices about which quotations to use and how to use them in an appropriate way. Rather than relying on memorised annotations or regurgitated teacher explanations, students can engage in active meaning making.

Neil Mercer (2014) argues that 'unproductive talk is often the outcome of students using the wrong ground rules—for example, implicitly following the rule 'keep your best ideas to yourself' rather than 'any potentially useful information should be shared and evaluated'. Conversely, he explains that when 'groups follow appropriate ground rules they are more likely to find good, creative solutions to problems. They learn how to use talk to get things done.' In the context of quotations, this gives students the opportunity to move beyond the action of passively taking notes and into collaborative exploration. They test their thoughts, refining them, developing reasoning skills and making more judicious choices when it comes to their writing. As Mercer states, when students 'use talk to reason together, they become better at reasoning on their own', improving their attainment across all subjects, not just in English.

How?

HACK #9.7: TURN AND TALK

Quotations hold the potential for rich discussion, yet are frequently relegated to brief annotations on whiteboards while students copy down the notes in their exercise books, never to be looked at again. One educator who emphasises the importance of dialogue in the classroom is Pritesh Raichura. His blog, *Bunsen Blue*, focuses on teaching and learning within the context of science, but he offers valuable strategies for educators across any subject discipline. One strategy I feel is particularly suited to the teaching of quotations is Turn and Talk.

Before engaging with Raichura's work, I had not fully appreciated the strategic potential of this approach in the context of discussing quotations.

Generating ideas: This method, probably the most used when it comes to Turn and Talk allows students the opportunity to consider their ideas, rehearsing their thoughts and refining their ideas with a partner. For example, a teacher might pose a question like, 'What does the phrase 'dead butcher' suggest about Macbeth's downfall from being 'brave'?' After providing wait time, a teacher could prompt with 'Tell your partner what you are thinking – 3...2...1, off you go!' This allows students to then share and build upon each other's ideas and expand their understanding. The more they engage with a quotation, the more likely they are to remember it.

Building fluency: Raichura's approach to explicit instruction adds a layer of questioning that ensures Turn and Talk is even more impactful. He says:

> 'My strategy for explicit instruction involves asking questions in three phases. **Phase 1** questions include firing out high-frequency 'checks for listening'. These are simple questions all pupils are expected to answer (either through choral response or 'all hands up cold calling) and serve to interrupt the loss of attention. **Phase 2** questions involve lots of rehearsal and give pupils a chance to grapple with or generate new ideas. The goal is to build understanding to the point where it is secure. **Phase 3** questions are 'checks for understanding' and their responses give the teachers feedback about whether to move on to the next part of the explanation or not.' (Raichura, 2023)

Let's think about how this method might work with a quotation from Simon Armitage's *Remains* (2008) as the foundation for discussion: 'he's here in my head when I close my eyes, dug in behind enemy lines'. In this quotation, the speaker of the poem is haunted by a man he has killed. Consider this example script below:

Phase 1 – Checking for listening (quick fire, factual questions)

> **Teacher:** [pointing to the board] Okay, everyone. Eyes on the board, Thank you. The quotation we're exploring first is: 'He's here in my head when I close my eyes, dug in behind enemy lines.' Let's consider what we understand on a literal level here. Whose head is the speaker talking about – his own or the man he killed?
>
> **Class:** [as part of a choral response] His own.
>
> **Teacher:** Who does he see when he closes his eyes?
>
> **Class:** The man he killed.

Teacher: Which word does Armitage use to show the man who was killed is difficult to remove from the speaker's mind?

Class: 'Dug'.

Phase 2 – Rehearsal and idea generation

Teacher: Let's now go a little further. Think for a second. What could the phrase 'dug in behind enemy lines' suggest about the soldier's mentality. I'll give you 10 seconds to think about that question.

[Teacher observes students thinking and offers wait time.]

Teacher: Now tell your partner what you think about the phrase 'dug in behind enemy lines'. What does this suggest about the soldier's mentality? You have 45 seconds to discuss. 3...2...1... begin.

[Students talk in pairs as teacher circulates.]

Teacher: Let's share some ideas. What did you and your partner discuss, Student 1?

Student 1: We discussed how it might mean the memory of the man he killed is stuck. It's part of his brain now and he can't escape it.

Teacher: Excellent. The memory is entrenched which means it would be difficult to remove. With that in mind, how could you connect your idea to the concept of 'enemy lines'?

Student 1: Maybe it means that his memory has become the enemy. Like, he's fighting his own trauma inside his own head.

Teacher: Great. It's not just about memory. It's the struggle against that memory. It's as if his mind has become a place of conflict itself. What are your thoughts, Student 2?

Student 2: It's like he's fighting himself.

Teacher: Interesting. Let's think about the term 'behind enemy lines' for just a moment. This is a military term that means you're in enemy territory. So what might it suggest if the speaker says the figure of the man he killed is 'dug in behind enemy lines?' What might this imply about how the speaker views his own mind?

[Pause for thinking time.]

Student 2: Maybe he feels his mind has become the enemy. He's at war with himself now.

Teacher: Great response. His thoughts, his memory and guilt are all enemy territory that feels inescapable. Maybe the trauma has completely overtaken him. He is stuck in enemy territory with no respite.

Phase 3 – Check for understanding (mini whiteboards and elaboration of responses)

> **Teacher:** Whiteboards out please. Answer the following question in two bullet points. 'What does the phrase 'dug in behind enemy lines' suggest about the soldier's mental state?' Keep your boards close to your chest when you have answered.
>
> [Students write their responses on their mini whiteboards.]
>
> **Teacher:** Everyone show me your boards in 3…2…1. And show me!
>
> [Teacher observes and narrates a few of the answers, correcting misconceptions and praising stronger answers.]
>
> **Teacher:** Brilliant. Can you please explain your thought process behind your answer, Student 3?
>
> **Student 3:** I wrote that his memory is buried deep inside him. Even when he shuts his eyes, he can't escape.
>
> **Teacher:** Well done. Student 4?
>
> **Student 4:** I wrote that it's about his guilt. He is stuck with his guilt and he can't get rid of it.
>
> [Teacher continues to ask follow-up questions to encourage a deeper understanding of the quotation.]

As this approach demonstrates, structured conversations around quotations can foster repeated exposure to key ideas, ensuring students remember the rich ideas being discussed, while encouraging whole-class participation and supporting rich, contextual understanding. Discussions like these create opportunities for all students to engage more deeply with the text, allowing them to construct meaning collaboratively and with confidence.

While this type of sequence could be applied to many areas of English teaching, I've found it especially effective when working with quotations. They serve multiple purposes: they anchor a student's argument, invite interpretation and are used to both support and challenge ideas. We place emphasis on quotations, perhaps a little too much at times, but it's what we do with these quotations that truly matter.

Raichura's sequence is powerful because it moves quotations beyond the realm of the whiteboard and rapid firing questioning. Rather than asking isolated questions like 'Why has Shakespeare used this verb?' or 'What does this suggest?', we can create a space for more meaningful exploration, simultaneously checking for understanding and probing deeper levels of analysis, helping students to not only remember quotations, but to truly own them.

Why?

Reframing how we approach quotations in the classroom is vital to deepen understanding. If we can get students to think about them as more than just textual evidence, but as windows into the writer's craft, the themes of the text and the context in which the work was produced, we can encourage greater responses when it comes to student articulation of interpretations. The collaborative, and more importantly, the critical exploration of quotations is vital in moving students beyond surface level analysis.

The approaches discussed here help shift quotations to becoming active sites of inquiry. They allow students to see how they can use quotations to make meaning instead of treating them as fragments to be memorised and deployed.

Quotations as part of rich, dialogic classroom practice not only help students to build analytical skill but also encourage a deeper appreciation of literature itself, one that cultivates curiosity and critical thinking. When we teach quotations in these ways, we're not just preparing students to meet a restrictive and somewhat limiting exam rubric, we're helping them to become thoughtful, reflective and judicious readers.

CHAPTER 10: SENTENCE STRUCTURES AND GRAMMAR

The aim of this chapter is not to provide a comprehensive guide to teaching every aspect of grammar. There are already texts that offer far more detailed approaches than I could attempt here. Instead, this chapter serves as an entry point for those teachers who may feel apprehensive about where to start with grammar teaching. It offers non-threatening, practical suggestions for how one could begin integrating grammatical concepts into a classroom, providing a set of tentative first steps before moving towards more complex instruction. With this in mind, please treat these hacks as a 'way in' to something that many are overwhelmed by. Grammar is an expansive and intricate subject, a strand of our specialism that cannot be distilled into its essential components within the confines of a single chapter. This chapter signposts key ideas, offering suggestions that might resonate with you in terms of 'where you are' with grammar teaching and teaching in general within your own contexts. This is not a chapter that will teach you the terminology of sentence structures. You won't find detailed discussions of anadiplosis (ending one sentence or clause with a word or a phrase that is then repeated at the start of the next sentence or clause), or polysyndeton (the use of multiple conjunctions in close succession). Instead, you'll find a gentle introduction to how one might go about exploring grammar through the lens of creative and academic writing.

Grammar instruction should not be viewed as a 'bolt on' to the curriculum. Too often, grammar is treated as a separate, standalone element to English teaching, rather than something intrinsic to it. But grammar is not a separate subject. It is deeply woven into the fabric of the discipline of English; we are not teachers of English and grammar. If anything, one could argue that we are teachers of English through grammar, and teachers of grammar through English. Grammar should not be 'othered'. As Jennifer Webb and Marcello Giovanelli (2023) state:

> 'Teaching grammar over time is about more than the activities you do in the classroom. It is about maintaining a culture of language awareness in the classroom. We should frequently expose students to grammar features in context, make deliberate use of precise language, and encourage students to do the same.'

In that spirit, the suggestions and strategies in this chapter should foster curiosity, build confidence and allow you to jump into cultivating a richer culture of grammar and language awareness in your classroom.

READING

What?

Grammar is often perceived as a rigid set of rules, something to be applied with the utmost precision. Break those rules and one risks committing linguistic heresy. But this traditional view can muddy the waters when it comes to exploring grammar's real purpose and potential. At its core, grammar should not be about policing correctness. It should be about making meaning. It is the system through which language structures and shapes and conveys thinking. When explored in the correct way, grammar can be a powerful tool for clarity and creativity, enabling students to make deliberate, informed choices in their writing. Why, then, is grammar frequently marginalised in English classrooms, segregated from everything else in the subject and rushed through to make space for other areas of a curriculum that might be deemed 'more important'?

Many students and, if we're being honest with ourselves, many teachers, find grammar intimidating. In the past I have hesitated to linger on it because I am afraid of getting things incorrect myself. Yet when grammar is integrated into a broader process of reading and writing it has the potential to empower our young people as communicators and thinkers.

One perspective that has really shaped my thinking when it comes to exploring grammar in the classroom comes from the University of Exeter's research into what they describe as the 'contested issue' of grammar instruction. They argue:

> 'The research we have carried out is underpinned by a view of the importance of teaching grammar in the context of children's writing, not as a body of separate knowledge learned for its own sake. Our research promotes the idea of Grammar as Choice, rather than grammar as being simply about rules and correctness. It focuses on being explicit about how language works, and about how different language choices construct meanings in different contexts, using the correct grammatical terminology as part of that explicitness.'

This is an important shift: looking at grammar as craft as opposed to grammar as correction. It requires us to reframe our approach, teaching grammar not in isolation but through the process of writing itself. This doesn't always happen. Too often, one becomes reactive when it comes to grammar, only going over something when a student stumbles: 'You're not sure how to use a semicolon? No worries. Let me quickly explain it.' Ad-hoc interventions, while well intentioned, will rarely lead to deep understanding. Planned opportunities to revisit and embed this knowledge are vital if students are to create schema.

The University of Exeter's research advocates for the explicit teaching of grammar as a means of exposing students to an awareness of the linguistic choices that might be available to them. This isn't just about knowing terminology, it's about developing a sense of agency within a writer. With that in mind, grammar instruction should be fully integrated into our schemes of work and our curricula as a whole, not as an afterthought, but as a strong foundation of how we support students to write with purpose.

To aid the explicit instruction of grammar, the University of Exeter proposes the LEAD principles, a set of guidelines designed to consider what strong grammar teaching should entail.

Principle	Explanation	Rationale
Links	Make a link between the grammar being introduced and how it works in the writing being taught.	To establish a purposeful learning reason for addressing grammar, and connect grammar with meaning and rhetorical effect.
Examples	Explain the grammar through examples, not lengthy explanations.	To avoid writing lessons becoming mini-grammar lessons, and to allow access to the structure even if the grammar concept is not fully understood.
Authentic texts	Use authentic texts as models to link writers to the broader community of writers.	To integrate reading and writing and show how 'real' writers make language choices.
Discussion	Build in high-quality discussion about grammar and its effects.	To promote deep metalinguistic learning about why a particular choice works, and to develop independence rather than compliance.

Figure 10.1 LEAD principles

With these principles, suddenly the intangible becomes tangible. I can already see how I might approach certain aspects of grammar teaching in my classroom. One of the most valuable aspects of these principles, in my opinion, is how clearly they foreground the reciprocal relationship between reading and writing, for students must come to understand that readers are writers and writers are readers. These roles are deeply intertwined. When students begin to see and appreciate how writers make intentional grammar choices, they become better equipped to consider the choices they themselves can make.

What strikes me the most about this approach is that it does not dictate how students should write. As the University of Exeter emphasises, grammar teaching should be about 'showing students the repertoire of choices available to them, and discussing how those choices create different meanings.' Debra Myhill pushes this idea further, stating:

> 'Grammar as choice is a purposeful and creative way to teach grammar. Using authentic texts, it shows developing writers how different grammatical choices change how their writing communicates to a reader. We see this as a way to empower young writers and help them understand the power of choice.'

Such an idea deeply resonates, a powerful reminder that writing is not just about correctness but about communication. At the heart of all effective communication lies intentionality. Is the message that we are delivering the message that is being received? When students are aware of the linguistic options available to them, they are more likely to write in ways that clearly express intended meaning.

In a way, the LEAD principles echo Alex Quigley's approach to vocabulary instruction, the notion that we cannot just have students copy something from the board and expect them to learn it but that they must *do* something with it: use it, manipulate it, discuss it, reflect upon it. Grammar, like vocabulary, can be learned through active engagement: writing, experimenting, revising, analysing and trying different approaches on for size.

If we reduce grammar to a rigid system of rules we will undermine a student's ability to appreciate how language and grammar can be artfully and intentionally messed with. Consider poetry as an example. Poets will often play with, or in some cases even defy, conventional grammar to create a particular effect. Poetic license is not a mistake but a choice and teaching students to recognise and identify these choices allows them to engage with the text on a deeper level, thinking about not just what a writer is saying but how they're saying it and why they need to express their ideas in that way.

This is ultimately what we want our students to do, not to fixate on punctuation marks in isolation but to recognise the significance of linguistic decisions: Why has the writer made this choice? How does it manipulate the way in which we read the text? What other choices could the writer have made? With that in mind, why is this choice the right one for the writer's intention?

So why do so many teachers find grammar difficult to teach? Ask ten teachers, and it's likely you'll receive ten different answers. For me, the difficulty stems from my own experience as a student. I don't remember being taught grammar in the ways that are emerging in our classrooms now. While today's renewed emphasis on grammar is not unwelcome, it can feel overwhelming, especially for teachers who are grappling with complex content they were never exposed to themselves. I remember grammar lessons as being occasional, isolated sessions: a dry hour on commas or semicolons that left me feeling disengaged. Yet treating grammar as a checklist clearly does not work. As Andrew McCallum (2016) from the English and Media Centre says: 'teaching students a long list of grammar terminology out of context has no impact on the quality of their reading or writing.' This is something I wholeheartedly agree with. McCallum goes on to say:

> '[Secondary English teachers] can focus on the how of grammar rather than the what [as the what is often covered in primary]. In their final GCSEs, students will be rewarded for demonstrating the ability to choose wisely from the range of grammatical options at their disposal and for commenting on aspects of language as they see fit. They will not definitively have to identify the perfect aspect of a verb or demonstrate they can use a reflexive pronoun.'

If we are to teach grammar in meaningful ways, we must first consider some hard truths regarding its misapplication. Grammar cannot be reduced to a checklist of features, yet under the pressure of high-stakes assessment, that's exactly what it risks becoming. Consider the AQA English Language GCSE, for example, where 16 out of 40 marks for writing are allocated to spelling, punctuation and grammar. This signals the importance of grammatical competence, but also creates potential pitfalls, the biggest being that grammar is taught merely to secure marks as opposed to supporting authentic communication. This is often seen in reductive instruction: 'Use two semicolons' or 'Ensure you are paragraphing for effect around three times.' Meaning is already lost if students are shoehorning these ideas into their work without proper thought for what they are actually trying to communicate.

This is precisely what the hacks I am about to discuss aim to avoid. It makes sense to start by examining how expert writers use grammar, not just correctly but intentionally and creatively too. Through close reading, students encounter grammar in its natural context: grammar that varies and adapts depending on its audience and purpose. The same punctuation mark, used across a variety of genres from a range of different voices, can teach more than any abstract rule.

To understand grammar is not simply to master a skill. It is to give students the tools not just to follow a conversation but to shape it critically, creatively and with confidence.

How?

HACK #10.1: APPLYING THE LEAD PRINCIPLES

This hack can be applied to any grammatical concept but its success depends on the use of authentic texts that model the feature in a meaningful context and the integration of grammar instruction within a thoughtful and considered, sequenced curriculum. These sorts of lessons should not exist in isolation but across Year 7 to 11 schemes of work, taught at appropriate points and revisited regularly.

Using the LEAD principles, we can teach grammar through four purposeful stages. These stages can work alongside broader text analysis too, to ensure grammar is not segregated from the rest of our subject.

Stage 1 – Language

Begin by explicitly introducing the grammatical focus that students will be looking at. Clearly name it, whether it's a focus on relative clauses, prepositional phrases, fronted adverbials or even a punctuation feature like a semicolon. Explain its meaning in accessible terms. Students need a solid understanding of the rule or structure in order to make informed choices about when and how to use it.

For example, if your focus was the subordinate clause, your explanation might look like this:

> A subordinate clause is a group of words that adds extra information to a sentence. It can't stand alone as a complete sentence – it needs a main clause to make sense. Let's look at an example: 'Although the cinema was crowded, we managed to find good seats.' Here, 'Although the cinema was crowded' is the subordinate clause. It contains a subject ('the cinema') and a verb ('was') but doesn't express a complete thought on its own.

Provide examples and non-examples to students to help them consider the concept they are being taught with confidence.

Stage 2 – Analysis

Once the concept has been introduced clearly, move into an analysis of an authentic text. An authentic text is a real piece of writing where the grammatical feature appears in context. This stage allows students to see the concept being used by a writer with more experience so they can think about what it is and also why it is being used. General questions one might ask to encourage students to explore the function of the grammar within the text include the following.

- What do you notice about what this concept does to our reading of the text?
- How does it shape meaning?
- How does it connect ideas or help you clarify information?
- What can you infer about the situation in the text from the grammar being used?
- What effect does the concept have on the tone or the pace or the voice?
- How does the grammar help the writer convey the message they wish to express to their readers?

This is more of an interactive stage and is grounded in discussion. Most importantly, connections between a writer's grammatical choice and its effect should be modelled explicitly by the teacher. For example, if the focus is on prepositional phrases, one might say:

> When you're writing a story or describing a place, help your reader picture it clearly by saying exactly where things are. You can do this by using prepositional phrases like 'under the table' or 'next to the door' to give clear visual details.

In this example, an appropriate authentic text might be the beautiful opening of Jon McGregor's *If Nobody Speaks of Remarkable Things* (2023), chosen because it perfectly models what I want students to understand, exposing them to a range of prepositional phrases that help model the creation of a vivid and sensory world:

> If you listen, you can hear it. The city, it sings. If you stand quietly, **at the foot of a garden, in the middle of a street, on the roof of a house**. It's clearest **at night**, when the sound cuts more sharply **across the surface of things**, when the song reaches out **to a place inside you**. It's a wordless song, for the most, but it's a song all the same, and nobody hearing it could doubt what it sings. And the song sings the loudest when you pick out each note. The low soothing hum **of air-conditioners**, fanning out the heat and the smells **of shops and cafes and offices across the city**, winding up and winding down, long breaths layered **upon each other**, a lullaby hum **for tired streets**.

From this authentic text, we can then not only show an example through specific contextual detail but also pave the way for deep discussion as to why particular choices work, to help 'develop independence rather than compliance' (University of Exeter). In this instance, more specific questions one might ask to instigate discussion could include the following.

- How do prepositional phrases contribute to the overall mood or imagery of the passage?
- Do any of the prepositional phrases repeat or build a rhythm? Why might the writer have done that?
- Which prepositional phrases are especially effective or poetic in this text? Why?
- Can you rewrite a sentence from the passage with different prepositional phrases? How does that change the tone or meaning?
- Does the author rely more on prepositional phrases or verbs/adjectives to create imagery? Why might that matter?

Although it is important that students understand the function of grammar, notice how the questions are much more focused on alerting students to the stylistic and expressive power of the grammar, rather than simply identifying it.

It might even be apt to then provide a second extract from a different writer that uses the same grammatical technique to consider the similarities and differences, giving students an appreciation of how grammar can be manipulated and changed depending on context and situation.

Stage 3 – Rehearsal

This stage is, strictly speaking, a writing technique, but I think it is useful in showing how reading and writing are intertwined. Students need to be moved from a phase of observation and consideration to experimentation. This stage, therefore, invites students to rehearse by deliberately practising using the grammatical concept being taught.

Offer students a purposeful writing task that encourages them to apply the grammar in context. This might include rewriting bland or underdeveloped passages to enhance them with the target grammatical structure. For example, students might be given a description where prepositional phrases are included. Conversely, they could be challenged to simplify an overworked passage by stripping away excessive prepositional phrases, prompting discussion about what is gained or lost in the process.

To summarise, these opportunities for rehearsal allow students a chance to play with language, to explore its possibilities, weigh its effects and articulate thinking. Through such deliberate practice, students begin to internalise not just the so called rules of grammar but its purpose too, how it can shape meaning and serve authorial intent. This sequence, using the LEAD principles as inspiration, supports this journey: first, students learn the grammar explicitly, then they see it used authentically, next it is analysed critically and finally, it is applied creatively through a series of rehearsals and writing opportunities.

HACK #10.2: QUESTIONS, NOT TARGETS

This is technically a writing hack, but I have placed it here because it springboards nicely from the previous strategy. The LEAD principles run with the idea of grammar as choice. With this in mind, this next strategy is about considering the ways in which we are asking students to think about how they are using grammar. Hack 10.2 has to come after the teaching of a grammatical structure but simply put it's this: change the targets/feedback we're communicating around grammar. We need to encourage options when it comes to grammar, not impose limitations by implementing checklists in class.

NOT: You should vary your sentence lengths to make your writing more interesting and fluent.

BUT: What effect does a short sentence have when it's placed between two much longer ones? How does it change the rhythm or impact of the paragraph?

These questions work not only when asking students to reflect on their own work but when they're thinking about writers' choices too. Sometimes I think we need to make the fact that students have choice explicit in order to understand that *other* writers have choice and it is our job as readers to debate why that choice has been made.

Let's consider two more examples.

NOT: You should use semicolons to join two related main clauses.

BUT: What difference does it make if you use a semicolon instead of a full stop or a conjunction? How does that change the flow or feel of the sentence?

NOT: Use fronted adverbials to add detail and variety to your writing.

BUT: What happens to the emphasis in a sentence when you move the time or place to the front? How does it draw your attention differently as a reader?

When students can *read* the grammar choices made by writers, they are better equipped to make deliberate, purposeful choices in their own writing. For those interested in developing this deeper understanding, I highly recommend exploring the University of Exeter's work in this area. Their approach is a genuine game changer.

HACK #10.3: PROVIDE COMMENTARY

Use authentic texts as opportunities to provide commentary on selected aspects of grammar, sentence structure or punctuation. The key word here is 'selected'. We don't want to interrupt the flow of class reading too often, especially when we're at a particularly good bit and students are fully engaged. Occasionally though, taking the opportunity to model opinions around grammar choices can be really useful. (e.g. 'I really like how the author has made this particular grammatical choice around X because it has made me consider Y.')

Through this, we can show students how to be selective, what to notice and comment on and how they, in turn, might use those tools in their own writing.

HACK #10.4: AVOID USING WORKSHEETS

This one might be a cheat, as it's only a few sentences long, but avoid using worksheets. You yourself as the teacher will have more to offer students than a worksheet that is clearly a 'bolt on' to the lesson; worksheets cannot model choices in the same way a teacher can. Worksheets cannot instigate and carry a debate in the same way a teacher can. Worksheets cannot ask questions in response to initial student answers in the same way a teacher can. Make students think hard when it comes to grammar, but make sure it is you that is making them think, not a worksheet that does not offer the authenticity of a real text to discuss and debate.

WRITING

What?

When it comes to grammar and writing, purpose is key. In academic writing, grammar functions to present ideas in a formal, logical manner that offers clarity. Grammar supports an authoritative voice and provides structure to the analytical ideas being expressed. In contrast, creative writing often uses grammar more fluidly and artistically. Writers may bend or break convention rules to create mood, rhythm or a distinctive voice. In this context, grammar becomes a tool for experimentation and expression, allowing students to explore language and 'try different ideas on for size'.

Recognising these differences can help students understand when they need to follow the conventions of academic or critical writing, and why they can take a more explorative approach in the context of creativity. This awareness will enable them to adapt their writing style appropriately, depending on their purpose and audience.

How?

HACK #10.5: CREATIVE IMITATION

One effective method for teaching grammar and sentence structure is through creative imitation in writing. Creative imitation involves taking something that already exists, whether that be a meticulously crafted sentence, paragraph or passage, and using it as a springboard to generate new and original work. It needs to be caveated with the fact that this is not about copying another writer's ideas or memorising sentence structures to regurgitate as and when the occasion calls for it. It is simply an apprenticeship model, a way of helping students experiment with grammar in a low stakes, low threat environment where they can explore without the fear of getting something wrong.

All good writers are thieves; the more we read, the more we unconsciously absorb the styles and strategies of other writers. This is exactly how I pitch the idea of creative imitation to students. This is not about plagiarism. It's about having the best writers model to us as novices how to write; as an apprentice learns by observing and replicating the techniques of their superior, students can benefit from emulating the language patterns of experienced writers as they tentatively take steps to find their own individual and authentic voice.

It is an entry point. Reading informs writing by building linguistic repertoire and while good readers can often become good writers, the transfer doesn't always happen naturally. We must make the bridge between the two explicit.

Here's a practical approach to using creative imitation in the classroom:

1. Begin by starting with a strong model. Choose a sentence that will generate lots of discussion, one where deliberate grammatical choices have been made that students can unravel through discussion. When I was first introduced to the concept of creative imitation as an NQT, we examined a sentence from Normal Lewis' *The Shaman of Chichicastenango* and so it seems pertinent to use that here.

> 'We hired a car and set out northwards through a landscape copied from China: bamboos brushed in on mist; the grey lace of precipices hung from mountain outlines in the sky; Indians dressed in coolie straw under the slant of rain; a stork in silhouette transfixed in a swamp; soft, melancholic, water-washed colours.' (Lewis, 1986)

As a side note, while evocative, the sentence itself echoes some outdated and problematic cultural references, invoking a term historically tied to exploitation that has derogatory and colonial connotations. We need to maintain the integrity of the structure because that's the purpose of the exercise, but we also need to address these concerns. A revised version, then, might look like this:

> 'We hired a car and set out northwards through a landscape reminiscent of China: bamboos brushed in on mist; the grey lace of precipices hung from mountain outlines in the sky; workers in traditional straw hats walking along rain-soaked paths; a stork in silhouette, frozen in a swamp; soft, melancholic, water-washed colours.'

The first task is to consider the sentence itself. I might ask the following questions.

> What do you notice about the sentence?
> What is effective about it?
> What do you think the writer is trying to achieve with the sentence?

These questions promote close reading and discussion, encouraging students to identify structural elements and choices, aligning with the LEAD principles, particularly around the emphasis on authentic texts and discussion and placing grammar in a meaningful and analytical context.

2. The next step is to parse the sentence. Identifying the grammatical structures can help students to consider the syntactic role of each clause.

Begin by examining the punctuation. In this example, students will identify the colon, semicolons, commas and the full stop. I often have students circle or highlight these marks and then discuss their functions. This lays the groundwork for understanding how grammar supports meaning. Take for example, the independent clause:

> 'We hired a car and set out northwards through a landscape reminiscent of China.'

Ask students what kind of clause it is, what role it plays in the sentence as a whole. What is its role in the sentence? Here it serves as the main clause, where it sets the scene for what follows. It could stand alone as a sentence because it is grammatically complete.

What follows, however, is a different kind of choice. Again, ask students to consider the differences between these clauses and the main clause. Ask them to think about the choice the writer has made to frame the remaining parts as poetic, descriptive fragments, a series of vignettes that enrich the scene through their snapshots of vivid detail. Grammatically, we might describe these as elliptical clauses (structures where words are omitted but the meaning remains clear). They are loosely connected by semicolons, used here for rhythmic effect. The semicolons allow the sentence to unfold in a layered manner.

By engaging in this kind of parsing, students move beyond identifying parts of speech or labelling sentence types for the sake of it. They begin to see grammar as craft, a set of deliberate choices made to help shape how language looks, sounds and feels on the page.

3. Next, I might ask students to consider their own version of this sentence, using the same concept but with a different location. This helps them begin to try the grammatical structures 'on for size' in a familiar and low threat way. I would model this first. Let's use my home town as an example:

> 'We hired a car and set out northwards through a landscape reminiscent of Ipswich: Tudor-beamed pubs leaning over narrow lanes; the spire of a medieval church catching in the mist; schoolkids in hoodies loitering by the war memorial; Town fans in blue and white streaming past shopfronts; soft, rain-blurred greys and weathered stone against a low East Anglian sky.'

Or perhaps a stimulus that doesn't describe a specific place:

> 'We hired a car and set out northwards through a landscape fractured by war: skeletal buildings scorched and leaning; the haze of smoke hanging low over cratered streets; children wrapped in blankets beside rusted tank husks; soldiers in makeshift uniforms crouched beneath broken signage; muted, dust-heavy colours smudged by ash and dusk.'

Provide a writing frame of the grammatical structures to help students access this for themselves.

> We hired a _____ and set out _____ wards through a landscape copied from _____ : _____ ; _____ ; _____ ; _____ ; _____ , _____ , _____ _____ .

This will help students slot in their own ideas with ease. Draw attention again to the structure of the sentence alongside the purpose of the punctuation and how the grammar helps control the flow of the piece. Ask students to share their responses.

HACK #10.6: FURTHER ACTIVITIES AROUND CREATIVE IMITATION

From here, the activity can branch off into multiple ideas to help students explore grammatical choices in greater depth.

1. Keep the structure of the sentence the same but change the lens. Rewrite the sentence to make the same place feel eerie or unsettling, magical or dream-like, industrial and gritty, etc.
2. Keep as many of the same words as you can but change the punctuation to see how it changes your reading of the text.
3. Give students another model sentence but cut it into strips so that they have to order it in the way they think is best, the only caveat being that the main clause goes first. From this, students can then discuss and debate their choice around the order of their elliptical clauses, justifying their rationale as to why they have placed what they have in the way they have.
4. Give students a list of elliptical clauses from the model (e.g. 'Workers in traditional straw hats walking along the rain-soaked paths') and ask them to expand the fragment into a full sentence (e.g. 'Workers in traditional straw hats were walking slowly along the rain-soaked paths, heads bowed against the drizzle.'). Students can then discuss the difference this makes in terms of the choice to present the clause as elliptical as opposed to a main clause.
5. On the other hand, you could ask students to zoom out, asking them to shrink a full sentence into an elliptical clause before asking them 'What changes when you expand or compress a sentence?' or 'Which version feels more poetic? Which gives more information?'

At this point, you could then ask students to write another sentence with the same grammatical structure but one that changes the concept completely. No cars, no travelling northward. Just a main clause followed by a series of elliptical clauses.

This allows students to try the grammatical structures in different contexts which is all round harder to do. Don't forget to model this and your thought process behind the creation of a main clause followed by the elliptical clauses. What might help is if you offer a theme for students to base their sentences on. For example, I might say 'Write a similarly grammatical structured sentence based around description of the weather'. For example:

> She stepped outside and braced herself against the storm's fury: clouds split open by sudden forks of lightning; trees thrashing wildly in the garden; bins tumbling down the street like dice; sirens wailing somewhere beyond the rooftops; loud, relentless, wind-whipped rain.

Other sentences and passages that I have used successfully with creative imitation include the following:

> 'It is spring, moonless night in the small town, starless and bible-black, the cobble streets silent and the hunched, courters'-and-rabbits' wood limping invisible down to the sloe-black, slow, black, crowblack, fishingboatbobbing sea.'
> Dylan Thomas, *Under Milkwood*. Useful for learning about the role of commas and for creatively imitating the use of commas to create lists.

> 'It is only with the heart that one can see rightly; what is essential is invisible to the eye'
> Antoine de Saint-Exupéry, *The Little Prince*. Helpful for learning about and creatively imitating the use of semicolons in place of the conjunction.

> 'I found him in the garage on a Sunday afternoon' to 'We shoved our heads in at the doorway with him.'
> David Almond, *Skelling*. Useful for showing students how nouns can be used to describe.

> 'The river tore the edges of the farm lands and washed whole acres down; it toppled barns and houses into itself, to go floating and bobbing away. It trapped cows and pigs and sheep and drowned them in its muddy brown water and carried them to the sea.'
> John Steinbeck, *East of Eden*. Useful for creatively imitating use of verbs, prepositions and use of semicolons.

HACK #10.7: CONTROL AND MANIPULATE CLAUSES

It is important we clearly differentiate for students the distinct demands of creative and academic writing. Our approach to the teaching of grammar in these contexts need not be drastically overhauled; creative imitation, for example, can be used in both a creative sense and an academic sense, but we must be certain our students are aware of their purpose in order to ensure they can produce some good writing that meets the demands of the task at hand.

English teacher Tom Needham (2018b) points out the term 'good writing' is inherently vague. What makes a piece of writing strong resists a fixed definition because it spans a broad range of styles and voices and purposes and to rigidly define it would be to risk reducing it to something mechanical and formulaic, stripping it of individuality. Nonetheless, Needham asserts there are teachable elements of good writing such as patterns and sentence structures that are frequently found in sophisticated texts. If students can master these, they can improve their technical proficiency (Needham, 2018b).

This brings us to our next hack: identifying and explicitly teaching sentence constructions that elevate writing beyond everyday communication. Needham argues that we should focus:

> 'on teaching the aspects of sentence construction that go beyond functional, everyday communication and usage – the kind of sentences that people rarely use in everyday communication, even in formalised, academic speech, yet are regularly found in high quality writing.'
> (Needham, 2018b)

These structures are not genre specific but can be applied broadly across analytical, descriptive and narrative writing. Repeated exposure and practice with these forms will allow students to make these a habitual part of their writing styles.

It is a hack that fits particularly well with the process of creative imitation. Students learn by having their teacher model particular sentence structures (perhaps found in example essays) before experimenting and imitating as they learn to gain control over their syntactic choices. Katie Ashford (2015) echoes this view, arguing 'great writing is characterised by the ability to control and manipulate clauses', which is exactly where this hack comes in.

Needham identified three types of sentence that can be taught explicitly in the classroom. With his kind permission, we are able to explore them here, considering how each can be used to enhance academic and creative writing.

Noun appositives

A noun appositive is a word or group of words that follows and renames another noun. It provides additional information, clarification, or description about that noun. The appositive may be short or more detailed.

> **Creative example:** Lena, a curious inventor with a knack for building odd machines from scrap metal, spent most of her days tinkering in the dusty shed behind her grandfather's house.

> **Academic example:** Macbeth, a brave and loyal Scottish general, is introduced at the beginning of the play as a heroic figure who fights valiantly for King Duncan.

This is really useful, particularly the academic example, because the grammatical structure here allows students to expand on their knowledge without it inadvertently creating an exposition dump. A sentence like this would be particularly useful for a topic sentence, or as part of a thesis statement, particularly when the focus of the extended written response is based around a character or characters.

Participle phrases

A participle phrase begins with a present or past participle (a verb form ending in -ing, -ed etc.) and functions as an adjective, modifying a noun or pronoun. These phrases often add detail, action, or description to a sentence.

> **Creative example:** Clutching a letter sealed in wax, Zara stepped into the clearing, her heart pounding with the weight of secrets she couldn't yet name.
>
> **Academic example:** Emphasising the tension between fate and free will, Shakespeare constructs Caesar's final moments using dramatic irony, highlighting the leader's arrogance as he ignores the warnings surrounding him.

Again, these types of grammatical structures are important because they help explain how or why something is happening. When viewed through an academic lens, participle phrases can be really useful when exploring authorial intent or writer's technique. In both a creative and academic sense, these types of sentences allow us to combine two ideas at the same time by reducing the amount of words that are needed, making arguments clearer and more succinct.

Absolute phrases

An absolute phrase is a word group that provides additional detail to a sentence. It typically begins with a noun or pronoun followed by a participle and may include modifiers or objects. Rather than directly modifying a specific word, it offers context to help set a scene or explaining the circumstances surrounding the main action.

> **Creative example:** The men, huge bags piled on their backs, walked with laboured steps. (Needham, 2018b)
>
> **Academic example:** *Tissue*, by Imtiaz Dharker, explores the fragility of human life and memory, the paper symbolising both vulnerability and resilience, inviting readers to reflect on the delicate balance between control and chaos.

Absolute phrases are useful because they add concise detail that deepens description without the need for creating a separate sentence. In academic writing, they allow complex ideas to be expressed succinctly and in creative writing, they enhance imagery and mood.

Thinking about the grammatical and sentence structures you want to explicitly teach your students is key. It doesn't necessarily have to be the ones that are listed here, although Needham's rationale shows that students won't go far wrong with learning these. Yes, we want students to be able to name these; a shared language is vital so that we can be really precise as to what we want from students during the rehearsal period. Students knowing what you want them to rehearse allows for detailed feedback where the success criteria is explicit and clear.

> 'Many of our students do not read widely and, in the absence of deliberate and focused practice, would be extremely unlikely to be able to use and manipulate these constructions ... When teaching these constructions for the first time – particularly the appositive and the absolute phrases – it is common to hear assertions that the examples don't make sense, or that they are grammatically incorrect, evidence of just how unfamiliar some students are with these type of sentences.'
> (Needham, 2018b)

If students can understand these grammatical structures, they are armed with tools ready to use in their own writing, increasing their sophistication and broadening their ability to be able to express themselves in the ways they both want and need.

HACK #10.8: UPGRADE YOUR SENTENCE

A final, highly effective sentence-structure hack is the 'upgrade your sentence' method, developed by Grainne Hallahan. It is something I use in my teaching each year and is a valuable tool for encouraging students to draft and redraft their initial ideas. It is something that can be used in both academic writing and creative writing.

Students start with a basic sentence and are guided through ways in which to elevate it. This might be by adding detail, varying structure or choosing more precise language to achieve a desired effect. Each 'upgrade' should be modelled by the teacher first, before students have a go at improving a different sentence.

In a creative context, a resource might look like Figure 10.2.

In an academic context, a resource might look like Figure 10.3.

One caveat is that students cannot use the same upgrade for every simple sentence. What this offers, however, is a way to rehearse different ways of upgrading so they can internalise these structures and employ them at the right time.

CHAPTER 10: SENTENCE STRUCTURES AND GRAMMAR

Sentence upgrades	Simile start: *Like the shadow of a vicious predator* looming overhead, the sky was dark and heavy with menace.	Verb opening: *Hanging* low and unmoving, the sky was dark with the weight of something coming.
Not only ... but ... The sky was *not only* dark, *but* heavy with the promise of something approaching.	**The sky was dark.**	**Fronted adverbial:** *In the stillness before the rain*, the sky hung low and dark with the weight of something coming.
Triple (noun) opening: *Shadows, silence, and stillness* filled the sky, dark and oppressive.	**So, so:** The sky was *so* dark, *so* thick with silence, that it felt as if the night itself was swallowing the world whole.	**Triple (adjective) opening:** *Distorted, unnatural, and suffocating*, the sky was dark.

Figure 10.2 Creative writing sentence upgrades

Sentence upgrades	**By + ing:** (Explains how the author achieves something.) *By showing* Macbeth's growing pride and paranoia, Shakespeare warns readers about the dangers of hubris.	**This shows that:** (Links evidence or ideas clearly.) Shakespeare uses Macbeth to warn against the dangers of hubris. *This shows that* unchecked ambition can lead to personal and political ruin.
Not only ... but ... (Shows multiple effects or consequences.) Shakespeare *not only* warns against the dangers of hubris *but* also shows how ambition can destroy relationships and order.	**Shakespeare uses Macbeth to warn against the dangers of hubris.**	**Fronted adverbial:** (Add an introductory phrase to give context or emphasis.) *Through Macbeth's downfall*, Shakespeare warns against the dangers of hubris.
Despite: (Use to show tension or complexity in the argument.) *Despite* his early success and bravery, Shakespeare presents Macbeth as a warning against the dangers of hubris.	**If... then...:** (Used to show cause and effect or hypothetical reasoning.) *If* a person gives in to hubris, *then* Shakespeare shows they are likely to face destruction, just as Macbeth does.	**Triple (adjective) opening:** (Builds tone and sets up the analysis.) *Ambitious, proud, and reckless*, Macbeth becomes Shakespeare's warning against the dangers of hubris.

Figure 10.3 Academic writing sentence upgrades

ORACY

What?

Oracy plays a vital role in the teaching and learning of grammar. When integrated into grammar instruction it can instigate meaningful discussions around language choices, such as comparing sentence structures or evaluating the impact of specific grammatical elements. Through oracy, students can articulate the meaning and reasoning behind a writer's (or even their own!) grammatical decisions before committing their ideas to paper.

Yet when all is said and done, for me, discussing grammar demystifies it. Exploring it together through low threat discussion helps students understand that grammar is not something to be feared. At its best, grammar teaching is more than the labelling of different methods. As I have already said before in this chapter, it should invite exploration into choice and how language works to create meaning. Oracy provides a path in this process, a way of allowing students to rehearse their reflections on intentions.

How?

HACK #10.9 EFFECTIVENESS OF SENTENCE STRUCTURE

When I think of grammar and sentence structure, I think of the debates it can instigate. It is worth emphasising one more time that grammar should not be confined to worksheets or reduced to dry exercises where we deny students a chance to have their say. Grammar and sentence structure can serve as really powerful springboards for rich conversations and creative thinking.

Sentence structure, for example, sounds uninspiring and, dare I say, quite boring, yet if we frame it in the right way, it can be very engaging. This strategy, inspired by Lindsay Skinner, and originally shared at PiXL English, offers teachers a way to teach sentence structure while sparking debate and imaginative responses from students. This activity can be adapted in many ways, but I've found it's really useful when planning a piece of creative writing based on a stimulus.

Give students an image on which you want them to base their creative writing. For this example, we will use the image in Figure 10.4

Figure 10.4 Times Square, New York

Normally, I would begin by asking students to list the things they can see as a way of considering different types of nouns, yet on reflection I feel this only provokes surface level discussion. As such, I turn my attention to full sentences, and encourage students to consider things in the picture that aren't necessarily immediately obvious. For example, can we think of any perspectives we could write from that are in the buildings? In a car? I'll put the image up and then give them four different types of sentences, accompanied by a question:

Which of these sentences is most effective at showing the frustration of the man inside a car?

1. Caught in the endless traffic, trapped in his roasting vehicle, he sighed.
2. He sighed, caught in the endless traffic, trapped in his roasting vehicle.
3. Caught in the endless traffic, he sighed, trapped in his roasting vehicle.
4. Trapped in his roasting vehicle, caught in the endless traffic, he sighed.

In an example like this, I might be teaching students about participial phrases, yet notice how I don't start with that. Instead, I'm leading with the effect of the sentences first, the atmosphere and tone they create. I'm leading with a discussion that everyone can access so as not to exclude those who might find the grammatical strand of the lesson harder to engage with. Yes, arguably knowledge of what a participial phrase is, is important. Students need to know it and recognise it in order to use it, but I would advocate for a shift that is needed in our grammar teaching. More discussion around effect is needed; the balance needs to realign.

In this case, you could ask students to write their chosen sentence down on their mini whiteboards so you can see that everyone has an opinion and everyone has made a choice before a conversation that might resemble the following:

> **Teacher:** Now, which of these sentences do you think is most effective at showing the man's frustration? There's no right answer here. I'm interested in your opinions and your justifications for your choices. Let's go with someone who picked sentence number 1. What are your thoughts?
>
> **Student 1:** I think the first sentence is effective because it builds up the situation before saying 'he sighed', so the sigh feels like a natural reaction to everything he is experiencing.
>
> **Teacher:** Good. So you're noticing how the sequence of the sentence builds tension. The writer has delayed the sigh so we're getting a stronger sense of cause and effect. Who saw it differently? What did you think...Student 2?
>
> **Student 2:** I preferred the second one because it starts with 'he sighed' which makes his emotion is the centre of the focus right away. We then learn why he's sighing so it feels more like we're in his head, I think.
>
> **Teacher:** So how is the focus different to what Student 1 said?
>
> **Student 2:** It's more of his internal focus. We feel the sigh as it happens so it makes it more emotional I think.
>
> **Teacher:** Excellent. You also put sentence 2, Student 3. What were your thoughts?
>
> **Student 3:** Well, I put sentence 2 because I didn't really like the others, especially number 3. The structure feels a bit disjointed. It breaks the fluency of the piece. It's too jumpy.
>
> **Teacher:** Great, Student 3. Pacing matters, doesn't it? Fluency matters, and we need to be really aware of that when deliberately constructing sentences for effect.

The script here shows the genesis of a discussion around effect and around grammatical choice. Of course, the students here could be going deeper, and the teacher needs to lead them down that path, but we can see the sorts of discussion we want to have through this example. Out of this then comes the actual teaching of the grammar or sentence structure which is the focus of the lesson, ready for students to use this in their own writing.

This approach could work with anything. Let's consider dashes for example. I might present students with these sentences.

1. He slammed his hands – hard – against the steering wheel, as if the noise could drown out his growing sense of helplessness.
2. He slammed his hands against the steering wheel – once, twice – as if the noise could drown out his growing sense of helplessness.
3. He slammed his hands against the steering wheel, the sound sharp in the confined space – and still, it wasn't enough–

Once again, I might ask students which sentence they prefer, all the while framing my questions so that they focus on the writer's choice of grammar. In this example, students might pick up on how the dashes in the first sentence emphasise the word 'hard', isolating it for force and emotion. They might even say the writer has chosen to use the dashes there to create a pause that mimics the physical jolt of the action. It conveys frustration but the intensity comes now with the impact. In the second, the dashes set off a rhythmic detail that interrupts the man flow, mirroring, perhaps, the frustration and repetition of the man's actions, adding to the emotional intensity. Or in the third sentence they might comment on how the dash at the end leaves the sentence open, echoing ongoing frustration and the need for relief that doesn't come. It suggests there is more emotion to come, feelings he either can't quite express or escape. This structure can also invite the reader to consider how that sentence might end, which can be powerful in narrative writing, as the writer gives the reader a choice in this scenario.

Whatever sentence or grammatical structure is discussed, ensure that students debate. Through debate, students consider a writer's different options. Through these different options, possibilities are exposed and students don't just learn about the 'what' of grammar, but the 'how' and, most importantly, the 'why'.

Why?

Grammar is misunderstood, but through no fault of its own. Rigid, prescriptive rules are not where the true value of grammar lies.

When grammar is taught in context, through authentic texts, reading and writing, students can begin to appreciate how language choices shape meaning and effect. Encouraging critical thinking about why authors make choices around grammar and sentence structures and how these choices influence a reader's experience can enable students to then transfer those insights into their own writing, making intentional decisions rather than relying on formulaic rules.

That is why I will always advocate for an approach to grammar that fosters and nurtures this sense of exploration. Classroom dialogue can build metalinguistic awareness, equipping students with the confidence to articulate the impact of their grammatical choices. Communication in our society is complex and clear, considered communication is more essential than ever before.

In conclusion, through a cycle of introduce, review and repeat, teaching grammar as a tool for shaping meaning prepares students for real-world communication. It is for this reason that we should rethink grammar instruction: to move beyond fear of getting things wrong (and therefore avoiding it all together) and to embrace language's power to inform, persuade and inspire, while promoting the role grammar and sentence structure plays in this too.

CONCLUSION

This book was written with the intention of supporting you, the English teacher, with a set of strategies, a set of classroom hacks that allow you to tackle some of the most demanding aspects of our subject. English is vast in scope, from decoding texts and mastering grammar, to fostering deep literary analysis and exploration of subtext. It is both rewarding and complex. Add that to the time pressures we are all under, varying levels of student literacy and increasing curriculum demands (to name but a few of the challenges!) and it becomes clear how necessary it is to have a bank of adaptable and effective approaches at our fingertips.

As we hope you can see, we have not set out to prescribe a single, 'correct' way to teach English. Instead, in your hands, you have a collection of flexible hacks to draw from, to change, to adapt in order to suit your own individual needs. Whether you are teaching reluctant readers or aspiring poets, supporting students with limited literacy skills or challenging high attainers with advanced analysis and literary criticism, our hope remains that these hacks help you to navigate the daily reality of English teaching with clarity and confidence.

Teaching English requires balancing the need for explicit instruction with the nurturing of voice, interpretation and personal opinion and response. It means making the complex clear while still allowing space for open-ended thinking, for exploring whether one likes or dislikes a text, for challenging interpretations and beliefs. It involves helping students become technically-skilled writers while also aiding them in finding joy and agency in the written word. Achieving such a balance is no mean feat, and despite what some may say, there is no one way of doing it.

These hacks should be treated as stepping stones, as gateways in, rather than fixed scripts. Some may be adopted fully, others might be tweaked, some may even be ignored completely! With thoughtful modelling, guided practice, scaffolded writing and rich, diverse reading experiences, we can help students to achieve academic success in English while developing the confidence to use what they've learned beyond the classroom.

Thank you for reading *Teacher Hacks: English*. We encourage you to return to it, whether you're planning a new unit or supporting a struggling learner, or just looking for a way in which to explain a new, tricky idea. Read it, use it, pass it on. We hope it helps as many people as possible.

Teaching is hard. It's hard because it matters and it matters every single day. Our work does not end when the bell rings. It follows us home, into our thoughts, our worries, our hopes. Every lesson, every word, every decision can make waves in a student's life in ways we might not always see or appreciate. The weight of such a responsibility is immense. We hope that *Teacher Hacks: English* helps you to navigate your lessons, your words, your decisions in the classroom. We hope, in some small way, that it supports or instigates a thought, an idea, a new way in to share the subject we all love with our students.

Bibliography

Counsell, C. (2018a). 'Senior curriculum leadership 1: The indirect manifestation of knowledge: (A) curriculum as narrative'. *The Dignity of the Thing*. Available at: https://thedignityofthethingblog.wordpress.com/2018/04/07/senior-curriculum-leadership-1-the-indirect-manifestation-of-knowledge-a-curriculum-as-narrative/

Counsell, C. (2018b). 'Taking curriculum seriously'. *Impact*. Available at: https://my.chartered.college/impact_article/taking-curriculum-seriously/

Crystal, D. (2007). *Words, words, words*. Oxford University Press.

Curtis, C. (2019). *How to Teach English*. Independent Thinking Press.

Deane, P. (2020). 'Building and justifying interpretations of texts: A key practice in the english language arts'. *Wiley Online Library*. Available at: https://onlinelibrary.wiley.com/doi/full/10.1002/ets2.12304

Department for Education. (2025) 'Supporting reading in secondary school: Guidance and workbook for all secondary school practitioners'. Available at: https://assets.publishing.service.gov.uk/media/680bacceb0d43971b07f5bba/Supporting_reading_in_secondary_school_for_all_secondary_school_practitioners.pdf

Didau, D. (2017). 'Everyone values critical thinking, don't they?'. *The Learning Spy*. Available at: https://learningspy.co.uk/featured/everyone-values-critical-thinking-dont-2/

Didau, D. (2018). 'How to explain... structured discussion'. *The Learning Spy*. Available at: https://learningspy.co.uk/literacy/how-to-explain-structured-discussion/

Didau, D. (2021a). 'How should writing fit into the English curriculum?'. *The Learning Spy*. Available at: https://learningspy.co.uk/featured/how-should-writing-fit-into-the-english-curriculum/

Didau, D. (2021b). 'How should we teach students to interpret texts?'. *The Learning Spy*. Available at: https://learningspy.co.uk/english-gcse/how-should-we-teach-students-to-interpret-texts/

Didau, D. (2022a). 'Using tenor, vehicle and ground to analyse metaphors'. *The Learning Spy*. Available at: https://learningspy.co.uk/english-gcse/using-tenor-vehicle-and-ground-to-analyse-metaphors/

Didau, D. (2022b). 'Implementing English: five useful teaching strategies'. *The Learning Spy*. Available at: https://learningspy.co.uk/english-gcse/implementing-english-five-useful-teaching-strategies/

Ducasse, A.M and Brown, A. (2022). 'Rhetorical relations in university students' presentations'. *Journal of English for Academic Purposes*, 63.

Dunlosky J., Rawson K.A., Marsh E.J., Nathan M.J. and Willingham D.T. (2013). 'Improving students' learning with effective learning techniques: Promising directions from cognitive and educational psychology.' *Psychological Science in the Public Interest*, 14(1), 4-58.

EEF. (2017) 'Improving children's learning by improving the quality of classroom talk.' Available at: https://educationendowmentfoundation.org.uk/projects-and-evaluation/projects/dialogic-teaching

EEF. (2021a). 'Teacher Feedback to Improve Learning.' Available at: https://educationendowmentfoundation.org.uk/education-evidence/guidance-reports/feedback

EEF. (2021b). 'Improving literacy in Key Stage 2.' Available at: https://educationendowmentfoundation.org.uk/education-evidence/guidance-reports/literacy-ks2

EEF. (2023). 'Communication and language approaches'. Available at: https://educationendowmentfoundation.org.uk/early-years/toolkit/communication-and-language-approaches

EEF. (2025a). 'Oral language interventions'. Available at: https://educationendowmentfoundation.org.uk/education-evidence/teaching-learning-toolkit/oral-language-interventions

EEF. (2025b). 'Metacognition and self-regulated learning'. Available at: https://educationendowmentfoundation.org.uk/education-evidence/guidance-reports/metacognition

Evans, R. (2023). 'Emotional literacy: A forgotten intelligence?'. *VNet Education CIC*. Available at: https://vnetcic.com/emotional-literacy-a-forgotten-intelligence/

Fahnestock, J. (2011). *Rhetorical style: The uses of language in persuasion*. Oxford University Press.

Fisher, D. and Frey, N. (2013). 'The gradual release of responsibility framework'. International Reading Association. Available at: https://keystoliteracy.com/wp-content/uploads/2017/08/frey_douglas_and_nancy_frey-_gradual_release_of_responsibility_intructional_framework.pdf

Flavell, J.H. (1979). 'Metacognition and cognitive monitoring: A new area of cognitive-developmental inquiry.' *American Psychologist*, 34(10), 906–911.

Frank, M. (2018). 'Morpheme Matrices'. *ATLAS Literacy*. Available at: https://atlasabe.org/wp-content/uploads/2019/04/Morpheme_Matrices-rev072120.pdf

Gibbs, S. and Helman, Z. (2022). *The trouble with English and how to address it: A practical guide to designing and delivering a concept-led curriculum*. Routledge.

Graham, S. and Hebert, M.A. (2010). *Writing to read: Evidence for how writing can improve reading. A Carnegie Corporation Time to Act report*. Alliance for Excellent Education.

Graham, S., Liu, X., Bartlett, B., Ng, C., Harris, K.R., Aitken, A., Barkel, A., Kavanaugh, C., Talukdar, J. (2018). 'Reading for writing: A meta-analysis of the impact of reading interventions on writing.' *Review of Educational Research*, 88(2),. 243-284.

Green, B., Molyneux, P. and Scull, J. (2022). 'Rhetoric, agency, pedagogy: A "new" perspective on language and literacy education'. *AJLL* 45,. 297–308.

Hass, C. and Flower, L. (1988). 'Rhetorical Reading Strategies and the Construction of Meaning.' *College Composition and Communication*, 39(2), 167–83.

Hattie, J. (2009). *Visible learning: A synthesis of over 800 meta-analyses relating to achievement*. Routledge.

Haynes, F. (2019). 'Structuring classroom talk'. *Class Teaching*. Available at: https://classteaching.wordpress.com/2019/06/17/structuring-classroom-talk/

Heal, J. and Berlin, R. (2025). *Mental models: How understanding the mind can transform the way you work and learn*. Hachette Learning.

Hebert, M., Bazis, P., Bohaty, J. J., Roehling, J., Nelson, J. R. (2021). 'Examining the impacts of the structures writing intervention for teaching fourth-grade students to write informational text.' *Reading and Writing*, 34, p. 1711–1740.

Henry, M. (2019). 'Morphemes Matter: A framework for instruction'. *International Dyslexia Association*. Available at: https://dyslexialibrary.org/wp-content/uploads/file-manager/public/1/Spring%202019%20Final%20Henry%20p23-26.pdf

Howard, K. (2019a). 'Physically, emotionally, psychologically: A three layer dissection of character'. *Says Miss*. Available at: https://saysmiss.wordpress.com/2019/03/26/physically-emotionally-psychologically-a-three-layer-dissection-of-character/

Howard, K. (2019b). 'What's not said: Subtleties in An Inspector Calls'. *Says Miss*. Available at: https://saysmiss.wordpress.com/2019/03/12/whats-not-said-subtleties-in-an-inspector-calls/

Howard, K. (2025). 'The Role of Rhetoric in Education'. *Says Miss*. Available at: https://saysmiss.wordpress.com/2025/02/13/curriculum-the-role-of-rhetoric-in-education/

Howe, C and Mercer, N. (2007). 'Children's social development, peer interaction and classroom learning'. *Primary Review Research Survey 2/1b*, University of Cambridge.

Howe, C., Hennessy, S., Mercer, N., Vrikki, M. and Wheatley, L. (2019) 'Teacher–student dialogue during classroom teaching: Does it really impact on student outcomes?' *Journal of the Learning Sciences*, 28(4–5), 462–512.

Hymes, D. (1974). *Foundations in sociolinguistics: An ethnographic approach*. University of Pennsylvania Press.

International Literacy Association. (2020). *Teaching Writing to Improve Reading Skills*. Available at: https://www.literacyworldwide.org/docs/default-source/where-we-stand/ila-teaching-writing-to-improve-reading-skills.pdf

Jenkins, S. (2025). 'Another way we are failing an entire generation: We must teach young people to speak'. The Guardian, 24 July. Available at: https://www.theguardian.com/commentisfree/2025/jul/24/schools-oracy-debating-failing-generation-teaching-public-speaking

Joyce, G. (2010). *The Silent Land*. Hachette Digital.

Kennedy, M. M. (2016). 'How does professional development improve teaching?'. *Review of Educational Research*, 86(4), 945-980.

King, S. (2000). *On writing: A memoir on the craft*. Hodder.

Kirschner, P. A., Sweller, J. and Clark, R. E. (2006). 'Why minimal guidance during instruction does not work.' *Educational Psychologist*, 41(2), 75–86.

Lee, E. (2018). 'Tips for answering AQA GCSE English Language Paper 1 Question 3'. *Madame Anglais*. Available at: https://madameanglaise.wordpress.com/2018/01/23/tips-for-answering-aqa-gcse-english-language-paper-1-question-3/

Lemov, D. (2024). *Doug Lemov's field notes*. Available at: https://teachlikeachampion.org/tag/disciplined-discussion/

Lewis, N. (1986). 'The Shaman of Chichicastenango' in *In Trouble Again: A special issue of travel writing*, edited by Bill Buford, p.173. Granta.

McBride, K. (2023). 'How oracy supports vocabulary development'. *Schools Week*. Available at: https://schoolsweek.co.uk/how-oracy-supports-vocabulary-development/

McCallum, A. (2016). 'Putting grammar teaching in context'. *English and Media Centre*. Available at: https://www.englishandmedia.co.uk/blog/putting-grammar-teaching-in-context/

McCourt, M. (2025). 'Stop designing 'relevant' curricula for the poor'. *EMaths*. Available at: https://www.emaths.co.uk/blog/general-education/item/stop-designing-%E2%80%98relevant%E2%80%99-curricula-for-the-poor

McGregor, J. (2023). *If nobody speaks of remarkable things*. Collins Modern Classics.

Mercer, N. (2003). 'The educational value of 'dialogic talk' in 'whole-class dialogue'. *New perspectives on spoken English in the classroom: Discussion papers*. p.74.

Mercer, N. (2013). 'The social brain, language, and goal-directed collective thinking: A social conception of cognition and its implications for understanding how we think, teach, and learn.' *Educational Psychologist*, 48(3), 148–168.

Mercer, N. (2014). 'Why teach oracy?'. *University of Cambridge*. Available at: https://www.cam.ac.uk/research/discussion/why-teach-oracy

Mercer, N. and Littleton, K. (2007). *Dialogue and the development of children's thinking: a sociocultural approach*. Routledge.

Meyer, B. and Ray, M. (2011). 'Structure strategy interventions: Increasing reading comprehension of expository text.' *International Electronic Journal of Elementary Education*, 4(1), 127–152.

Millard, W. (2021). 'Oracy after the pandemic'. *The Centre for Education and Youth*. https://cfey.org/reports/2021/04/oracy-after-the-pandemic/

Miller, R.T. and Pessoa, S. (2016). 'Where's your thesis statement and what happened to your topic sentences? Identifying organizational challenges in undergraduate student argumentative writing'. *Wiley Online Library*. Available at: https://onlinelibrary.wiley.com/doi/10.1002/tesj.248

Mills, K. (2009). 'Floating on a sea of talk: Reading comprehension through speaking and listening'. *International Reading Association*. Available at: https://www.gearyschools.org/pages/uploaded_files/14.pdf

Mohamad, H.R. (2022). 'Rhetorical devices for rhetorical appeals to logos, ethos and pathos in ENL and ESL research abstracts: A contrastive analysis of the rhetoric.' *Malaysian Journal of Social Sciences and Humanities*, 7(3), e001314.

Myatt, M. (2021a). 'Thinking about curriculum intent'. *Mary Myatt*. Available at: https://www.marymyatt.com/blog/thinking-about-curriculum-intent

Myatt, M. (2021b). 'Walking the talk'. *Mary Myatt*. Available at: https://www.marymyatt.com/blog/walking-the-talk

Myatt, M. (2022a). 'How rich vocabulary helps pupils to learn the curriculum'. *Mary Myatt*. Available at: https://www.marymyatt.com/blog/how-rich-vocabulary-helps-pupils-to-learn-the-curriculum

Myatt, M. (2022b). 'English overview'. *Mary Myatt*. Available at: https://www.marymyatt.com/english-overview

Myhill, D. (n.d.) 'Grammar as choice'. *University of Exeter.* Available at: https://www.exeter.ac.uk/research/centres/languageandliteracy/grammar-teacher-resources/grammaraschoice/

Nagy, W. E. (1988). *Teaching vocabulary to improve reading comprehension.* International Reading Association.

National Literacy Trust. (2011). 'Literacy: A route to addressing child poverty?'. *National Literacy Trust* Available at: https://nlt.cdn.ngo/media/documents/2011_11_11_free_research_-_literacy_and_poverty_review_2011_nkvmmAk.pdf

Needham, T. (2018a). 'Explicit vocabulary teaching 1: What and how?'. *Thoughts about teaching.* Available at: https://tomneedhamteach.wordpress.com/2018/02/05/explicit-vocabulary-teaching-1-what-and-how/

Needham, T. (2018b). 'Teaching phrases 4: An overview of absolute phrases'. *Thoughts about teaching.* Available at: https://tomneedhamteach.wordpress.com/2018/01/29/teaching-phrases-4-an-overview-of-absolute-phrases/

Needham, T. (2020). 'Is explicit instruction the right approach?'. *Thoughts about teaching.* Available at: https://tomneedhamteach.wordpress.com/2020/09/14/is-explicit-instruction-the-right-approach/

Needham, T. (2022). 'Teaching AQA Language Question 3?'. *Thoughts about teaching.* Available at: https://tomneedhamteach.wordpress.com/2022/06/09/teaching-aqa-language-question-3/

Ofsted. (2022). *Research review series: English.* Available at: https://www.gov.uk/government/publications/curriculum-research-review-series-english/curriculum-research-review-series-english

Ofsted. (2024). *Telling the story: the English education subject report.* Available at: https://www.gov.uk/government/publications/subject-report-series-english/telling-the-story-the-english-education-subject-report#part-b-secondary-english

Oracy Education Commission. (2024). *We need to talk: The report of the Commission on the future of oracy education in England.* Available at: https://oracyeducationcommission.co.uk/wp-content/uploads/2024/10/Future-of-Oracy-v23-web-13.pdf

Orwell, G. (2008). *1984.* Penguin Books.

Parker, K. (2022). 'Hinterland knowledge: everything you need to know'. *TES,* 28 June. Available at: https://www.tes.com/magazine/teaching-learning/secondary/hinterland-knowledge-everything-teachers-need-know

Piaget, J. (1959). *The language and thought of the child.* Routledge.

Pryke, S. (2019). 'Laying the foundations for talking about structure: AQA English Language – Paper 1, Question 3'. *An English Teacher's Notebook.* Available at: https://englishteachersnotebook.blogspot.com/2019/10/laying-foundations-for-talking-about.html

Pryke, S. (2022). 'High think/high participation ratio in English – Ideas, thoughts and musings'. *An English Teacher's Notebook,* Available at: https://englishteachersnotebook.blogspot.com/2022/10/high-thinkhigh-participation-ratio-in.html

Pryke, S. and Staniforth, A. (2022). *Ready to teach: A Christmas carol.* John Catt.

Quigley, A. (2018) 'Vocabulary Knowledge and the Frayer Model'. Available at: https://alexquigley.co.uk/vocabulary-knowledge-and-the-frayer-model/

Quigley, A. (2021). 'Three Pillars of Vocabulary Teaching'. Available at: https://alexquigley.co.uk/three-pillars-of-vocabulary-teaching/

Quigley, A. (2024a). 'Mighty morphology – 5 resources'. Available at: https://alexquigley.co.uk/mighty-morphology-5-resources/

Quigley, A. (2024b). 'Why word consciousness matters'. Available at: https://alexquigley.co.uk/why-word-consciousness-matters/

Quigley, A. and Coleman, R. (2018). 'Improving literacy in secondary schools: Guidance report'. EEF. Available at: https://d2tic4wvo1iusb.cloudfront.net/production/eef-guidance-reports/literacy-ks3-ks4/EEF_KS3_KS4_LITERACY_GUIDANCE.pdf

Rackley, L. and Bradford, T. (2022). 'Joyful noise and abatement: idle chatter and the undercommons of oracy education'. *Literacy*, 56, 191–198.

Raichura, P. (2023). 'Turn and talk'. *Bunsen Blue*. Available at: https://bunsenblue.com/2023/12/30/turn-and-talk/

Raichura, P. (2025) 'Choral Response and 'I say, you say''. *Bunsen Blue*. Available at: https://bunsenblue.com/2025/02/08/choral-response-and-i-say-you-say/

RCSLT. (2021). *The centrality of spoken language to developing literacy and numeracy skills*. Available at: https://www.rcslt.org/wp-content/uploads/2021/12/Language-and-Literacy-briefing_2nd-December-final-version-006.pdf

Rees, J. (2024). 'Explaining Ofsted's definition of 'cultural capital': A comprehensive guide'. *The National College* Available at: https://nationalcollege.com/news/ofsted-cultural-capital-guide

Resnick, L.B., Asterhan, C.S.C. and Clarke, S.N. (2015). *Socializing intelligence through academic talk and dialogue*. American Educational Research Association.

Rice, M. et al. (2024). 'Promoting inference generation: Using questioning and strategy instruction to support upper elementary students'. *International Literacy Association*. Available at: https://ila.onlinelibrary.wiley.com/doi/full/10.1002/trtr.2353

Robinson, M. (2013). *Trivium 21c: Preparing young people for the future with lessons from the past*. Independent Thinking Press.

Roediger, H.L. and Karpicke, J.D. (2006). 'Test-enhanced learning: Taking memory tests improves long-term retention.' *Psychological Science*, 17(3), 249–255.

Rosenshine, B. (2012). 'Principles of instruction research-based strategies that all teachers should know'. Available online at: https://www.teachertoolkit.co.uk/wp-content/uploads/2018/10/Principles-of-Insruction-Rosenshine.pdf

Rupley, W.H., Nichols, W.D., Mraz, M., Blair, T.R. (2012). 'Building conceptual understanding through vocabulary instruction'. *Reading Horizons: A Journal of Literacy and Language Arts*, 51(4), 299–312.

Schraw, G. and Dennison, R.S. (1994). 'Assessing metacognitive awareness.' *Contemporary Educational Psychology*, 19(4), 460–475.

Sedita, J. (2024). 'Making inferences to support comprehension'. *Keys to Literacy*. Available at: https://keystoliteracy.com/blog/making-inferences-to-support-comprehension

Shanahan, T. (2016). 'Relationships between reading and writing development.' in C. A. MacArthur, S. Graham and J. Fitzgerald (Eds.), *Handbook of writing research* (2nd ed.). Guilford Press.

Shanahan, T. and Shanahan, C. (2008). 'Teaching disciplinary literacy to adolescents.' *Harvard Educational Review*, 78(1), 40–59.

Shelby, K. (2021). 'Purpose, audience, tone, and content'. *English Composition Handbook*. Available at: https://open.ocolearnok.org/woscenglishcomp/chapter/6-1-purpose-audience-tone-and-content/

Sherrington, T. (2013). 'Great Lessons 1: Probing'. *Teacher Head*. Available at: https://teacherhead.com/2013/01/22/great-lessons-1-probing-questions/

Simon, R. (n.d.). 'Oracy across the curriculum: The evidence'. *Voice 21*, Available at: https://voice21.org/oracy-across-the-curriculum-the-evidence/

Smith, R., Snow, P., Serry, T., Hammond, L. (2021). 'The role of background knowledge in reading comprehension: a critical review'. *Reading Psychology*, 42, 2021, 214–240.

Standford University. (2026). 'Teaching Writing'. Available at: https://teachingwriting.stanford.edu/

Sweller, J., Ayres, P. and Kalyuga, S. (2011). *Cognitive load theory*. Springer.

Sweller, J., van Merriënboer, J. J. and Paas, F. (2019). 'Cognitive architecture and instructional design: 20 years later.' *Educational Psychology Review*, 31(2), 261-292.

Tailor B. (2016). 'Rhetoric and oracy in the Classics classroom.' *Journal of Classics Teaching*, 17(33),. 14-21.

TES Resources. (2026). *Mathew-Lynch's Shop*. Available at: https://www.tes.com/teaching-resources/shop/Mathew-Lynch

The Junto Institute. (2024). 'The Junto emotion wheel'. *The Junto Institute*. Available at: https://www.thejuntoinstitute.com/2024/08/28/emotion-wheels/

The Reading Agency. (2024). 'The state of the nation's adult reading: 2024 report'. *The Reading Agency*. Available at: https://readingagency.org.uk/adult-reading-research-report-2024/

The Reading Agency. (2026). 'Reading facts'. Available at: https://readingagency.org.uk/our-work/our-research/reading-facts/

Thomas, D. (2024). 'Growing oracy focus could benefit maths teaching'. *TES*, 1 May. Available at: https://www.tes.com/magazine/analysis/secondary/growing-oracy-focus-could-benefit-maths-teaching

Thompson, R.F. (1973). 'Teaching literary devices and the reading of literature'. *Journal of Reading*, 17(2), 113-118.

University of Exeter. (n.d.). 'The grammar as choice pedagogy.' *University of Exeter*. Available at: https://www.exeter.ac.uk/research/centres/languageandliteracy/grammar-teacher-resources/grammaraschoice/thegrammarforwritingpedagogy/

Voice 21. (2023). 'Voicing vocabulary'. *Voice 21*. Available at: https://voice21.org/wp-content/uploads/2023/09/The-Voicing-Vocabulary-Report.pdf

Voice 21. (2024). 'How oracy supports vocabulary development'. *Voice 21*. Available at: https://voice21.org/how-oracy-supports-vocabulary-development/

Vygotsky, L.S. (1962). *Thought and language*. MIT Press.

Vygotsky, L.S. (1978). *Mind in society: The development of higher psychological processes*. Harvard University Press.

Webb, J. (2018) 'Challenge for all: #PracPed18'. *Funky Pedagogy*. Available at https://funkypedagogy.com/challenge-for-all-pracped18

Webb, J. (2022) 'Visualise metaphor'. *Funky Pedagogy*. Available at https://funkypedagogy.com/wp-content/uploads/2022/11/VISUALISE-Metaphor-FINAL.pdf

Webb, J. and Giovanelli, M. (2023). *Essential Grammar* Routledge.

Wellington, J. and Osborne, J. (2001) .*Language and literacy in science education*. Open University Press.

Wiliam, D. (2011). *Embedded formative assessment*. Solution Tree Press.

What Works Clearinghouse. (2016). 'Teaching secondary students to write effectively'. *Institute of Education Sciences*. Available at: https://ies.ed.gov/ncee/wwc/Docs/PracticeGuide/508_WWCPG_SecondaryWriting_122719.pdf

Whittaker, F. (2016). 'Campaign demands support for speaking skills after teachers describe training 'barriers''. *Schools Week*. 8 November. Available at: https://schoolsweek.co.uk/campaign-demands-support-for-speaking-skills-after-teachers-describe-training-barriers/

Wood, B. (2018). 'Why I No Longer PEE'. *Just a Teacher Standing in Front of a Class*. Available at: https://justateacherstandinginfrontofaclass.wordpress.com/2018/10/28/why-i-no-longer-pee/

Yothers, B. (n.d.). 'Thesis statements in literary analysis papers'. *Resources Final Site*. Available at: https://resources.finalsite.net/images/v1620142357/smhsorg/a4wyrtz3qk9seylmaqr3/Thesis_statement_handout__1.pdf

Zwiers, J. (2019). *Next steps with academic conversations : new ideas for improving learning through classroom talk*. Stenhouse Publishers

Photo credits

Photos reproduced by permission of: **p.43** © Denysiuk Natalia/Shutterstock.com; **p.87** © Everett Collection/Shutterstock.com; **p.97** © Igor Faun/Shutterstock.com; **p.209** © Skreidzeleu/Shutterstock.com.